G000150351

VANISHING SENSIBILITIES

FRONTISPIECE Jean François Janinet (1752–1814), Liberty (wearing victor's laurels, she holds a Phrygian cap and Hercules's club; at her feet lies a vanquished many-headed serpent; a sphinx guards her throne), 1792, aquatint engraving after Jean Guillaume Motte, Louvre, Paris; Photo: Michèle Bellot; Réunion des Musées Nationaux / Art Resource, NY. By kind permission.

Für die Liebe flicht der Himmel gnadenreich den Siegeskranz.

—*ALFONSO UND ESTRELLA*, act III, no. 28

Vanishing Sensibilities

SCHUBERT, BEETHOVEN, SCHUMANN

Kristina Muxfeldt

OXFORD
UNIVERSITY PRESS

OXFORD
UNIVERSITY PRESS

Oxford University Press, Inc., publishes works that further
Oxford University's objective of excellence
in research, scholarship, and education.

Oxford New York
Auckland   Cape Town   Dar es Salaam   Hong Kong   Karachi
Kuala Lumpur   Madrid   Melbourne   Mexico City   Nairobi
New Delhi   Shanghai   Taipei   Toronto

With offices in
Argentina   Austria   Brazil   Chile   Czech Republic   France   Greece
Guatemala   Hungary   Italy   Japan   Poland   Portugal   Singapore
South Korea   Switzerland   Thailand   Turkey   Ukraine   Vietnam

Copyright © 2012 by Oxford University Press

Published by Oxford University Press, Inc.
198 Madison Avenue, New York, New York 10016

www.oup.com

Oxford is a registered trademark of Oxford University Press
All rights reserved. No part of this publication may be reproduced,
stored in a retrieval system, or transmitted, in any form or by any means,
electronic, mechanical, photocopying, recording, or otherwise,
without the prior permission of Oxford University Press.

Library of Congress Cataloging-in-Publication Data
Muxfeldt, Kristina.
Vanishing sensibilities: Schubert, Beethoven, Schumann / Kristina Muxfeldt.
   p. cm.
Includes bibliographical references and index.
ISBN 978-0-19-978242-0 (alk. paper)
1. Music—19th century—History and criticism. 2. Beethoven, Ludwig van,
1770–1827—Criticism and interpretation. 3. Schubert, Franz, 1797–1828—Criticism and
interpretation. 4. Schumann, Robert, 1810–1856—Criticism and interpretation. I. Title.
ML196.M98 2012
780.943′09034—dc22   2010051245

Publication of this book was supported by the John Daverio Endowment of the American
Musicological Society and the Publications Endowment of the American Musicological Society, supported
through the National Endowment for the Humanities.

1 3 5 7 9 8 6 4 2

Printed in the United States of America
on acid-free paper

For Charles Rosen

Contents

Credits for Music Examples

MUSIC EXAMPLES IN chapter 1 from *Alfonso und Estrella* are based on the following edition and reproduced with kind permission:

"No. 3 Chorus and Ensemble - Andantino: Laß dir danken für die Gaben - act one"

from: Franz Schubert: Alfonso and Estrella, Romantic Opera in three acts, Libretto: Franz von Schober, D 732, Vocal Score based on the Urtext of the New Schubert Edition by Catherine & David McShane, BA 5540a, page 39: measure 91–99, page 41: measure 111–115 © Bärenreiter-Verlag Karl Vötterle GmbH & Co. KG, Kassel

"No. 17 Chorus and Aria - Allegro molto: Es sei sein Blut vergossen

(Es falle Mauregat)- act two"

from: Franz Schubert: Alfonso and Estrella, Romantic Opera in three acts, Libretto: Franz von Schober, D 732, Vocal Score based on the Urtext of the New Schubert Edition by Catherine & David McShane, BA 5540a, page 242–244: measure 473–509 © Bärenreiter-Verlag Karl Vötterle GmbH & Co. KG, Kassel

"No. 7 Chorus and Aria - Allegro moderato: Es schmückt die weiten Säle - act one"

from: Franz Schubert: Alfonso and Estrella, Romantic Opera in three acts, Libretto: Franz von Schober, D 732, Vocal Score based on the Urtext of the New Schubert Edition by Catherine & David McShane, BA 5540a, page 86–87: measure 92–115, page 88–89: measure 145–151 (vocal line only: set above the vocal line for verse 1), page 90–91: measure 181–187 (vocal line only: set above the vocal line for verse 2) © Bärenreiter-Verlag Karl Vötterle GmbH & Co. KG, Kassel

"No. 10 Finale - Adagio: Was wird ich nun beginnen - act one"

from: Franz Schubert: Alfonso and Estrella, Romantic Opera in three acts, Libretto: Franz von Schober, D 732, Vocal Score based on the Urtext of the New Schubert Edition by Catherine & David McShane, BA 5540a, page 131–133: measure 132–149 © Bärenreiter-Verlag Karl Vötterle GmbH & Co. KG, Kassel

Music examples in chapter 2 from *Der Graf von Gleichen* are based on the following edition* and reproduced with kind permission:

"No. 8 Finale - Recitative and Aria: Himmel was mußt ich hören?"

from: Franz Schubert: Der Graf von Gleichen, Neue Ausgabe sämtlicher Werke, Serie II: Bühnenwerke, Band 17, D 918, Vorgelegt von Manuela Jahrmärker, BA 5552, page 58–59: measure 1–32 © Bärenreiter-Verlag Karl Vötterle GmbH & Co. KG, Kassel

"No. 5c - Duet: "Ich wünscht um dich zu schmücken die Erde kahl zu pflücken"

from: Franz Schubert: Der Graf von Gleichen, Neue Ausgabe sämtlicher Werke, Serie II: Bühnenwerke, Band 17, D 918, Vorgelegt von Manuela Jahrmärker, BA 5552, page 42: measure 1–8 © Bärenreiter-Verlag Karl Vötterle GmbH & Co. KG, Kassel

"No. 20b - Duet: "Wohl an! Sprich zu dem frommen Kinde"

from: Franz Schubert: Der Graf von Gleichen, Neue Ausgabe sämtlicher Werke, Serie II: Bühnenwerke, Band 17, D 918, Vorgelegt von Manuela Jahrmärker, BA 5552, pages 127–128: measure 33–42 © Bärenreiter-Verlag Karl Vötterle GmbH & Co. KG, Kassel

*In addition to the *NSA* the author gratefully acknowledges the other editions consulted in the preparation of the *Der Graf von Gleichen* excerpts:

Richard Kramer, "Posthumous Schubert," *19th Century Music*, 14, no. 2 (1990): 197–216.

Franz Schubert: Der Graf von Gleichen; Oper in zwei Akten (D 918); Erstveröffentlichung der Handschrift des Komponisten aus dem Besitz der Wiener- Stadt und Landesbibliothek, text by Eduard von Bauernfeld, ed. Ernst Hilmar, with an essay by Erich W. Partsch. Vol. 2 of *Veröffentlichungen des Internationalen Franz Schubert Instituts* (Tutzing: Hans Schneider, 1988).

Acknowledgments

FIRST AND FOREMOST, my thanks go to Suzanne Ryan, without whose vision and expertise this book never would have come into print. To her energetic staff at Oxford, to my production editor Erica Woods Tucker, to Sue Marchman who made the index, and to Donna Wilson, who prepared the music examples, I am much indebted.

Critical financial support for this project came from West European Studies at Indiana University, Yale University's Morse Fellowship and A. Whitney Griswold fund, and an American Musicological Society publication subvention. Colleagues at numerous archives and libraries provided kind assistance. Special mention is due the Gesellschaft der Musikfreunde in Vienna, the Wienbibliothek im Rathaus, the Österreichisches Theatermuseum, Stift Kremsmünster, the Thüringisches Landesmusikarchiv, the archive of the Deutsches Nationaltheater in Weimar (now at the Hauptstaatsarchiv), the Angermuseum in Erfurt, and the Beinecke Rare Book and Manuscript Library at Yale University. Lutz Mager provided the jacket photo of "Nebensonnen" (taken at the "blaue Stunde" near Hede in Sweden). For permission to revise two chapters previously published I am grateful to *Journal of the American Musicological Society* and *19th Century Music* and Camden House press graciously let me adapt a few paragraphs from an essay I wrote for a collection on German Romanticism.*

* Kristina Muxfeldt, "Schubert, Platen, and the Myth of Narcissus," *Journal of the American Musicological Society* 49 (1996): 480–527; and the subsequent colloquy: "On 'Schubert, Platen, and the Myth of Narcissus,'" *Journal of the American Musicological Society* 50 (1997): 225–27; "*Frauenliebe und Leben* Now and Then," *19th Century Music* 25 (2001): 27–48; "The Romantic Preoccupation with Musical Meaning" in *The Literature of German Romanticism*, Camden House History of German Literature, vol. 8, edited by Dennis F. Mahoney (Rochester: Camden House, 2004), 251–272.

The anonymous readers for the Press and the members of the publications committee of the American Musicological Society have my sincere gratitude for their trouble. I owe special thanks to Scott Burnham who read the entire manuscript with profound insight and the most generous spirit. Richard Kramer's unstinting support reaches back for decades. His own probing scholarship has been an inspiration to me since my undergraduate days and the critical refinements he introduced at various stages have made this into a much better book. Maynard Solomon shared his insights freely and encouraged mine from the first time that we met. A brief version of chapter 1 was first presented at a symposium honoring his work and influence. I am deeply indebted to Charles Rosen for all his sage advice and stimulus.

The themes in this book have occupied me for many years, inevitably spilling into my teaching and conversations with colleagues, students, and friends. Occasions to test these ideas at visiting colloquia or conferences happily have also been plentiful. I cannot properly acknowledge in this space everyone who truly deserves my thanks but, in addition to those already mentioned, I have enjoyed frequent lively exchanges about this material with Kofi Agawu, Kathryn Alexander, Paul Berry, Martha Calhoun, Phil Ford, Michael Friedmann, Paula Gabbard, Roman Ivanovitch, Karen Lazar, Eva Linfield, Vera Micznik, Massimo Ossi, Ellen Rosand, Elizabeth Schulze, and Ayana Smith. Previous editors have contributed much to the substance and shape of these ideas. They are James Hepokoski, Paula Higgins, and Dennis F. Mahoney. Betsy Sabga and Daniel Melamed offered generous personal support at a critical time. Practical assistance came from Angela Beeching, Chris Holmes, Giovanni Zanovello, and my brother Jost Muxfeldt.

Charles Rosen's wit and friendship have sustained me through the entire process. Had he not kept after me, there would not be this book.

Notes to the Reader

BECAUSE OF THE general availability of scores for the Beethoven symphonies, score examples to accompany discussions of these works are not given here. Examples are provided for most of the other works discussed in the text.

English translations are given for all essential quotations from German sources. The original language appears directly in the text whenever practical and when its tone is particularly to be savored (*italics* when it is helpful to imagine the words spoken or sung). Otherwise, translations appear in the notes along with other commentary for readers who are curious to know more.

Prologue: The Historian

The pleasures of historical reflection ignite when we stumble upon traces of those once vibrant concerns that have shaped the achievements and thinking of a past era, and something clarifies that has been bothering us all along. It is exhilarating when a fortuitous encounter with such faded passions allows us to see beyond the constructs and tempers of our present age to glimpse conditions of life in another time, or, indeed, to bring to greater awareness the reflexes of our own age.

We can cultivate these discoveries not only by immersing ourselves in the cultural accomplishments and language of the past—without which there is nothing to stumble upon—but, just as important, by learning to notice in ourselves and our contemporaries the symptoms of intellectual evasion, signs that we are skimming over, or fitting into habitual critical models, those things that strike us as puzzling, maybe even alienating, about the past: they are just what should draw our most intense and sympathetic focus. The more we become aware of the forces channeling thinking in our time, the better able we are to imagine the pressures that conditioned creative thought in the past and to distinguish differing ambitions (or ways of coping) within it.

I begin with these words about method because the tension between modern critical perspectives and past sensibilities is a persistent concern in these essays on Schubert, Beethoven, and Schumann. Written over a period of a dozen years or so, nearly all of them were sparked by something that stood out in recent critical reception—a difficulty in explaining peculiar features of a piece, dismay at ideological forces discovered in it, or even a pattern of appreciative response. Too often I found myself unable to reconcile critical reaction with my own experience of the music, and it seemed that we were losing touch with the sensibilities of the past: taking at face value what was meant as theatrical send-up, hearing as parody what came from the heart, or perhaps merely assuming that everybody in another age heard the tone of an utterance in the same way (or, to complicate things still further, that even a single person heard it always in the same way). Just imagine a historian a few hundred years from now coming upon a loose page of the script for an episode of the post-9/11, anti-Bush sitcom *Whoopie*, a show that regularly defused ethnic stereotypes by giving them vent. And imagine the consequences if our historian were to extract from this merely a few "quotes" (as so many today call any snippet of verbal material), or if she mistook its deadpan humor for matter-of-fact expression, or if the historical background she had assembled around it were off by a presidency or two! How accurately, then, could this same historian tell our present day from the period flavor of a show like *Mad Men*? Or distinguish what must have been the realities of 1962 corporate and suburban life from its distillation into hour-long segments of a television drama? Frightening to think. It could go the other way around, too, of course, with the spotlight turned on the cultural critics. Say, if our historian got to wondering why it was that so many academic authors in the long late-twentieth century routinely, even obsessively, demonstrated their disdain for the sup-posed ignorance of earlier generations by placing scare quotes around their words? Just *listen* to how that sounds. Could they really have been convinced they were so much wiser back then (when their own technologies for revisiting the past still were in an in-fancy)?

This is a cautionary tale, some version of which I have held in mind as I have tried to make vivid more of the forgotten conditions and passionate concerns once addressed by music now two centuries old, music that for some of us grows only more captivating as time goes by, especially as we set side by side projects that were successful in their own day with others that failed. And we really have only just begun to excavate the worlds they came from! The chapters on Schubert and Schumann each focus on a single piece involving both music and text. Those texts range in scope (two operas, a song cycle, a song) and in subject matter, but every one of these works posed uncommon challenges to societal norms—theirs, and in altogether different ways again, to ours. They address po-litical freedom, marriage *à trois*, a woman's perspective (marriage again), and, more obliquely, same-sex passion. Nothing is more unstable, and yet can appear so firmly entrenched, as our present ideas about matters of identity and taste, or, come to think of it, about anything else that falls squarely into today's statistical normal. How fortunate that we have music to extend our vantage point. In its "reading" of a text a musical setting may direct our attention to cultural references no longer immediately understood: nowhere have I learned better how to read poetry than by way of song, which is like having a friend from an earlier time standing over your shoulder as you read, pointing out things on the page with eyes shining and a smile.

The two Beethoven essays take up broader currents of reception. I have included a brief interlude on striking gender imagery in nineteenth-century perceptions of Beethoven, a telling measure of changing sensibilities. Musicians who first resisted Beethoven could end up enthusiasts "like the partisans of Greek love" Carl Friedrich Zelter once observed, and later underwent this very conversion. It is good to know about him that he could change his mind (even with some of the old reservations still intact). More critically, by zooming in on the preoccupations of three such very different musical personalities as Schubert, Beethoven, and Schumann—two whose careers partially overlapped and a third whose music was deeply indebted to both of them—it is easier to gauge the significance of recurring themes, seeing how individual attitudes and ambitions fit with broader generational tendencies. Histories that imagine a uniform past, less diverse or less complex than life in the present, generally lose my attention fast, and I hope that the shifting focus of these essays will contribute to a livelier and more three-dimensional picture of trajectories of thought within the age.

At the beginning of the volume are studies of two Schubert operas, neither of which came to performance during the composer's lifetime, and both of them based on libretti crafted by friends of his. I explore the culture of Viennese censorship as a shaping force, as something that can tell us about such things as plot continuity, performance demeanor, and audience reaction in an age when sophisticated modes of indirect expression were cultivated as a matter of survival. Most everyone in 1820s Vienna knew that it was only a matter of time before the old social hierarchies collapsed, even as Prince Klemens von Metternich, the minister of state, led a determined campaign to suppress political dissent through police surveillance and tight censorship control. Through all this the theater remained the most public forum available for presenting views (naturally only indirectly) on such pressing social questions as the nature and limits of liberty, the definition and regulation of marriage, or the arbitrary authority of a legal system still bound up with ancient canon law. The contemporary fascination with medieval legend, ancient myth, and historical drama reflects these circumstances because displacing stories into distant times and places was a way for playwrights, librettists, and composers to air controversial positions before a captive public and to stir private debate. Such fictional projections let one exaggerate outmoded social beliefs and attitudes that persisted in the modern world. To the same end, all manner of musical emphases, even something as simple as a performer's tone of delivery, could be used to emancipate fleeting meanings from a libretto's script.

Alfonso und Estrella's libretto was cobbled together from a variety of sources, its characters drawn from an episode in medieval Spanish history, during several weeks of intense creative collaboration between Schubert and Franz von Schober and it successfully cleared the hurdle of the censor's desk. One stellar model for achieving this challenging goal with social criticism still intact was Mozart opera, which had enjoyed a comeback on Vienna's stages in the years around 1820 and remains a mainstay on ours today. I invoke Mozart's work in these pages not because I want to suggest that Schubert necessarily owed more to these classics than to other popular stage works that have fared less well over time, but because this is a shared part of our musical heritage that lets us vividly imagine the experiences of contemporary theatergoers who drew connections across the repertory, much as dedicated moviegoers do now (especially with those films they regard as instant classics). If we knew nothing more of *Figaro* today than its libretto, we never would have guessed how much more subversive was this production than the play of Beaumarchais, banned in Mozart's Vienna, from which it was adapted. Merely excavating the libretti of productions that once were talked about obviously is not enough. We need performances (at least of some). Finding commercially viable venues for performing "specialty interest" stage works—inventing them if need be—will surely be a defining challenge for musicians and scholars in this still young century of ours.

In contrast to *Alfonso und Estrella*, Schubert took up the composition of *Der Graf von Gleichen* only after the libretto had been banned. This project has generally been treated as a puzzling curiosity in Schubert scholarship, although, thankfully, we now have an edition of the manuscript draft and, in recent years, several completions have been performed. (Regrettably, of the two performances available on record today, neither is true even to the libretto. One freely alters its language, the other has made drastic cuts.) Strictly speaking, unfinished works can have no reception history, at least can have had no public impact in their own time. But the ambition of this opera project, and the forceful statement it was designed to make, becomes evident from a comparison with the numerous versions of the story that had been successfully brought to the stage before Schubert and Eduard von Bauernfeld decided to weigh in on the conversation. Long before Schubert seized upon it for the subject of his last opera, this fashionable story, based on a thirteenth-century legend, had become a vehicle for airing arguments about the proper and legal basis for marriage, ever—or so it seems—a conceptual cornerstone of society.

Marriage is a central theme in Schumann's *Frauenliebe und Leben* as well. My focus here is on the disjunction between modern misgivings about a male-authored song cycle that sets forth a woman's perspective on memorable milestones in her life, and the avant-garde musical aesthetic that made possible Schumann's moving portrayal of the widow's frustrated memory in the postlude. (A version of this study appeared in print a few years ago. I have updated a good many things, keeping intact the original structure as much as possible, and have added to it a postscript with some newer thoughts about performance history.)

While these scenes from a woman's life have seemed like a period piece now for well over a century, the cycle did reflect certain strains of forward social thinking in its own day. Schumann's songs point to the future—ours, in fact, which holds marriage more ideal than ever, even if, overall, our understanding of the terms of the contract has shifted. Chamisso's poems themselves are retrospective, told in the voice of a grandmother, by which he implicitly evoked his mother's generation even as he reflected on modern times. (From this angle we might compare his Woman—and Schumann's—to Max Ophuls's Contesse Louise, brilliantly portrayed by Danielle Darrieux in *The*

Earrings of Madame de . . ., a film from 1953 set around the turn of the century when Ophuls himself was a small boy. Here, too, the layers of historical representation are not easily disentangled: Which manners from 1895 had left palpable traces on 1953 experience, for example?)[1] Of course, Schubert's vision of a consensual three-way union in *Der Graf von Gleichen*, had it been completed, would have been a far greater provocation to society than Schumann's *Frauenliebe* songs, but both works championed a growing ideal of marriage by individual choice and willing consent, an expectation that rose to a rallying cry in the women's emancipation movement of the 1850s. I bring this out not to be perverse but because it helps explain the widespread appeal of the poems in their time. Marriage: the goal of romantic love. Unions long had been contracted for other reasons, serving mainly patrilineal interests, and arranged by third parties (a situation that fueled countless eighteenth century opera plots and plays). Even the new laws allowing court challenges to paternal wishes still kept economic barriers in place, as Robert Schumann and Clara Wieck experienced. Just a few short decades later, the very fact that anyone should be forced to make an appeal in court for permission to marry had come to seem intolerable.

"Music Recollected in Tranquillity: Postures of Memory in Beethoven" is intended as a companion to the *Frauenliebe* essay, exploring technical precedents for Schumann's surprising portrayal of interiority in the figure of "everywoman." Memory is a subject of renewed interest in the sciences and humanities today (as it was for the Romantics), and its role in the music of Beethoven has been remarked upon with some regularity, although rarely worked out in great detail. Stimulated by these suggestions, I was fascinated to note the many different varieties and forms of memory we can discern and Beethoven's imaginative techniques for distinguishing them. This is not the place for an extended treatment of the subject either, but it seems useful to linger over a few instances that show the even greater experiential precision in Schumann's portrayal of a surviving spouse's memory, with its powerful fusion of consolation and despair—all inspired by a vivid identification with Chamisso's woman. At any rate, I see no reason why we must keep Schumann's song cycle locked into discussions about gender portrayal alone.

At the end, we return to Schubert, and to the oldest of the essays in this volume, which brings to the fore again the devastating police action that left its mark on *Alfonso und Estrella*, seen now from a different angle. I have updated a few things here as well, bringing in brief replies to some of the public reaction these ideas have provoked. My study of Schubert's Platen song "Du liebst mich nicht" was conceived in the wake of Maynard Solomon's groundbreaking biographical investigation into Schubert's sexuality. A flurry

---

1. This is further complicated in the film by one anachronous detail: Louise fainted during the Lisbon earthquake, her husband relates, but this took place in 1755! (It is the subject of a famous poem by Voltaire, friend to another Madame de ***; Ophuls's film title trails off because Louise's family name is only ever spoken when we are out of hearing range.) Even earlier in the film a thick historical texture permeates the action at the Paris opera, as the lost earrings (*oreilles*) are sought in vain to the strains of "J'ai perdu mon Euridice" of Gluck.

of responses to his proposal appeared in the 1990s, grappling with what this might mean
for an understanding of the music. I thought it more profitable to turn the question
around: What did discourse about same-sex passion sound like in the early nineteenth
century, and how did Schubert engage the subject? The Platen song sprang to mind
because its resonance with the myth of Narcissus long had struck me. What provoked the
historical detective work was the misfit I perceived between previous attempts to explain
(or explain away) the song's surprising rhetoric and my own instinct that Schubert's drastic musical emphases point to exactly the terms needed to grasp the referential background of Platen's poem, mythic and psycholgical.

In a climate of repressive censorship composers could take pleasure in reinforcing prohibited political or social meanings that operated just beneath the radar of full awareness.
There was a long tradition of this in music for the stage, as we shall explore in the opera
studies. Plus, censorship was not only a powerful shaping force but at times itself an un-
dercurrent of meaning in early nineteenth-century Viennese theater, opera, and song.
Just think of the Venetian gondolier in Schubert and Johann Mayrhofer's "Gondelfahrer"
who all alone is still awake at midnight and standing watch as the others slumber
peacefully—like the solitary boatman whose duty it was to enforce the ancient Venice
curfew, safeguarding the city's Christian population during the hours between sundown
to sunrise from residents of the Jewish ghetto (this ordinance was lifted only in 1797
when Napoleon's troops came through). That goes two ways in a poem written by a freethinking, yet apparently dutiful censor in the employ of an autocratic state in which
tolerance for divergent beliefs was fast eroding: atheism was now a serious charge, Freemasonry legal no longer, dreams of self-determination and nationhood the ultimate
threat. (Naturally, the poem's imagery can also be read in cosmic terms: the boatman who
ferries souls to a final rest, or in any number of other provocative ways.)[2] It helped such
indirect meanings to thrive, of course, that music was widely admired for its abstraction
and that even its sheer beauty could distract. Much more work is needed exploring the
historical and social conditions that shaped 1820s sensibilities before we will have an ac-
curate picture of this music's functioning in its own time: how convenient it was, though,
that interest in the opacity of musical meaning should have flourished among Romantic
critics at this precise historical moment when open expression was so hampered.

Throughout this book I have tried to refrain from over interpretation when the historical documents themselves capture the dynamic of the situation: What was novel or eccentric or even reckless? What was widely accepted? What was public? What was hidden?
What was on a path distant from our world? What was delightfully modern? I do not

---

2. David T. Bretherton offers an intriguing interpretation connecting these songs to Italian freedom fighters in
the 1820s in "The Shadow of Midnight in Schubert's 'Gondelfahrer' Settings," *Music and Letters* 92 (2011):
1–42. To my ears, Schubert's partsong (D 809) invites oblique hearing even more than the solo setting (D
808): among other oddities, the midnight chimes from St. Mark's in Mayrhofer's poem are heard only to strike
"six" in the partsong.

necessarily assign privileged status to the understanding of contemporaries. The reactions of modern observers—whose interests may lie closer to our own—can sometimes provide as good or an even sharper focus on the motivations of the past, drawing out tendencies less apparent or less noteworthy to contemporaries. At other times the very alienation expressed by modern observers is a clue that conditions necessary to understanding vanishing mind-sets have been buried or forgotten. Recognizing this, we should check the impulse to turn our distant forebears into easy targets of our disapproval, for they are even less able to answer back than are the merely geographically distant cultures that we study. (This is not to say, of course, that we ought not be critical.) These problems become acute when our conversations turn to the social structuring of gender, whose outgrowth or separation from nature was an impassioned topic of debate in the early nineteenth century, and which has continued to gather momentum and political force in our time, rapidly transforming expectations and coloring how we weigh the social arguments of the past. Here it seems to me especially important to position creative ambitions in the intellectual currents of their own time. What once seemed radical can become normative with time; what once seemed ordinary can appear distorted and extreme in another age. We cannot do justice to a complex past—its successes, its failures, and its unrealized hopes—if we are afraid to lose ourselves in another world. These critical essays, accordingly, represent my own effort to trace a path back in time, to hear life's color in some impressive musical ruins (or sometimes, sadly, only promising torsos), so caringly preserved for us by generations of selfless editors and dedicated performers. Without their painstaking efforts, projects such as this one would not have been conceivable.

I have sketched historical situations (and modern ones) as much as possible with first-hand testimony, using letters, diaries, reviews, essays, and other records of past conversations, however fragmentary, to bring distant concerns back into earshot. Sometimes an abundance of directly pertinent testimony has not come down, however, or the surviving documents do not address exactly the questions we are asking today. This is a problem with all historical reconstruction, and those difficulties are further magnified when social or commercial pressures discouraged the creation of written records in the first place. For several of the studies in this book I have had to travel farther afield for evidence that is necessarily circumstantial, turning, for example, to Franz Grillparzer's run-ins with censorship and the reception of Johann Wolfgang von Goethe's *Stella* to help situate Schubert's *Der Graf von Gleichen*, or to early nineteenth-century views on women's literary ambitions to show how a project like Schumann's *Frauenliebe und Leben* fit into broader tendencies. My goal has been to restore to awareness lately neglected directions of thought around significant musical projects by three major voices in early nineteenth-century cultural life by listening in on the conversations they were a part of. This means that I have been more concerned to illuminate possible, plausible avenues of reception in the age, and to identify the mechanisms of communication involved, than to set down a firm vision of what must have happened.

VANISHING SENSIBILITIES

Words do not constitute an overt act; they remain only in idea. When considered by themselves, they generally have no determinate signification, for this depends on the tone in which they are uttered. It often happens that in repeating the same words they have not the same meaning; this depends on their connection with other things, and sometimes more is signified by silence than by any expression whatever. Since there can be nothing so equivocal and ambiguous as all this, how is it possible to convert it into a crime of high treason? Wherever this law is established, there is an end not only of liberty, but even of its very shadow.

—CHARLES-LOUIS DE SECONDAT, Baron de Montesquieu, *The Spirit of Laws*

I

Liberty in the Theater, or the Emancipation of Words

OLD FRIENDS

O ewige Nacht! Wann wirst du schwinden? Wann wird das Licht mein Auge finden? (Eternal Night! When will you finally pass away? When will my eyes meet the light?) Tamino's language conspicuously is veiled, and a cryptic choral voice replies, "Bald Jüngling, oder nie" (soon, young man, or never). Hearing that Pamina still lives, Tamino picks up his flute. The beasts in the forest may be enchanted, but alas, Pamina does not hear. *Höre! Höre mich*! he cries, listens intently, then turns away in dejection: "umsonst" (no use). The singer has only to look out into the audience in search of Pamina for these words to take on a resonance beyond the onstage plot, cutting through the theater's imaginary fourth wall. "Umsonst:" it is we who have not heard Tamino's cry. The oblique language and puzzling turns of Schikaneder's plot long have provoked political interpretation: heard as a direct appeal to the audience, "hear me!" is an invitation to read against the grain of the officially approved libretto.

Other such moments in *The Magic Flute* spring to mind. Recall, for another, Pamina's blazing words *"Die Wahrheit,* sei sie auch verbrechen" (the truth, and were that a crime), her reply to Papageno's "what shall we say?" when they are caught fleeing Sarastro's realm. And consider Sarastro's response to Pamina's plea for mercy after she confesses her "criminal" effort to escape Monostatos's wicked lechery and Sarastro's power: "zur Liebe will ich dich nicht zwingen, *doch* [his voice drops down a tenth] *doch geb' ich dir die Freiheit nicht"* (I shall not force your love, but I will not grant you freedom). Mozart evidently expected these words to offend the ears of

enlightened audiences even then, for the menacing range sets in relief the contradictions inherent in "benevolent autocracy" as a power structure.[1]

Words break free of the situation on stage in another way in *Don Giovanni*'s first-act
finale with the abrupt shift from E♭ to a brilliant C major as the masked guests enter the
ballroom and cries of "viva la libertà" break out all around. Mozart's exhilarating trum-
pet-and-drums martial rhetoric carries us away even as we realize how nonsensical this is
as a party greeting heard a dozen times over (the stage action freezes for rather too long).
The words refer to the "Maskenfreiheit" of the ballroom, the license to party in ano-
nymity, but Mozart's music draws something more from the moment with a rousing military style that called up the fervent hopes for political liberty that filled the air after the
American Revolution. Liberty meant something different to each of the actors who lifted
a glass in her name—after all, it could serve the interests of the libertine as well as of the
nobles scheming to expose him. This leads to social chaos at the ball, where tension from
the din of three orchestras in conflicting meters playing dances associated with the upper,
middle, and lower classes builds to a huge storm cloud, saturated and ready to burst, and
Zerlina's lightning screams confirm the breakdown of society's rules and the fears this
aroused. The censors eventually took notice of the passage, for the words were changed to
"viva la società" in Habsburg-friendly Italy during the 1820s.[2] Joviality replaced liberty,
likewise, in Viennese performances given in German translation: "Es lebe die Freiheit, die
Freiheit soll leben!" became "Es lebe die Fröhlichkeit, die Fröhlichkeit soll leben!"[3]

Music's sheer beauty may *distract* us from hearing in similar fashion the very first words
that Beethoven's Leonore sings: "wie groß ist die Gefahr; wie schwach der Hoffnung
Schein" (how grave is the danger; how weak the rays of hope, or "how weak the sem-
blance of hope"). Leonore already has been introduced in spoken dialogue as the young
lad Fidelio, the intriguing stranger who has earned the quiet admiration of the prison
warden and his daughter. After divisi violas and celli have established the intensity of
feeling, Marzelline begins the canon "Mir ist so wunderbar" accompanied by pizzicato
strings and intertwining clarinets and flutes that mask Leonore's plainly different words.

1. In a probing monograph about power dynamics on the late eighteenth-century stage, Ivan Nagel explores
   many such cases of pleading for mercy and the granting of clemency. Ivan Nagel, *Autonomy and Mercy:
   Reflections on Mozart's Operas*, trans. Marion Faber and Ivan Nagel (Cambridge, Mass.: Harvard University
   Press, 1991). Originally published in German: Ivan Nagel, *Autonomie und Gnade: Über Mozarts Opern*
   (Munich: Carl Hanser Verlag, 1988).
2. Pierluigi Petrobelli, "Don Giovanni in Italia," *Analecta Musicologica* 18 (1978): 36. Also cited in Julian Rushton, *W. A. Mozart: Don Giovanni*, Cambridge Opera Handbooks (Cambridge: Cambridge University Press,
   1981), 140.
3. *Don Giovanni* received its first Viennese performance in German translation in 1792 in Schikaneder's Freihaus-
   theater. W. E. Yates, *Theatre in Vienna: A Critical History, 1776–1995* (Cambridge: Cambridge University Press,
   1996), 26, 139. A stimulating discussion of this passage appears in an exchange of letters between Robert Marshall
   and Charles Rosen, "What Mozart Meant: An Exchange," *New York Review of Books*, 6 December 2007. See also
   Anthony Arblaster, *Viva la Libertà: Politics in Opera* (London: Verso, 1992), 13–44. Long before, of course, we had
   Rosen's comments in *The Classical Style: Haydn, Mozart, Beethoven* (New York: Norton, 1971), 94–95, 322–25.

We strain to make out what she sings, but the counterpoint obscures the goal of each thought, rendering "Gefahr" and "Schein" inaudible. With Rocco's entry, Leonore's words briefly are exposed as they dart through the texture in an inner voice—"wie groß, wie groß ist die Gefahr"—their natural declamation subordinated to the need for rhythmic momentum and to imitation of Marzelline's gestures. The canon is the one number that Joseph von Sonnleithner added to Jean-Nicolas Bouilly's original libretto, no doubt in part to satisfy a local Viennese fashion for operatic canons.[4] It was inserted into the libretto's exposition, whose main task it is to establish the characters' relations to one another for the audience. Here Leonore stands before us as Fidelio in the disguise she must maintain before the other characters on the stage. This gives the illusion that we are privy to her inner thoughts and aware, with her, of the dangers that lurk within the plot. But this is a French revolutionary story displaced into sixteenth-century Seville out of political necessity, a pressure ever present for the early nineteenth-century Viennese theatergoer who would have been surprised to see recent politics portrayed directly. (The temporal displacement, significantly, is made only in the German adaptations of Bouilly's *Léonore ou L'amour conjugal*, not in the French original, which Christine Siegert's study of multiple German translations of Bouilly's libretto for Cherubini's *Les deux journées* has shown belongs to a larger pattern of suppression in libretti crafted for Vienna.)[5] Much like the appearance of the masked guests in *Don Giovanni*, Leonore's disguise is a transparent illusion within the illusion acted on stage. When Jaquino finally enters into the quartet (still standing apart from the others, as the stage direction specifies), his seething anger is masked by the classically balanced, unreactive melody that treats "my hair stands on end" no differently from "she loves him, it is clear"; but Beethoven takes care that we shall hear Jaquino's words at the end of the exquisite canon, giving him a rhythmic patter

---

4. On the Viennese opera canon, see Heinrich W. Schwab, "'Mir ist so wunderbar.' Zum Kanon auf der Opernbühne," in *Von der Leonore zum Fidelio: Vorträge und Referate des Bonner Symposions 1997*, ed. Helga Lühning and Wolfram Steinbeck, Bonner Schriften zur Musikwissenschaft 4 (Frankfurt: Lang, 2000), 235–48, and Dorothea Link, "The Viennese Operatic Canon and Mozart's 'Così fan tutte," *Mitteilungen der Internationalen Stiftung Mozarteum* 38 (1990): 111–21.

5. Helmut C. Jacobs, "Jean Nicolas Bouilly (1763–1842) und die Genese des Leonorenstoffes: 'Léonore ou L'amour conjugal' als 'Fait historique' der Revolutionszeit," *Archiv für Musikwissenschaft* 48 (1991): 216; Christine Siegert, "Brüderlichkeit als Problem: Zur Rezeption von Luigi Cherubinis *Les deux journées*," in *Early Music: Context and Ideas II*, International Conference in Musicology, 11–14 September 2008, ed. Zofia Fabiańska, Alicja Jarzębska, Wojciech Marchwica, Piotr Poźniak, and Zygmunt M. Szweykowski (Kraków: Jagiellonian University, 2008), 306–35. Siegert demonstrates that the two versions of Cherubini's opera adapted for Vienna by Georg Friedrich Treitschke and for the Theater an der Wien systematically blunted all references to political turmoil and made far more significant alterations than did other German translations of this story set during the seventeenth-century Fronde rebellion. In the Viennese productions the wicked Cardinal Mazarin was stripped of his ecclesiastical affiliations (as he was in Catholic Munich) and transformed into a minister of state. Ironically, in later years this alteration might actually have encouraged spectators to catch a glimpse of their own minister of state in the figure of Mazarin. (It would be interesting to know about productions in which he became a non-ecclesiastical figure how they dealt with the "et incarnatus est" music that Cherubini used to accompany the Italian soldiers' expression of loyalty to Mazarin.)

that cuts through the texture: *Mir fällt kein Mittel ein, mir fällt kein Mittel ein, mir sträubt sich schon das Haar, der Vater willigt ein, mir wird so wunderbar, mir fällt kein Mittel ein.* Rocco, he fears, is going to grant Marzelline and Fidelio the necessary consent to marry. This is the situation within the plot. But "der Vater" also was a commonplace contemporary usage for the emperor. If we substitute this meaning, it gives an independent coherence to the words—"I can come up with no solution, I can come up with no solution, my hair stands on end, the father gives his consent, how fantastical all this seems, I can come up with no solution!" *Mir*, however, "fällt ein Mittel ein" (despite Jaquino's avowals to the contrary): here is a recipe for circumventing the censors! The escaping words of course would have carried different associations at the 1805 premiere when the city was occupied by French troops and freedoms won under Joseph II were fast eroding (for the young Emperor Franz was easily swayed by the savvy politicians at his court); at performances of the 1814 revision or when the canon alone was performed before the assembled heads of state attending the Congress of Vienna; and again at the 1822 revival when Austria effectively had become a police state under Metternich. One might imagine that a subversive hearing would have been most widely tempting at the 1822 production; nevertheless, the potential always was there. Here, I will note only in passing that seated in the audience for both the 1814 production and the November 1822 *Fidelio* revival was Franz Schubert, and that two of the 1822 cast members also performed Schubert partsongs at the Gesellschaft der Musikfreunde that year: they were Jakob Wilhelm Rauscher, the Jaquino, and Johann Nestroy (Don Fernando), who went on to become Austria's greatest comic playwright and political satirist. Moreover, the Schubert champion Johann Michael Vogl originally was slated to sing Florestan in 1822 (he had been Pizarro in 1814). If anyone was in a position to delight in Beethoven's dangerous attitudes, they surely were.[6] In any case, it is important that the canon to some degree always stands apart from the time and situation of the opera, as Helga Lühning too has remarked.[7] This prepares us to listen so to speak à

---

6. We find reverential uses by the dozen of "der Vater" for the emperor in Joseph Rossi, *Denkbuch für Fürst und Vaterland* (Vienna: J. B. Wallishauser, 1814), a commemorative volume celebrating the emperor's triumphant return from Paris following Napoleon's surrender and the signing of the allied treaty in May 1814. Nicholas Mathew examines Beethoven's role in official celebrations surrounding this event in "Beethoven's Political Music, the Handelian Sublime, and the Aesthetics of Prostration," *19th Century Music* 33 (2009): 110–50. He aligns the message of Beethoven's Ninth Symphony with spectacles mounted by the state when he describes a performance of Handel's "Thunder Chorus" this way: "They sang a newly written text to the chorus that transformed it into a kind of Ode to Joy—the repeated word 'Freude' (joy) in each verse coinciding with Handel's rousing vocal melismas" (121). We should be clear, however: Beethoven's "Ode to Joy" is just as far removed from the sentiment of this political poem as is the Handelian original.

7. Helga Lühning, ed., *Leonore: Oper in zwei Aufzügen von Ludwig van Beethoven: Das Libretto der Aufführung von 1806* (Bonn: Beethoven-Haus, 1996). She writes: "Das einzige Stück, für das Sonnleithner in Bouilly's Libretto weder Vorlage noch Anregung fand, ist das Quartett *Mir ist so wunderbar*. Und ausgerechnet dieser *Canon* ist, wie keine andere Nummer der Oper, durch eine einzigartige dramatisch-musikalische Gestaltungsidee geprägt, die sie der Handlungssituation vollkommen enthebt" (23). Lühning returns to the matter in "Über die unendlichen Augenblicke im *Fidelio*," *Bonner Beethoven Studien* 4 (2005): 111–20. Here

gauche when, later, in the first-act finale, a male chorus of prisoners sings a ten-minute hymn to freedom. And in the quintet that joins the chorus at the end of the act, after a chastened Rocco has eased his mind over the role he is to play in Pizarro's plot against Florestan by urging that the other prisoners be let free (showing himself willing to sacrifice one to save many, a most undemocratic principle), Jaquino's words once more cut through the jumble of hushed voices: "if only I could understand what everyone is saying!" he sings as we ourselves are straining to hear (this was added in 1814).[8]

The strategies differ, but in each of these situations in *The Magic Flute*, *Don Giovanni*, and *Fidelio* the predisposed hearer is encouraged to associate words with events beyond the fiction on the stage. For brief moments, something grabs hold of our attention (a style that is out of place, conspicuous word repetition, or simply the angle of a performer's delivery), inviting us to reflect on forbidden things, the real-world restrictions that shape expression on the stage. Parallels with the here and now suggest themselves, then quickly evaporate. In none of these situations has there been an explicit break in character or change of address (as we find, for example, in the banquet scene in Giuseppe Gazzaniga and Giovanni Bertati's *Don Giovanni Tenorio* where Pasquariello and Don Giovanni raise a toast to the ladies of Venice).[9] To be most effective, and indeed to have gotten past the

---

she examines more closely how the canon is made to stand apart, noting that this "free zone" is created by music's power alone ("Die Musik schafft sich den Freiraum ganz allein und trotzdem auf so überwältigende Art, dass sie die Zweifel an der dramatischen Legitimation des Quartetts vergessen lässt" [113]).

8. This technique is spoofed in a comic trio in Joseph Weigl's 1809 *Die Schweizerfamilie* (a strangely uneventful and seemingly apolitical plot in which an idyllic miniature Switzerland is erected within "German" borders). A letter has arrived, filling the Count, Durmann, and Paul with anticipation. Paul, the tenor, teases the audience with his silly repetitive patter: "Man muß doch jedes Ding entfalten, will man davon den Inhalt sehn" (should one wish to see the content of *any thing*, one must first unfold it). This either hints at a secret meaning or is absurd for stating the obvious over and over. When finally it is opened, the letter is a letdown (reporting that there is no news to report), and all suspense raised by the trio is instantly deflated. We celebrate the dramatic power of *Fidelio*, especially the denouement in the quartet "Er sterbe!" that builds to an unprecedented level of tension before Leonore draws her pistol. Weigl's ultra-naive lyric opera aims for the exact opposite, a kind of antidrama at every turn. Anna Milder premiered both the heroic Leonore and Emmeline, the exaggeratedly mawkish Swiss teenager deranged by her yearning for the echoing valley where Jakob Fribourg stayed behind. The Count, who adores these common people, spares no labor or expense to ensure that they will remain on his land: a perfect facsimile of their Swiss village, enclosed by a high wall, is built on stage. Quite incredulously, Till Gerrit Waidelich finds in the fictional creation Emmeline merely a true mirror of the sensibility of a "typically naive girl in *Biedermeier* times." See his essay "'diese in Tönen geschriebene Liebesgeschichte, welche wie keine mehr den Namen einer deutschen *Volksoper* verdient': Zur Rezeptionsgeschichte von Joseph Weigls *Schweizer Familie* in Biedermeier und Vormärz," in *Schubert: Perspektiven*, 2 (Stuttgart: Franz Steiner Verlag, 2002), 180–81. (By the same token, then, I suppose Julia Roberts's superbly portrayed Vivian Ward in the sentimental rags-to-riches Hollywood picture *Pretty Woman* must be an equally "authentisches Abbild" of a 1990 call girl's sensibility? I think not: when this film was released, I had a New York neighbor from whose window came blasting the theme song at the same hour every night until, thankfully, he finally grew tired of it.)

9. Paolo Gallarati has noted that Mozart in fact tends to maintain the autonomy of the world represented on stage, addressing the audience only rarely for an effect of comic alienation. He attributes Mozart's sensitivity here to his familiarity with spoken theater. "Mozart and Eighteenth-Century Comedy," in *Opera Buffa in Mozart's Vienna*, ed. Mary Hunter and James Webster (Cambridge: Cambridge University Press, 1997), 108–9.

censors in the first place, such doubled moments capable of calling to mind contemporary events (perhaps only semiconsciously) must stand out without straining the coherence of the fictional representation. Alternatively, nonsense must appear to rule throughout.

DIE VERKEHRTE WELT

At the start of Ludwig Tieck's 1798 play *Die verkehrte Welt* (The World Upside-Down) the Epilogue steps forward and begins: "Now gentleman, how did you enjoy the play?" Tieck designated his work "a historical play in five acts" (ein historisches Schauspiel): it is an eyewitness account of a lifetime's theatrical practice. Writing about the *Leonore* operas, Helmut C. Jacobs observed that "historical" events or anecdotes came to mean not only those events from the distant past that could be held as a mirror to the contemporary world but also current events to which one had been an eyewitness.[10] Tieck's play turns a wide-angle lens to the theater itself. This can be hilarious, as when the innkeeper quizzes the stranger who asks for a room: "you are surely from the old school, isn't that right? A man of the old stamp, perhaps translated from the English?"[11] Numerous oblique references to contemporary political events are slipped in: the play is an eyewitness in this double sense, addressing both current affairs and eighteenth-century stage trends. When the curtain first rises, another stage is revealed within the stage, and an audience is seen watching it. In the opening scene a poet-playwright bickers with one of his characters, Skaramuz, who does not see why the poet should control the proceedings.[12] When the poet reproaches him he replies *Ich höre nichts*! "I hear nothing: Mr. Poet, see how I cover my ears!" *Aber das Stük*! "But the play!" exclaims the poet. *Was Stük! Ich bin auch ein Stük und ich habe auch das Recht mitzusprechen.* "What play! I too am a play, and have the right to my own say-so. Or do you think I haven't got my own will, that the illustrious Sir Actor always is forced to do what you command? Oh, but Sir, how very quickly the times sometimes do change." A short while later a member of the audience, Grünhelm (green helmet), objects that audiences expect to be entertained, not subjected to such quarreling, and to show the poet how this is done he begins to sing "Der Vogelfänger bin ich ja" from *The Magic Flute*. The audience cheers, and Grünhelm addresses the poet, "Nun? Sehn sie mein Herr, das ist nur eins von meinen *Mitteln*" (Now what do you think of that, dear Sir? And this is but one of my methods)!

10. Jacobs, "Jean Nicolas Bouilly (1763–1842) und die Genese des Leonorenstoffes," 208.

11. For more on this passage I can recommend Peter Szondi, "Friedrich Schlegel and Romantic Irony, with Some Remarks on Tieck's Comedies," in *On Textual Understanding and Other Essays*, trans. Harvey Mendelsohn, foreword by Michael Hays, Theory and History of Literature, vol. 15 (Minneapolis: University of Minnesota Press, 1986), 57–74.

12. Scaramuccia is the commedia dell'arte character from whom Leporello is also partly descended. These literary roots are explored in Charles C. Russell, *The Don Juan Legend before Mozart: With a Collection of Eighteenth-Century Opera Librettos* (Ann Arbor: University of Michigan Press, 1993).

The division between stage and audience constantly is reset in Tieck's play, forcing us to stay alert if we are to follow the actors' movements across the theatrical space. Grün-helm longs to try out what he has learned as a theatergoer, but Pierrot, tired of his life on the other side, decides to take a giant leap across the footlights "as if from the famed Leucadian rock," hoping either to die or to be transformed into a spectator by this stunt. In this inverted world the stage is a confining place where roles are locked in place: free-dom lies beyond. A string of plays-within-plays is performed in the second act, prompt-ing one character to ask, "what if it turned out that we too were in a play?" At one point the theater machinist shows off his talents with a spectacular thunderstorm that leaves the actors drenched without warning and furious. The audience would be disappointed if the show had no storm, he explains, and reveals how it is done: "I've got some rosin dust which I blow across a light source: this makes lightning; at the same moment an iron ball is rolled upstairs 'und das bedeutet dann den Donner'" (and then that means thun-d-d-der). All these self-conscious scenes and chaotic plots produce a grand non-sense in which every theatrical convention, contemporary plot archetype, and machin-ist's trick is laid bare. Everyone, we realize, has his own agenda. Hidden behind several layers of theatrical illusion is a plot about a young couple terrified to ask the girl's father to let them marry and the father is so moved by their performance that he gives his consent. The couple, played by the tragic muse and a young man we have just encountered as "the stranger" have resorted to putting on a play about another pair seeking parental consent to marry, leaving the young man with twinges of guilt over this underhanded portrayal of their own situation. The domestic became a safe haven for portraying the political.[13]

This all must have seemed even funnier to late eighteenth-century and early nine-teenth-century audiences, who were accustomed to arbitrary displays of power and rigid censorship control from absolutist rulers increasingly on the defensive. Even Mozart's famous joke from the glockenspiel in the pit during *The Magic Flute*'s opening run—when Papageno's magic bells suddenly displayed a mind of their own and Schikaneder had no choice but to improvise a reply on the spot—is raised to a higher power when we consider that the Viennese authorities, along with extending censorship to the theater (originally in 1770), absurdly had tried to ban extemporization to prevent performers from adding back in what the censors had struck.[14]

Mere gesture or pantomime could carry ideological messages too, of course, and these were even harder to regulate. The Leucadian leap that Tieck's Pierrot hoped would transform him from an actor into a spectator refers to an expiatory rite of Apollo whereby criminals were thrown from the Leucadian cliffs into the sea, feathers tarred to their

---

13. We see this reflected again some years later in the censor's alteration of the title for Schubert's 1823 opera *Die Verschworenen* (The Conspirators) to *Der häusliche Krieg* (The Domestic War). A charming little comedy based on Aristophanes's *Lysistrata*, it encourages women to take political action, prescribing a surefire path to victory: they must band together and withhold sex until their husbands agree to stop fighting wars.

14. Yates, *Theatre in Vienna*, 9.

limbs. If they survived the fall, they were let go free. If not, they got to know another form of freedom. Partly for philosophical reasons and partly because this leap of faith allowed for high-tech stagecraft and sound effects, it began to appear on stages everywhere: a character might plunge from a tower onto a cushioned platform out of sight from the audience, with a delayed crash backstage, or perhaps a realistic illusion might be created with the pulley-operated ropes that Italian theater machinists had used to simulate flight since the seventeenth century. In Franz Grillparzer's *Sappho*, a smash hit at the Burgtheater in 1818, Sappho plunges from the Leucadian cliff to cure herself of her unrequited passion for Phaon, who has abandoned her for a younger, more conventionally feminine Melitta (following a performance in Dresden, however, there were complaints that Phaon played the part "too close to Grillparzer's intent," arousing the indignation of the audience).[15] Moments before she throws herself from the cliff, the other characters see a strange look of clarity and contentment come over her. Something similar occurs in Schubert and Johann Mayrhofer's song "Atys" (1817), where the ending is changed from the Catullan original to allow for a deadly plunge after Attis is overcome with longing for an irretrievable past. No direct mention is made of the source of his anguish: in a fit of madness he has castrated himself to serve the goddess Cybele and now has come to regret that act. The song ends with the longest postlude Schubert ever wrote, a return of the music from the song's opening now in the piano alone, heard as if from another world.[16] Fiction and reality came together twenty years later when Mayrhofer, a longtime censor, took his own leap of faith from the top floor of the censorship office, transforming himself from an actor on the world's stage to a spectator from the beyond.

When Tieck revised *The World Upside-Down* for publication in *Phantasus* (3 vols., 1812–16), he removed all the overt political commentary and added an introductory

---

15. Norbert Fuerst, *Grillparzer auf der Bühne: Eine fragmentarische Geschichte* (Vienna: "Manutiuspresse" Wulf Stratowa Verlag, 1958), 43. In act 4 Sappho still cried out in solitary despair: "protect me, ye Gods, from myself. The dark spirits in my innards have wakened and rattle the iron bars of my prison" (und rütteln an des Kerkers Eisenstäben).

16. In a probing review of Ruurrd R. Nauta and Annette Harder, eds., *Catullus' Poem on Attis: Texts and Contexts* (Leiden: Koninklijke Brill, 2005), Jane Lightfoot unexpectedly brings in Schubert ("Matrons without Stains," *Times Literary Supplement*, 22 July 2005). She admires Caroline Kroon's "text linguistic" approach for its insight into how the poem achieves its effect through repetition, "all sources of which—lexical, phonetic, syntactic, metrical, thematic—are inventoried, together with diligent attention to the use of tense, narrative pace, clause-types and sentence connectives. The effect that emerges is one of 'swaying' backwards and forwards between a number of themes, especially the theme of wandering, and perhaps even that of repetition itself." This reminds her that in 1817 Schubert wrote a song about Attis using a poem by his friend, "the homosexual poet and classicist manque Johann Mayrhofer, which is clearly based on Catullus' original. Mayrhofer all but drops the theme of castration, but concentrates on that of loss and estrangement from home; at the end of the poem his Attis plunges from a height into the woods, presumably to his death." She believes that Schubert understood the aesthetic of the Catullan original, even if he may not have known it directly, pointing to the song's "mesmeric triple time, . . . the sense of swaying conveyed by modulations between A minor and major, and . . . the ABA structure whereby a central passage of passionate declamation is enclosed by hypnotic outer sections. Attis' opening lament and eventual death thus take place to the same trance-like melody."

symphony and musical interludes, whose content is paraphrased in words: in stark contrast to the whimsically changing plots of the spoken play, the most sustained arguments in vivid poetic imagery sound through this music, leaving the poet-playwright distressed to find himself so moved by music's "noble nonsense." The overture, marked *forte*, builds to a striking cadence: *Gebt acht! Gebt aber auf die rechte Art acht! hört zu! hört zu! zu! zu!! zu!!!* (Pay attention! Pay the right sort of attention! Listen close! Listen close! close! close!! close!!!)

Tieck's play celebrates a mode of attention that we do not often bring to this repertory today. *The World Upside-Down* encouraged contemporary listeners to hear what the sheer sounds of words and the eloquent speech of music had to say, and it urged them to pay close heed to those fleeting meanings that arise in the moment, downgrading the concern for plot coherence or character development. Winfried Menninghaus in fact sees in this "poetics of nonsense" and the related idea of "das wunderbare" a critical and undervalued tendency in Romantic aesthetics, best exemplified, perhaps, in Tieck's *Puss in Boots* (in which play one audience member remarks to his neighbor at intermission that this is a *Magic Flute* imitation and they even roll out the sets for the trial by fire and water) and *Bluebeard's Seven Wives*. Drawing on formulations by Novalis and Tieck he writes:

> We call *wunderbar* those "elements" or "objects" of poetry that obey no justification or derivation, but which simply "are there all of a sudden, without cause." Or in the words of Ludwig Tieck: *wunderbar* is "everything in which we perceive an effect without knowing its origin" and which in this sense is "incomprehensible" to our causality-oriented mode of thought.[17]

Part of the fun of this in the theater was to tease audiences with the possibility of a hidden sense, often one that had a political edge. Another fine example presents itself in one of the musical episodes in *The World Upside-Down*, a rondo between acts 3 and 4 with the refrain "here there is no sense" that culminates in an aesthetic manifesto:

> From the mosquito to the elephant, to say nothing of the human being, everything is first and foremost there for its own sake. Why should it not be so with our thoughts, which are prior to their deployment? Why not also for our moods and joys and laughter (*Laune und Lust und Lachen*) and with a world turned

---

17. "Wunderbar heißen solche 'Elemente' oder 'Gegenstände' der Poesie, die keiner Begründung oder Ableitung gehorchen, sondern einfach 'da [sind], auf einmal, ohne Veranlassung.' Oder mit Ludwig Tiecks Worten: wunderbar heißt 'alles, wo wir eine Wirkung ohne eine Ursache wahrnehmen' und was insofern für unser Kausalitäts-orientiertes Denken 'unbegreiflich' ist." Winfried Menninghaus, *Lob des Unsinns: Über Kant, Tieck und Blaubart* (Frankfurt: Suhrkamp Verlag, 1995), 56. For an English translation of his book, see Winfried Menninghaus, *In Praise of Nonsense: Kant and Bluebeard*, trans. Henry Pickford (Stanford, Calif.: Stanford University Press, 1999).

upside-down? Just invert it one more time, and you'll bring the right-side up, and then you no longer will be tempted to say: here there is no sense!

THE CULTURE OF VIENNESE CENSORSHIP AND METTERNICH

I

The use of the theater to refract recent events was a well-established tradition on Vienna's stages by the early nineteenth century, as it was, indeed, throughout Europe, and the techniques that creative ingenuity devised to combat censorial control evolved steadily, not unlike slang usages that mutate as soon as they are widely understood. W. E. Yates has argued that the role of Viennese theater censorship shifted over time, starting out in the 1770s as an educational tool at the court to model good speech and manners and only gradually becoming an instrument of political oppression hostile to Enlightenment ideas. This distinction is somewhat tricky to maintain—although the restrictions certainly changed over time and censorship increased—since to promote some things means inevitably to suppress others, and this rarely is benign.[18] Nevertheless, it is helpful to consider that censorship exerted pressure not only by what was forbidden but also by what officially was encouraged—or even coerced.

Even in those productions that appeared superficially to be consonant with the state's interests, double-pronged meanings were possible: the bombastic displays of patriotism that swept across Austria after Napoleon's defeats cannot all have been motivated by a simple heartfelt love of country, even if some people will have been content to take them at face value. This at least is what is implied by Wenzel Tomaschek's report that Beethoven declared his *Wellington's Victory*, op. 91, to be a "folly, and that he liked it only because with it he had thoroughly thrashed the Viennese."[19] A similar false tone at the close of Grillparzer's play *König Ottokars Glück und Ende* a decade later left the censors uneasy. It

---

18. Yates, *Theatre in Vienna*, 9–10. A memorandum from 1770 by Joseph Sonnenfels, the director of the court theater, stated that censors were to restrict everything "that offends in the slightest against religion, the state, or good manners, all obvious nonsense and coarseness, that is, everything unworthy of a capital city and the seat of a court" (10). The very first item on this list already contradicts a fundamental principle of the French Enlightenment, the separation of church and state, and with it the atheist leanings of many of its most influential thinkers. Although Sonnenfels has been called "the herald of Enlightenment thought in Austria," he clearly supported censorship restrictions. See also Werner Ogris, "Die Zensur in der Ära Metternichs," in *Humaniora: Medizin—Recht—Geschichte* (Berlin: Springer Verlag, 2006), 243–56. A wealth of information on Austrian censorship practice was already assembled in a fascinating monograph published in the year censorship was lifted. [Dr.] Adolph Wiesner, *Denkwürdigkeiten der Oesterreichischen Zensur vom Zeitalter der Reformazion bis auf die Gegenwart* (Stuttgart: Verlag von Adolph Krabbe, 1847). Austrian censorship statutes from 1781 to 1902 are accessible online at http://www.univie.ac.at/medienrechtsgeschichte/statutes. html (accessed 18 August 2010).
19. Alexander Wheeloch Thayer, *Thayer's Life of Beethoven*, revised and edited by Elliott Forbes (Princeton, N.J.: Princeton University Press, 1967), 565.

ends with the cast kneeling down to cry, "Hail! Hail—Austria!—Hail!—Habsburg forever!" to the accompaniment of trumpets and cheers.

Stringent control was exercised over all forms of public expression once Prince Klemens von Metternich became the de facto head of state during the Congress of Vienna (he was chief minister from 1809), and especially after he appointed the ironfisted Count Josef Sedlinitzky his chief of police in 1815. Spies found their way in everywhere, and even private gatherings were not safe from infiltration. The city's paterfamilias, the emperor Franz, retreated from an active role in affairs of state, meddling only rarely, until before long he had become little more than a figurehead. "Habsburg forever!" could ring disingenuous, therefore, not only because it appeared obligatory but because hailing the Habsburgs might be heard as an affront to Metternich, a call to the imperial family again to take charge—much as, in the revised *Fidelio* of 1814, Rocco's quick-thinking show of patriotism ("des Königs Namenstag ist Heute!") at once condemned and shielded him from the wrath of Pizarro. Rocco's patriotic loyalty to the king is portrayed by Georg Friedrich Treitschke and Beethoven as an opportune weapon against tyranny.

Although Metternich's skill at diplomacy during the Congress may have been widely admired, his ruthless, underhanded methods of manipulating those around him quickly made him into a despised figure. Looking back upon these events in 1828, Charles Sealsfield (formerly the Austrian monk Karl Postl, who fled Metternich's Austria for the United States in 1822) had these words to say about Prince Metternich in his book *Austria as It Is: Or Sketches of Continental Courts*: "Never has there been a man more detested and dreaded than Metternich. From the Baltic to the Pyrenees, from the boundaries of Turkey to the Borders of Holland, there is but one voice heard respecting this Minister—that of execration."[20] A few pages later, Sealsfield paints a vivid picture of Metternich's methods. Following a description of his graceful physical appearance, we read (in charmingly faulty English and French):

> No man turns these gifts to better advantage. With a grace, a *sens gêne*, not in the least incumbered by any of those drawbacks, religion, morality, or principle,—he will entertain a circle of fifty and more persons in the most charming manner,— enter into dissipation and the follies of his equals and superiors; but, at the same time, while administering to the pleasures and vices of others, will form his schemes on their frailties and hobby-horses. In the art of penetrating the weak side of his superiors, and, what is still more, of making himself necessary to their frailties, he is absolutely a master.[21]

---

20. Charles Sealsfield, *Austria as It Is: or Sketches of Continental Courts: By an Eyewitness* (London: Hurst, Chance, 1828; reprint, Whitefish, MT., Kessinger Publishing, n.d.), 144 (chapter 6). A critical edition with German translation, substantial commentary, and documents, edited by Primus-Heinz Kucher, was published by Böhlau Verlag in Vienna in 1994. I refer to the page numbers of the original edition, reprinted in facsimile by the internet-based rare books publisher, Kessinger Publishing.

21. Sealsfield, *Austria as It Is*, 148–49.

A harsh wind blew across the Habsburg domains under Metternich's rule, which continued to 1848, and the more tolerant era of Joseph II came to seem like a distant golden
age.[22] All forms of entertainment, public and private, were affected by this just as was the
business of everyday life. Against this general historical backdrop we may now turn our
attention to a narrower sequence of events surrounding the composition of Schubert and
Franz von Schober's opera *Alfonso und Estrella*.

II

In his documentary biography of Schubert, Otto Erich Deutsch described the poet
Johann Senn (1795–1857, pseud. Bombastus Bebederwa) as "one of the first and most
severely punished victims of the new measures adopted by the Austrian Police Chief
Count Josef Sedlinitzky."[23] In January 1820 the police raided a gathering of students at a
farewell celebration for one of their comrades, Alois Fischer, who was about to leave
Vienna because his stepfather had died. After a spy was recognized and expelled from the
group, the police came to fear that some kind of conspiracy was under way. Schubert
escaped the incident with only a black eye after mouthing off to the authorities, and
Franz Bruchmann, another friend who was present, soon departed for the University of
Erlangen—despite an 1819 order forbidding Austrian students from leaving the country.
But Senn was thrown in jail, where he languished for fourteen months before being
exiled to Tyrol, without ever having been charged with a crime. From prison he produced a ninety-two-page document of agitated gibberish that confounded the authorities. Later, in Innsbruck, he was shunned and charged with being an atheist.[24] In a letter
to the Innsbruck police chief, dated 24 February 1823, Sedlinitzky maintained that Senn
had been banished for his participation in a student organization (a *Burschenschaft*) and
for his fanatical embrace of such "phantoms of the mind" as citizenry and a system of
representation.[25] Nationhood was *the* liberal cause among German intellectuals in the

---

22. Lothar Höbelt, "The Austrian Empire," in *The War for the Public Mind: Political Censorship in Nineteenth-
Century Europe*, ed. Robert Justin Goldstein (Westport, Conn.: Praeger, 2000), 214.

23. Otto Erich Deutsch, *Schubert: Die Dokumente seines Lebens*, Franz Schubert, *Neue Ausgabe sämtlicher Werke*,
ser. 8, suppl. vol. 5 (Kassel: Bärenreiter Verlag, 1964), 88: "[Senn war] ... eines der ersten und am schwersten
bestraften Opfer der neuen maßnahmen des österreichischen Polizeidirektors, Josef Graf Sedlinitzkys."

24. See Moriz Enzinger, "Franz v. Bruchmann, der Freund J. Chr. Senns und des Grafen August v. Platen: Eine
Selbstbiographie aus dem Wiener Schubertkreise nebst Briefen," *Veröffentlichungen des Museum Ferdinandeum in Innsbruck* 10 (1930): 117–339. Alois Fischer wrote to Franz v. Bruchmann about the accusations of
atheism in a letter of 18 February 1823, 306–7. Enzinger gives 20 January 1820 as the date of the celebration
for Fischer. The police report justifying Senn's arrest is dated 25 March 1820.

25. Moriz Enzinger, "Zur Biographie des Tiroler Dichters Joh. Chrys. Senn," *Archiv für das Studium der Neueren
Sprachen* 156 (1929): 169–83. "[Er wurde] wegen fanatischer Hinneigung zu den Hirngespinsten von Volk-
sthum und Repräsentativ System von hier abgeschafft" (176). Letters of warning flew among police chiefs in
the spring of 1823, when Senn joined the army and went with his regiment to Trento in northern Italy, in the
vicinity of recent uprisings by freedom fighters against Austrian rule (178–79).

1820s, and some Austrian students, Senn included, were feared to be willing to die for it.[26] Some months after the police raid, Schubert moved out of the rooms he had been sharing with the poet Johann Mayrhofer, and their friendship grew more distant: Mayrhofer earned his living as a censor, after all. He must have been put on the spot by the behavior of his hotheaded younger friends, even though as a freethinking scholar of classical literature and a poet himself, Mayrhofer often took up controversial psychological themes in his work—always treating them obliquely and with the expected decorum, however. Censorship restrictions had been relaxed briefly in 1809–10 to permit scholars greater freedom: this privileged class evidently learned to tread lightly.[27]

Reverberations of the incident long have registered in Schubert scholarship whenever events can be directly linked to Senn's name: Schubert published settings of Senn's poetry in the summer of 1823, his first song opus without a dedication, as Walther Dürr has remarked.[28] It included unpublished poems by Schubert's close friend Franz von Schober and by August von Platen, whom Bruchmann met not long after arriving in Erlangen. (The four songs in op. 23 are the magnificent "Selige Welt" and "Schwanengesang" on poems of Senn, Schober's "Schatzgräbers Begehr," and "Die Liebe hat gelogen" by Platen. This last and the Platen song "Du liebst much nicht" are taken up in chapter 6.) Shortly before this, on 28 February 1823, Sedlinitzky wrote to the Innsbruck constable with concern that Schober's poetry breathed the same "pernicious tendency" (*verderbliche Tendenz*) as Senn's.[29] Two years earlier (in 1821), on the Christmas Eve following Senn's banishment, the police had barged in on a celebration at the home of the actor Heinrich Anschütz, where a Christmas tree in the window (a Protestant custom) caught their eye, and Schubert was reprimanded for playing dance music during the holy season: he evidently believed that he was the target of their action.[30]

---

26. For an illuminating picture of the progress this cause had made by midcentury, see Celia Applegate, "Robert Schumann and the Culture of German Nationhood," in *Rethinking Schumann*, ed. Roe-Min Kok and Laura Tunbridge (New York: Oxford University Press, 2010), 3–14.

27. On one occasion, however, his work was judged to have crossed a line: Eduard Freiherr von Feuchtersleben withheld from his edition of Mayrhofer's poetry the libretto for Schubert's opera *Adrast* after much advice and "in consideration for the majority of the audience." Ilija Dürhammer, *Schuberts literarische Heimat: Dichtung und Literaturrezeption der Schubert-Freunde* (Vienna: Böhlau Verlag, 1999), 228. For more on this opera, see Elizabeth Norman McKay, "Schubert and Classical Opera: The Promise of Adrast," in *Der vergessene Schubert: Franz Schubert auf der Bühne*, exhibition catalog, österreichisches Theatermuseum, ed. Erich Wolfgang Partsch and Oskar Pausch (Vienna: Böhlau Verlag, 1997), 61–78.

28. Walther Dürr, "Lieder für den verbannten Freund: Franz Schubert und sein Freundeskreis in Opposition zum Metternich-Regime," in *Zeichen Setzung: Aufsätze zur musikalischen Poetik* (Kassel: Bärenreiter-Verlag, 1992), 135–40.

29. Enzinger, "Zur Biographie des Tiroler Dichters Joh. Chrys. Senn," 177.

30. Otto Erich Deutsch, *Schubert. Die Erinnerungen seiner Freunde* (Leipzig: Breitkopf & Härtel, 1957), 189–90. Schubert had gotten to know Anschütz's brothers Eduard and Gustav through the *Unsinnsgesellschaft* that met regularly in 1817. The "Grüne Tanne" was the inn where the first of the German *Burschenschaften* met and their biggest rally took place on the 300th anniversary of Martin Luther's posting of his theses.

Schubert and his friends thus found themselves in direct conflict with the authorities, going well beyond the ordinary frustrations with censorship that everyone in Metternich's Vienna complained about endlessly. Our only freedom of thought, Grillparzer grumbled, was the freedom to "keep our thoughts to ourselves."[31] More colorfully, Nestroy's Ultra in the 1848 satire *Freiheit in Krähwinkel* (Freedom Comes to "Crow's Corner") looked back upon the era of Metternich as a time when "we even had freedom of thought, so long as we kept them to ourselves. For there was a kind of dog ordinance for thoughts; you were permitted to have them on a leash, but as soon as you let them go, they bludgeoned them to death." (Ultra's most devastating critique takes the form of a little song maintaining that art got dumbed down during these years.)[32] Around the time that Metternich's special assembly met to ratify the 1819–20 Carlsbad Decrees, the editor of the *Wiener Zeitung*, Josef Karl Bernard, joked with Beethoven that "at the congress they now are drafting a law regulating how high the birds may fly and how fast the hare may run!" Soon after, Bernard reports, "Abbé Gelinek calls you 'a second Sand: you gripe about the Emperor, the Archbishop, and the Minister; you'll end up on the chopping block yet.'"[33] And when Grillparzer and Beethoven met to discuss a prospective opera in 1823, their conversations drifted quickly to censorship. Grillparzer envied music's relative freedom from the restrictions choking the verbal arts: "If they only knew what was on your mind when you compose," reads one tantalizing entry in a conversation book. A few years later he wrote: "words are proscribed; good thing that tones, the exponential representatives of words, still are free." Christophe Kuffner, the editor of a

---

31. W. E. Yates, *Grillparzer: A Critical Introduction* (Cambridge: Cambridge University Press, 1972), 12. Also quoted in Höbelt, "The Austrian Empire," 218.

32. Johann Nestroy, *Freiheit in Krähwinkel* (1848). A good edition is *Johann Nestroy: Stücke 26/I*, ed. John R. P. McKenzie, Johann Nestroy Sämtliche Werke, Historisch-kritische Ausgabe, ed. Jürgen Hain, Johann Hüttner, Walter Obermaier, and W. Edgar Yates (Vienna: Jugend und Volk, Edition Wien, Dachs Verlag, 1995). Ultra's speech is the great monologue in act 1, scene 7, where he reflects that "right and freedom are a pair of meaningful words; but only in the singular are they infinitely great. That is why they have always been given to us only in the worthless plural form." This qualified freedom of thought comes at the end of a list of such individually granted freedoms as Billiard- and *Maskenfreiheit*. His list calls up a clause in the 1810 censorship code, which expressly stated that no one may be held accountable for mere thoughts—so long as they are kept to oneself. Nestroy had more extensive contact with Schubert than is generally recognized. See Peter Branscombe's "Schubert and Nestroy (mit einem Seitenblick auf die Familie Unger)" in *Schubert und seine Freunde*, ed. Eva Badura-Skoda, Gerold W. Gruber, Walburga Litschauer and Carmen Ottner (Vienna: Böhlau, 1999), 279–90.

33. Karl Ludwig Sand's murder in Mannheim of the playwright and professor August von Kotzebue, a former liberal suspected of spying on the student *Burschenschaft* for the Russian czar, clearly led to reactionary paranoia, leaving someone as politically outspoken as Beethoven (and German to boot) open to absurd suspicions. For Bernard's remarks, see Ludwig van Beethoven, *Ludwig van Beethovens Konversationshefte*, issued by the Deutsche Staatsbibliothek Berlin, ed. Karl-Heinz Köhler and Grita Herre, with the aid of Günter Brosche, vol. 1 (Leipzig: VEB Deutscher Verlag für Musik), 308, 488, 339. The remark about the birds is misattributed to Beethoven in Höbelt, "The Austrian Empire," 218. The circumstances around Sand's murder of Kotzebue are fleshed out in the critical notes to Ludwig Tieck, *Phantasus*, ed. Manfred Frank, Schriften, vol. 6 (Frankfurt: Deutscher Klassiker Verlag, 1985), 1386.

literary magazine, remarked that now even a *Don Juan* opera would be banned by the censors were it newly composed.[34]

Through all this, the stage remained the most public platform available for airing controversial positions before a large audience. In this climate, as in others similar—say, in Hollywood under the Hays code—sneaking something past the censors became a sport, a way to delight audiences, leading to what Walter Obermaier has called "the public's passionate addiction to discovering hidden meanings."[35] (We have indirect confirmation of this in Tieck's ironic *Puss in Boots*, act 3, scene 6, where an enlightened ruler, having foolishly transformed himself into a mouse, is eaten by the cat, which subsequently announces: "Freedom and Equality! The Law has been devoured." A light goes off for one member of the audience: "Halt! A revolutionary piece. I sense allegory and mysticism in every word! Halt! Halt! Now I must go back and think over everything again, re-experience it, so that I may grasp all the angles, the profound allusions, the religious depths!") The authorities understood all this and even tolerated it to a point: when the Theater an der Wien was in danger of folding in 1806, Emperor Franz stepped in to forbid it. In Yates's words, "He stressed the usefulness of the theater as a political vent: if the audience were safely being entertained, they could not be on the streets hatching revolution."[36] This naturally works both ways: if the authorities were in the theater to monitor compliance with the rules of entertainment, they also could not be out harassing the city's residents. The stage is the perfect diversion. Like Papageno's bells, it casts its magic spell over everyone, including the authorities, putting time on hold:

Das klinget so herrlich, das klinget so schön! La-ra-la la la la-ra-la la la la-ra-la!
Nie hab' ich so etwas gehört und gesehn! La-ra-la la la la-ra-la la la la-ra-la!

ALFONSO UND ESTRELLA

I

In late summer 1821, a few months after Senn's sentence was handed down, Schubert and Schober retreated to the countryside to work on a "grand opera" together. Although *Alfonso und Estrella* was fully drafted by about six months later, and the libretto approved by the censor, the opera never came to performance during Schubert's lifetime. Johann

34. Ludwig van Beethoven, *Ludwig van Beethovens Konversationshefte*, ed. Karl-Heinz Köhler and Dagmar Beck, with the help of Günter Brosche, vol. 3 (1823), 288; vol. 9 (1826), 215, 219. "Den Musikern kann doch die Censur nichts anhaben[.] Wenn man wüßte was Sie bei Ihrer Musik denken!" "Die Worte sind verpönt; glücklich, daß die Töne, die potenzirten Repräsentanten der Worte noch frey sind!"

35. Walter Obermaier, "Schubert und die Zensur," in *Schubert-Kongreß Wien 1978 Bericht*, ed. Otto Brusatti (Graz: Akademische Druck- u.Verlagsanstalt, 1979), 119: "der vom Publikum geradezu leidenschaftlich betriebenen Deutsucht" is his formulation.

36. Yates, *Theatre in Vienna*, 22.

Michael Vogl, intended as Froila, evidently declined the role (he had sung the twin brothers Franz and Friedrich Spiess in Schubert's *Die Zwillingsbrüder* only two years prior). Vogl, who was nearing the end of his stage career, voiced misgivings about the direction of the opera and did not lend his support to it at the Kärntnertortheater, which was for Schubert not only a disappointment but an embarrassment, since announcements about an upcoming opera by him already had appeared in the press. In fact, the earliest mention we have that Schubert was working on a grand Romantic opera is in an April 1821 report (printed in June) in the *Dresdner Abend-Zeitung* by Ignaz Franz Castelli (later the librettist for *Der häusliche Krieg*). Anna Milder thought the opera unsuitable for Berlin too ("they are accustomed here to highly tragic grand opera or French comedies," she wrote), and she let it be known that she would have preferred a role crafted specifically for her. A score was also sent to Carl Maria von Weber in Dresden, and Ludwig Tieck expressed his interest in it to Schober.[37] Schubert himself declared *Alfonso und Estrella* his best opera, equaled only by *Fierabras* later,[38] and long even after Franz Liszt had put on a mangled production of the work in Weimar in 1854—with massive cuts and newly composed Wagnerian transitions to facilitate the action—Schober held to the memory that Ludwig Tieck, Matthäus von Collin, and Friedrich Schlegel all had praised the poetic worth of his libretto.[39] Discerning company this is, and somewhat surprising. Their admiration can have had little to do with the elaboration of the plot as such, since the happenings are only loosely, and somewhat forcibly, molded into a familiar opera plot-archetype that ends in forgiveness with the promise of a better future in the hands of a new generation, symbolized by a worthy couple. The litmus test for worthiness is key in stories ending with a succession of power: in *The Magic Flute*, the requirement is for courage and obedience along the path to illumination; in *Idomeneo*, it is a demonstrated willingness to sacrifice for others; in *Alfonso und Estrella*, a natural love of freedom and a

---

37. The most detailed account of Schubert's frustrated plans is in Till Gerrit Waidelich's monograph, *Franz Schubert: Alfonso und Estrella: Eine frühe durchkomponierte Oper. Geschichte und Analyse* (Tutzing: Hans Schneider, 1991), 29–34. There is more in Waidelich's "Joseph Hüttenbrenners Entwurf eines Aufsatzes mit der ersten biographischen Skizze Schuberts (1823) und zwei Fragmente eines ungedruckten Schubert-Nachrufs (1828)," *Schubert-Perspektiven* 1 (2001): 37–73; esp. 53, where we learn that the opera had been accepted by the censor. Evidently there was a performance for friends at the piano that impressed Weigl. Castelli's report from Vienna, printed in the 29 June 1821 issue of the Dresden paper, is excerpted in Deutsch's documentary biography without the 23–26 April date, for which we must turn to Till Gerrit Waidelich, ed., with preliminary work by Renate Hilmar-Voit and Andreas Mayer, *Franz Schubert: Dokumente 1817–1830*, vol. 1, *Texte: Programme, Rezensionen, Anzeigen, Nekrologe, Musikbeilagen und andere gedruckte Quellen*, Veröffentlichungen des Internationalen Franz Schubert Instituts, ed. Ernst Hilmar (Tutzing: Hans Schneider, 1993), documents 108, 85.

38. This according to Leopold von Sonnleithner's 1829 biographical sketch, quoted by Waidelich, *Franz Schubert: Alfonso und Estrella*, 16.

39. Deutsch, *Erinnerungen*, 178 [2nd ed., 239]. Schober's recollection is in a letter to Schubert's nephew Heinrich in 1876. He acknowledges that the libretto has many faults but holds to the memory that Tieck, Schlegel, and Collin praised it highly "als Gedicht." Liszt's revisions are discussed in detail by Waidelich, *Franz Schubert: Alfonso und Estrella*, 41–46. See also Allan Keiler, "Liszt and the Weimar Hoftheater," *Studia Musicologica Academiae Scientarum Hungaricae*, T. 28, Fasc. 1/4 (1986): 431–50.

peaceful temperament—a preference for the hunt over waging war—along with respect earned by accomplishment. Because Schubert's operas are not so often performed, it will be helpful to recall the plot:

Living *incognito*, Froila, the beloved lawful king of Oviedo, raises his son Alfonso in an idyllic valley, waiting for an opportunity to take back the throne from Mauregato, who stole it from him with the aid of his brutish, ambitious general Adolfo. Alfonso, champion in all games of war and song, yearns to know what lies beyond the valley he is forbidden to leave. His father seals a promise to free him by giving his son an heirloom chain, and later gives him a sword and a horn. Mauregato has a daughter, Estrella, whom Adolfo, the general, wishes to possess. Seeing that his daughter does not care for Adolfo, Mauregato invokes an old prophecy that only he who brings back Eurich's chain will marry Estrella. Sometime later, she loses her way in the forest on a hunt and meets Alfonso, who gives her his chain as a keepsake. Adolfo plots to overthrow Mauregato, threatening to take Estrella by force. Alfonso comes rushing to the rescue (*"Zurück!"*) and defends her father too, aided by his loyal hunting companions, who fly to his side at the call of his horn ("Ich, *ich* will euer Führer sein!"). Froila realizes his son loves the daughter of his arch enemy and forgives Mauregato. The crown is passed to Alfonso and Estrella.

Since there is little contemporary reception to work with, we can gauge only indirectly what effect the opera might have made in the 1820s. Ever since Liszt's production, complaints about the libretto's disregard for convention, oddities of declamation, and the static quality of some of the scenes, especially the lengthy celebrations in the first act, have plagued the opera's reputation. Eduard Hanslick found the characters to be "wooden marionettes,"[40] and many later commentators have noted the absence of psychological development and a lack of genuine passion between Alfonso and Estrella. Waidelich characterizes Estrella as "fast 'irreal,'"[41] which fits as well how Estrella describes Alfonso to her father in the aria "Herrlich auf des Berges Höhen" (no. 21): she knows not his name but sees him suffused in light, the power of his heavenly songs forcing dark forests to listen and the unmoving cliffs to resonate. (He is a present-day Orpheus, like Tamino.) And Helga Lühning remarks that in Adolfo's act 1 aria "Doch im Getümmel der Schlacht" (no. 8), Schubert's calculated placement of awkward initial stresses in nearly every line creates "a striking amalgam of desire and tumultuous warring that practically tramples over Schober's text." Probably, she notes, this was done with a glance at Monostatos's

---

40. Cited by Waidelich, *Franz Schubert: Alfonso und Estrella*, 104; the remark comes from an 1884 review of J. N. Fuch's production (155).
41. Waidelich, *Franz Schubert: Alfonso und Estrella*, 106.

grotesque wooing of Pamina. By this "grandiose exaggeration" of the text,[42] Adolfo becomes a caricature of evil. Estrella stands her ground: "Nimmer! nimmer!" she cries defiantly, like some silent film heroine. Not unlike Tieck's Skaramuz, Apollo, or Puss in Boots, these characters are mere silhouettes onto which we may project political personalities (as Friedrich Dieckmann has proposed, about which more shortly).

Just as striking is the way the narrative often hangs by a thread: its puzzling turns of logic (or, better, its absent logic) even have led to speculation—meanwhile disproved—that additional recitative or spoken dialogue must have gone missing. In fact, we now know that the directorship of the theater also felt more elaboration was needed and that Schober refused on the grounds that this would compromise the unity of his libretto.[43] Lühning sums up the resulting effect nicely. "Schubert's numbers lack the shadows that they ought to cast," she writes, recalling, with Liszt, "Peter Schlemihl's wundersame Geschichte" (Adalbert von Chamisso's story about a man who has no shadow).[44] Her essay calls for a reassessment of the opera's generic affiliations in the hope that this will let us shake off those persistent critiques traceable to Liszt's production, in which we now may recognize a misguided effort to squeeze Schubert's opera into an alien mid-nineteenth-century dramatic mold.

The puzzling contradictions derive as often from the music as they do from the text, or sometimes from a disjunction between the two. Why, when the curtain first rises, is everyone sneaking about in the dark to mysterious B♭-minor music with *unisono* writing and pizzicato bass ("Still noch decket uns die Nacht"), concerned not to waken "the father," who will rise in a magnificent formal recitative and aria that compare the rays of his former crown to those of the sun? ("Sei mir gegrüßt, o Sonne," no. 2). And why is it when the hush-hush peasant's music from the opening scene yields to ceremonial displays of affection for Froila that Schubert's cheerful music is filled with local yodel tunes ("Laß dir danken," in no. 3, shown in two excerpts in ex. 1.1), an odd choice for a story cast in the Spanish Middle Ages?[45] Thomas A. Denny draws attention to the overlap of patriarchal

---

42. Helga Lühning, "Schubert als Dramatiker: *Alfonso und Estrella* Vorurteile, Mißverständnisse und einige Anregungen zu einer Neuorientierung," in *Schubert und das Biedermeier: Beiträge zur Musik des frühen 19. Jahrhunderts; Festschrift für Walther Dürr zum 70. Geburstag,* ed. Michael Kube, Werner Aderhold, and Walburga Litschauer (Kassel: Bärenreiter-Verlag, 2002), 25–43, here 35–36 ("Schubert hat daraus, wohl ein wenig auf Monostatos' groteske Werbung um Pamina schauend, eine eigenartige Verbingung aus Begierde und Kriegsgetümmel gemacht und dabei Schobers Text regelrecht plattgetreten"). Liszt's essay "Schuberts Alfons und Estrella" appeared in the *Neue Zeitschrift für Musik* in 1854. It is reprinted in Franz Liszt, *Sämtliche Schriften,* vol. 5, *Dramaturgische Blätter,* ed. with commentary by Detlef Altenburg, Dorothea Redepenning, and Britta Schilling (Wiesbaden: Breitkopf & Härtel, 1989), 62–67.

43. Waidelich, "Joseph Hüttenbrenners Entwurf," 53: "die *Direction* habe einige [*sic*] reichhaltigere Ausschmückung im Buche gewunschen, wozu sich aber der Hr. Verfasser, weg. der hiedurch zerstört werdenden Einheit in seinem Werke nicht herbeyließ."

44. Lühning, "Schubert als Dramatiker," 31.

45. Had he needed one, Schubert might have found a precedent for this musical ploy in Mozart's *Abduction from the Seraglio,* where Belmonte's opening aria to Constanze, "Hier soll ich dich denn sehen," is joined by an Austrian wedding band at the climax: "und bringe mich zum Ziel."

EXAMPLE I.I Franz Schubert, *Alfonso und Estrella*, D 732, act one no. 3, Andantino, "Laß dir danken," 91–99 and 111–115. Vocal score, based on Bärenreiter edition, BA 5540a. By kind permision.

EXAMPLE 1.1. (*continued*).

and solar metaphors in Schubert's ceremonial music for name days, including those for his own father; for the emperor; for Josef Spendou (his family's benefactor); and for Salieri. Denny speculates that since the role of Froila was crafted for Vogl, these displays may have doubled as a tribute to the singer himself: the "real time" pacing certainly encourages these words to float free of the plot.[46] Finally, who are all the "Freunde" who swear allegiance to Adolfo and vengeance to the man whom Froila earlier has decried as a "dreadful tyrant," and why does this relatively minor character suddenly take on such enormous musical proportions?

Some of these things quite plausibly could have come about not just from inexperience but because Schubert and Schober were using the opera to vent their rage at Metternich's

---

46. Thomas A. Denny, "Archaic and Contemporary Aspects of Schubert's *Alfonso und Estrella*: Issues of Influence, Originality, and Maturation," in *Eighteenth-Century Music in Theory and Practice. Essays in Honor of Alfred Mann*, ed. Mary Ann Parker (Stuyvesant, N.Y.: Pendragon Press, 1994), 249–50. (For an intriguing exploration, incidentally, of Spendou's role in Schubert's family, see Maynard Solomon, "Schubert: Family Matters," *19th Century Music* 28 1 2004]: 3–14).

EXAMPLE 1.2   Franz Schubert, *Alfonso und Estrella*, D 732, act two, no. 17, "Es falle Mauregat!", 473–509. Vocal score, based on Bärenreiter edition, BA 5540a. By kind permission.

policies. Imagine their satisfaction in having assembled on stage in the middle of the second act a big male chorus of conspirators to denounce the villain whose three-syllable name just happens to begin with M! "Our pact has been sealed, we move swiftly on to act. Let his blood be shed; Let topple Mauregat!" "Er falle, er falle!" everyone cries as the music comes crashing down at the end of the ten-minute scene. Indeed, Mauregato's name is *shortened* to three syllables for the cathartic chorus (as shown in ex. 1.2). The events leading up to the scene feel contrived, raising our suspicion that any excuse for a conspirators' chorus would have served. This is but one of several striking places where events "just happen" with little preparation.

EXAMPLE 1.2 *(continued)*.

Not long before the conspirators assemble on stage we might also have found ourselves wondering, as did Friedrich Dieckmann, how it is that Alfonso gives away his chain (and, with it, his father's promise) to Estrella, a woman he has just met and whom he has little prospect of ever seeing again. Dieckmann compares the ancient power of Eurich's chain to Sarastros's *Sonnenkreis*.[47] He does not clarify where the power of the chain comes from: Eurich, the fifth-century king of the Spanish Visigoths, reputedly was responsible for the oldest Germanic code of law—before which the only legal benchmark was

---

47. Friedrich Dieckmann, "Die Überlistung der Konterrevolution," in *Gespaltene Welt und ein liebendes Paar: Oper als Gleichnis* (Frankfurt am Main: Insel Verlag, 1999), 177.

EXAMPLE I.2 *(continued)*.

"Gewohnheitsrecht" (customary practice)![48] As the cases of Senn and many others make clear, due process remained a distant dream in Schubert's time when justice routinely was left up to the discretion of Metternich's chief of police. Alfonso sings a spirited duet with Froila (the *più presto* of no. 6) proclaiming the chain his talisman, the shining star that will guide his way. For the tortured but clever Mauregato it serves a different purpose. An opportune ancient prophecy provides the means to stave off Adolfo's claim: only he who returns the missing chain shall wed Estrella ("Ein Mittel noch . . . nur wer die Kette Eurichs wiederbringt, die noch vom alten Königsstamme fehlt, wird mit Estrellen feierlich vermählt").

Other elements of the story resonate with life in early 1820s Vienna. A law forbids Alfonso from leaving his idyllic valley, just as Austrian students were barred from leaving

48. Karl Zeumer, "Geschichte der Westgotischen Gesetzgebung," in *Neues Archiv der Gesellschaft für ältere deutsche Geschichtskunde zur Beförderung einer Gesamtausgabe der Quellenschriften deutscher Geschichten des Mittelalter,* 32, no. 1 (Hamburg and Leipzig: Hahn'sche Buchhandlung, 1897), 419–516. Liszt describes him as "Saint Eurich," but the libretto states that Eurich's chain belonged to the old family of kings. See also Waidelich, *Franz Schubert: Alfonso und Estrella,* 111–12, and Michael Kohlhäufl, *Poetisches Vaterland: Dichtung und politisches Denken im Freundeskreis Franz Schuberts* (Kassel: Bärenreiter, 1999), 241. Kohlhäufl observes that King Eurich may have provided a model for the future nation, noting, significantly, that Eurich's code of law was independent of Rome.

the country after the Carlsbad Decrees were issued (or, for that matter, as Senn was banished to Tyrol). In the corrupt city an evil ruler has usurped the power of the beloved King Froila, whom no one has seen for so long that he is believed to be dead ("Er ruht wohl lange schon im Grabe, Ihn hat kein Auge mehr geseh'n"): heard in relation to an absent Emperor Franz, the naive tone of these words to the conspirators only underscores their irony. In the end, Mauregato's conscience eats away at him—for his theft of the crown and for his readiness to sacrifice his daughter Estrella to his ambition (there is little doubt, after all, that in this Spanish-medieval fictional world the code of honor between two men of stature will trump Estrella's revulsion at a forced marriage to Adolfo should he fulfill the prophecy)—and when Froila, the beloved king, appears before Mauregato bathed in the flattering rays of Christian forgiveness, the rogue monarch returns the crown. The demeanor in all this might be seen as a nineteenth-century harbinger of "camp," that stylized mode of ironic exaggeration that blossomed in the early twentieth century.

Nearly all the opera's characters are plucked from history: Alfonso the Chaste (who lived from 759 to 842) was the son of Fruela, whose illegitimate half brother, Mauregato, seized the throne.[49] Friedrich Dieckmann finds in the opera's quasi-historical drama only the thinnest possible cover for a story about the turmoil in the French political arena between 1790 and 1815, events that were deeply imprinted on the European imagination and had fueled many an earlier opera plot. Froila resembles the deposed Bourbon king Louis XVIII in this scenario, and Mauregato is a stand-in for Napoleon. Alfonso recalls Napoléon François Joseph Charles Bonaparte, Duke of Reichstadt, the ten-year-old offspring of a politically expedient marriage (arranged by Metternich) between Marie Louise of Austria and Napoleon. The figure of Napoleon's young son, speculates Dieckmann, "undoubtedly excited the imagination" of Vienna's intellectual youth, appearing to them as a figure of hope.[50]

II

In 1821 the emperor's grandson was being raised at court, tutored by Matthäus von Collin, a professor of the history of philosophy and aesthetics and the highly respected editor of the *Wiener Jahrbücher der Literatur*, a journal that in Peter Skrine's words was founded in 1818 "specifically under the direct auspices of Metternich to provide a subsidized organ for the expression and discussion of ideas congenial to the Restoration State and in line with its guiding principles." Skrine cautions, however, that "to jump to obvious conclusions and accusations of axe-grinding would in Collin's case be unwise. [He] was discreet,

---

49. Waidelich reproduces early nineteenth-century sources recounting this episode in Spanish history. The libretto only loosely matches any of them. Waidelich, *Franz Schubert: Alfonso und Estrella*, 307–11.

50. Dieckmann, "Die Überlistung der Konterrevolution," 173. When he died of tuberculosis at age twenty-one in 1832, there were rumors that Napoleon's son had been poisoned by Metternich's police.

trusted, and had access to the higher echelons of society and government, but he was also a keen, thoughtful observer of the way man functions as a political animal." Friedrich Schlegel characterized Collin in a letter to his wife Dorothea as "by far the best mind, and richest in feeling, of all those present here."[51] For a decade Collin also served the censorship office, but he quit his duties there in 1820, having grown increasingly distressed at the conditions faced by Austrian writers and artists.[52] Around the same time he began hosting gatherings that brought Schubert into close contact with such influential men of the theater as Count Moritz von Dietrichstein and Ignaz von Mosel, and Schubert set a number of his poems.

Collin himself wrote a cycle of plays on the medieval House of Babenberg and was deeply fascinated by the genre of historical drama. In the critical essay that he devoted to the subject in Schlegel's *Deutsches Museum* he extolled the Shakespearean examples of the genre above all others, a passion he shared with Ludwig Tieck, for whom he also had great admiration. Historical drama, for Collin, is defined by a single-minded devotion to accuracy and truth in the representation of events and characters, without other motivations entering in (such as the praise of God): it arises from a sensibility of doubt, not belief, he maintains. Accuracy of historical detail—a painstaking adherence to the facts of the case, which he sees as an ambition in some French drama—is no guarantee that "the historical style" will be achieved. Genuine historical drama, like Shakespeare's, will ring true even when the events portrayed are pure inventions of the mind (and this commitment to veracity of character, Collin argues, puts Shakespeare fundamentally at odds with a Romantic disposition, even though his themes sometimes are Romantic).[53] Skrine traces Collin's interest in historical drama to August Wilhelm Schlegel, who first had called for "a cycle of plays in which, as in Shakespeare's histories, the events of the national past, poetically evoked, would illuminate the present and suggest the future destiny of the nation."[54] In all likelihood Schubert and Schober's *Alfonso und Estrella* was conceived in some awareness of these trends, and Collin may well have played an even greater role: we still do not know where librettist and composer came upon the medieval historical subject matter.

---

51. Peter Skrine, "Matthäus von Collin and Historical Drama," *Modern Language Review* 78 (1983): 597–98. "Er is doch von allen hiesigen bei weitem der beste und gemütsvollste" (8 January 1820). Skrine's insightful essay gives a detailed account of the interweaving plots of Collin's historical cycle and Grillparzer's *Ottokar*.

52. Susan Youens, *Schubert's Late Lieder: Beyond the Song Cycles* (Cambridge: Cambridge University Press, 2002), 4–7.

53. Matthäus von Collin, "Über das historische Schauspiel," in *Deutsches Museum*, 9th issue (1812): 193–213, a journal edited by Friedrich Schlegel. In 1821–22 Schubert's friend Franz von Bruchmann (also a friend of Collin's) made a similar effort to grasp Goethe's relationship to Romanticism as is documented in his correspondence with August von Platen. Their relationship is explored further in chapter 6. Grillparzer thought the idea of historical drama based on fictional subjects absurd, and he blamed Ludwig Tieck for the fashion. Franz Grillparzer, *Dramen 1817–1828*, ed. Helmut Bachmeier, Franz Grillparzer *Werke in sechs Bänden*, vol. 2 (Frankfurt: Deutscher Klassiker Verlag, 1986), 848–50 (an extract, "Über Geschichte, Zeit und historisches Drama," from the 1853 *Selbstbiographie*).

54. Skrine, "Matthäus von Collin and Historical Drama," 598–600.

Obvious parallels exist between the opera's historically remote plot and Dieckmann's early nineteenth-century overlay, but just as many obvious contradictions spring to mind, not the least of which is that with Napoleon's death in May 1821 it no longer would have been possible to construe the conciliatory ending as a policy recommendation. At the opera's denouement Mauregato, overcome with guilt, fears that Froila's ghost has come for retribution ("No ghost, I am alive," Froila assures him). One is reminded here of Hamlet's scheme to expose his uncle's guilt by staging a play with details of his father's murder woven in: "The play's the thing / Wherein I'll catch the conscience of the King." My own instinct is that in 1822 the opera might have invited parallels with events still more recent and closer to home than Dieckmann's proposal of 1790–1815, but that *no* reading can be sustained consistently—just as Mozart's explosion of martial rhetoric in *Don Giovanni* only fleetingly called up the revolutionary fervor of the 1780s. The beauty of the method, after all, lies in the fact that while one listener might discover in Mauregato traces of Napoleon's character, another will be put in mind of Metternich: this preserves the essential deniability. That Napoleon and Metternich could be interchanged is less bizarre than first it seems. One was a brilliant military strategist, the other a gifted diplomat; each man used his distinctive talent to seize vast political power (and, curiously, they both also took math and fencing lessons from the same professors at Strassbourg).[55] Certainly, my aim here is not to decode once and for all what Schubert's opera meant so much as to understand *how* it was designed to stimulate political engagement in its own time. The ambition to summon current events—by allowing music's own bearing and rhetoric to carve independent meanings from the libretto's words—would account for at least some of the opera's anomalies.

Franz Grillparzer's play *König Ottokars Glück und Ende* (1823), about a thirteenth-century Bohemian king whose brilliant career suggested parallels with Napoleon, was ultimately shielded from censorship because Ottokar's downfall had led to the rise of the Habsburgs—a gift from heaven, Grillparzer called it in private. Discontinuities in the shadow narrative, therefore, moments where an analogy with the present is strongly suggested then immediately taken back, may just point to oblique intentions. This being so, it should not surprise us that coming right on the heels of Schubert's chorus of enraged conspirators, even before its full import has had a chance to sink in, there follows a touching portrayal of Mauregato's affection for his daughter Estrella: he is not as wicked as all that, life is complex, and the stage is set for Froila's forgiveness later.

Further strategies for deflecting censorial attention are hinted at in Grillparzer's autobiography and in the diaries of Joseph Schreyvogel, the chief dramaturg of the Burgtheater, who had taken a position as censor, according to Grillparzer, "for the sole purpose of stamping as many good works as possible *admitittur*." The situation was more complicated

---

55. Clemens von Metternich, *Metternich: The Autobiography, 1773–1815* (Welwyn Garden City, Ravenhall Books, Linden Publishing, 2004), 4.

than that. It was a coup for Sedlinitzky when the liberal-minded Schreyvogel agreed to work part-time for his office in 1817. For Schreyvogel, the position brought not only the chance to steer decisions but also a salary, a state pension, and respect in influential social circles, putting him in line for the directorship of the Burgtheater. Frustrations soon took over, and by 1823 Schreyvogel's authority was considerably scaled back, but he was determined to stay in the good graces of the imperial family and to keep the job long enough to collect his pension.[56] Schreyvogel knew well how to comply with restrictions just enough to bring a play to performance (resorting, that is, to judicious preemptive self-censorship), while remaining respectful of the author's intent. Better, he thought, completely to cut away minor characters belonging to the clergy than to alter their station in order to avoid the "ticklish" ban on portraying religious institutions or persons. In 1815, when concerns were raised that Adolph Müllner's play *Yngurd* might bring to mind Napoleon, he knew exactly where to intervene: any innuendo distinguishing between an acquired crown and one gained by birthright had better be softened if it seemed to favor the former. It was risky enough that the hero was the son-in-law of a king and that his career, like Napoleon's, had ended badly.[57]

In one famous act of defiance, Grillparzer merely manipulated the duration of applause by declining to take a bow when summoned by the crowd—a story he relates with glee in his autobiography. For a time there had been a ban on civil servants' receiving applause, which was to be reserved for heads of state. The emperor understood the affront, and Grillparzer was called in to the Police Bureau the next day (there is more on this incident in chapter 2, note 21). This interaction may cast an indirect light on the contemporary reception of *Alfonso und Estrella*'s overture, which begins with the depiction of a revolutionary storm: the double-dotted, bare-octave D minor, conjuring severe old authority, and menacing *forte* to *piano* timpani rumbles clearly herald the growing tempest (using expressive topics similar to those in Idomeneo's "Fuor del mare," which Vogl sang in 1819).[58] When the failed opera's overture was recycled for the first performance of *Rosamunde* in December 1823, the crowd went wild, and it had to be repeated.

---

56. Josef Schreyvogel, *Josef Schreyvogels Tagebücher 1810–1823*, ed. Karl Glossy, Schriften der Gesellschaft für Theatergeschichte, 3 vols. (Berlin: Verlag der Gesellschaft für Theatergeschichte, 1903), introduction, and vol. 2, especially, 280–389.
57. Schreyvogel, *Josef Schreyvogels Tagebücher*, vol. 2, 429–32 (Glossy's critical notes).
58. Andreas Liess, *Johann Michael Vogl: Hofoperist und Schubertsänger* (Graz and Cologne: Verlag Hermann Böhlaus Nachf., 1954), 200. Associations may bleed from one opera role to another, just as happens when we recognize our favorite actors in different roles in the movies. Between 1819 and 1821, just prior to Schubert's *Alfonso und Estrella* project, Vogl was cast in a wide variety of roles, from Gluck's tragic Orestes to Graf Wallstein in Weigl's dialect "Conversationsoper" *Die Schweizerfamilie*. During this time he could be heard in four Mozart operas—*Idomeneo, The Marriage of Figaro* (the Count), *The Abduction from the Seraglio*, and *The Magic Flute*. Vogl also took the part of Mikéli in Cherubini's *Der Wasserträger* (*Les deux journées*), a work that offered a perfect model for exploiting an incident in the historical past to critique contemporary politics.

This would not have been the first time that Schubert's friends orchestrated a noisy show of support at a public performance, as Waidelich reminds us about the premiere of *Die Zwillingsbrüder* in the Kärntnertortheater.[59] (Not coincidentally, perhaps, the mismatched overture was replaced when *Rosamunde* was first published in the mid-nineteenth century.) Even more remarkably, given that the opera never came to performance, a four-hand version already had been published *as* the overture to *Alfonso und Estrella* in 1826, suggesting that news of the opera had spread widely.[60] Opening *Alfonso und Estrella*'s third act is a full-fledged battle symphony, a Goyaesque scene representing the carnage of war. Just in case we do not understand the meaning of all the percussive bashing and the piccolo shrieks, a boy and girl flee the battle, describing the horrors we have just heard: corpses are strewn everywhere, and chilling screams are heard as the hoards catch up to fleeing citizens. (Even the composer of *Les Huguenots* might have been impressed by this vivid portrayal of battling factions!) It was a convenient fiction of Romantic aesthetics that music's meanings were infinite and untranslatable: at least where illustrative music was concerned, expressive conventions were sufficiently ingrained that a serious mismatch between music and dramatic situation eventually would make itself felt. What could be exploited, of course, was the inevitable time lag in widespread comprehension.[61]

III

Froila, Mauregato, and Alfonso all have a basis in Spanish history, but Estrella is drawn from some other sphere, long a puzzle for Schubert scholars. Colin Smith, a hispanist, makes the intriguing suggestion that Schubert's opera is based on the play *La estrella de Sevilla*, attributed to Lope de Vega: "Seville in particular vibrates operatically to a dangerous degree. To the well-known canon may be added Schubert's little-performed *Alfonso und Estrella* (1821), based on the Spanish Golden Age play *La estrella de Sevilla*, and Massenet's *Chérubin* (1905), which develops the characters invented by Beaumarchais and da Ponte."[62] Smith does not elaborate; however, like the Estrella in *The Star of Seville* (a story cast in the twelfth century but understood as a commentary on the rule of Philip II, the sixteenth-century Spanish Habsburg king) the identity of Schubert's Estrella is unstable, flickering between corporeal presence and celestial ideal. (Lope de Vega's

---

59. Waidelich, "Josef Hüttenbrenners Entwurf," 37: "Bei Schuberts erster öffentlicher Präsentation im großen Rahmen, der Uraufführung der Posse *Die Zwillingsbrüder* im Kärntnertortheater, waren seine Freunde, nach einhelligem Zeugnis der Journalisten, als Clacque geradezu unangenehm aufgefallen."

60. Waidelich, *Franz Schubert: Dokumente 1817–1830*, vol. 1, documents 374, 269.

61. Linguistic barriers function similarly, and when Domenico Barbaja took over the Kärntnertortheater and the Theater an der Wien from late 1821 to 1826, German-language opera gradually was driven from the stage.

62. Colin Smith, "'Ma in Spagna son già mille e tre': On Opera and Literature," *Modern Language Review* 91 (1996): 37. *Der Stern von Sevilla* was banned by the Viennese censors in 1826 for its depiction of a murderous prince. Alice M. Hanson, *Musical Life in Biedermeier Vienna* (Cambridge: Cambridge University Press, 1985), 43.

EXAMPLE 1.3 (discussed on p. 33) Franz Schubert, *Alfonso und Estrella*, D 732, act one, no. 7, chorus and aria, Allegro moderato, 92–115 and vocal line 145–151; 181–187. Vocal score, based on Bärenreiter edition, BA 5540a. By kind permission.

Estrella is "the metaphorical light that leads to truth," in the words of James Mandrell.)[63] Alfonso knows her from a song that his father sings: when a knight pursues the heavenly vision to the edge of a cliff and tries to lock her in his embrace, he plunges to his death.

---

63. James Mandrell, "Of Material Girls and Celestial Women, or, Honor and Exchange," in *Heavenly Bodies: The Realms of* La Estrella de Sevilla, conference proceedings from an international symposium on *La estrella de Sevilla* held at the Pennsylvania State University, 1992, ed. Frederick A. De Armas (Lewisburg, Pa.: Bucknell University Press; London: Associated University Presses, 1996), 148–49. Mandrell builds on an essay by

EXAMPLE 1.3 *(continued).*

Harlan H. Sturm and Sara G. Sturm, "who speak first of Estrella's 'symbolic role' as the light leading to recognition of a higher order, and they conclude that, in terms of astronomy, 'the play's title, *La estrella de
Sevilla*, has double significance, for Seville itself is a star which will guide the King. The play is in this sense
about a king who must learn the true nature of monarchy from his subjects themselves.'" In another stimulating essay in this volume Melveena McKendrick supplies this background: "In the 1570s, several decades
before *La estrella de Sevilla* was written, the Escobedo affair had implicated the most catholic of kings,
Philip II, in a reason-of-state scandal that outraged the misinformed and caused great anguish to Philip
himself when he discovered that he had been manipulated by his treacherous advisor Antonio Pérez (to
whom don Arias bears more than a passing resemblance)." Melveena McKendrick, "In the Wake of *Machiavelli—Razón de Estado*, Morality, and the Individual," 88. "Reason of state" allows that breaking the law and
restricting rights is justifiable when the security of the state (or the authority of its ruler) hangs in the balance. *The Star of Seville* circulated widely in German translation in the early nineteenth century, and, indeed,
Grillparzer deemed Lope de Vega his favorite author.

"What a beautiful story, father," is young Alfonso's curious response to the violent end of the ballad of the cloud maiden—this critical story-within-the-story that became one of the casualties of Liszt's production (and echoes of which, in Schubert, surfaced again as "Täuschung"—Delusion—in *Winterreise*). Froila's song reignites Alfonso's passion for the hills and the cliffs on the outskirts of his home, which are "auf einmal neu und wunderbar." He breathes more easily in the open air: "im *freien* ist mir wohl!" Moments later, when Estrella appears, lost in the wilderness, he thinks she is the cloud maiden.[64] "Who are you?" Alfonso marvels. *We* already have heard her, accompanied by a women's hunting chorus (she is Diana), in a sad air with a breathtaking vocal turn at the climax of each strophe, a kind of sonic somersault, or lassoing yodel, whose declamation gets progressively more absurd: pure voice as an emblem of freedom (ex. 1.3, score on pp. 31–32):[65]

Es schmückt die weiten Säle	Adorning spacious halls
Des Goldes eitle Pracht,	Is all the idle pomp of gold,
Doch meine bange Seele	Yet fearsome Night
Umhüllet düst're Nacht.	Enshrouds my anxious soul.
[Zur Jagd, zur Jagd!	[To the hunt, to the hunt!
Die frohe Jagd befreit die Brust.]	The merry hunt frees the heart.]
Guitarrentöne hallen,	The music of guitars rings out,
Der Blumen fülle lacht,	A wealth of flower blossoms laugh,
Und Balsamdüfte wallen,	And soothing scents linger on,
Mein Herz umhüllt die Nacht.	But Night enshrouds my heart.
Ach, was mein Herz begehret,	Ah, my heart's desire
Ist freundlich, zart und still,	Is friendly, sweet, and calm,
Nie wird es mir gewähret	Never will I be granted it
Im blendenden Gewühl.	Amid the glist'ning tumult.

Later, her father envisions her on the battlefield, a protective angel fluttering in the wind (not unlike Florestan's vision in the dungeon of Leonore). And with Alfonso she sings a C-major battle hymn—about the coming of dawn—that will bring to mind the "Marseillaise" ("Schön und herrlich seh ich's tagen," no. 28; Alfonso and Estrella see one another striding across the battlefield in the second stanza: "Ja ich seh dich im Getümmel schreiten in der Hoheit/Hoffnung Glanz"). She is Liberty. The revolutionary hymn was banned throughout Europe after 1792, but this could not prevent some of its distinctive features from appearing in new melodies (musical resemblance, after all, is difficult to

---

64. Her arrival is presaged by a distinctive clarinet theme, reminiscent of the echoing shepherd's call in Weigl's *Die Schweizerfamilie* by which Emmeline feels Jakob Fribourg's ("free citizen") proximity before his arrival.

65. Goddess of the hunt, and twin to Apollo, Diana exacted a promise from her father, Zeus, never to force her to marry against her will. Her priestesses took a vow of chastity.

litigate).[66] At Notre Dame Cathedral in Paris, declared a "temple of reason" in 1793, statues of Liberty had even replaced statues of the Virgin for a time, and Liberty was a commonplace figure on English stages, where she could be openly named.[67] In Vienna, however, the authorities were sufficiently paranoid that even a shipment of tins from France with "liberty" stamped into a seal was confiscated.[68] Just as the words "viva la libertà" would have conjured up different things for Lorenzo da Ponte (banished from Vienna in the early 1790s),[69] for Johann Senn, or for Sedlinitzky, everyone has a different picture of Estrella. The coarse political mercenary Adolfo sees in her a "sweet snake" and threatens to take her by force to the "despised altar of marriage"—an image that was especially potent at a time when consent in marriage was a topic of serious legal reform, whose urgency was reflected on stages everywhere (compare the four images of "liberty" shown in fig. 1.1, noting especially the many-headed serpent that Le Clerc's Liberty has conquered and how closely Delacroix's figure matches Diana's pose in the marble; the Velázquez Madonna wears a crown of stars). Allusions to forced marriage (or else consent withheld) became a symbol of tyranny, domestic and more broadly political.[70] The same theme is at the heart of Schubert's opera *Die Zwillingsbrüder.*[71] Now the ancient prophecy too comes into sharper focus: Liberty will consent to be chained only to the one who returns the rule of law. Give me Liberty, or give me death: might some listeners have understood in Alfonso's response to the knight's deadly plunge at the end of the ballad of the cloud maiden a reference to the Leucadian "leap of faith" familiar from Tieck or from Grillparzer's *Sappho*?

66. Matthew Head has explored woman as a figure of freedom in Beethoven's work, including Klärchen in *Egmont*, Leonore, and Leonore Prohaska, in the work of the same name for which Beethoven wrote incidental music in 1815. Matthew Head, "Beethoven Heroine: A Female Allegory of Music and Authorship in *Egmont*," *19th Century Music* 30 (2006): 97–132. "Precisely because women were subject to severe constraints on their publications," he writes, "heroines who 'broke through' those constraints emblematized freedom from prescribed roles and identities. What better image to represent an author's movement from servant to 'free' artist than a woman acting with heroic self-determination?" (100–101).

67. For an account of the English situation, see David Worrall, *Theatric Revolution: Drama, Censorship, and Romantic Period Subcultures 1773–1832* (Oxford: Oxford University Press, 2006). Chapter 4, "Theatrical Subcultures: Fireworks, Freemasonry, and Philip de Loutherbourg," traces a fascinating prehistory of themes later taken up in *The Magic Flute*.

68. Ogris, "Die Zensur in der Ära Metternichs," 246. He does not say, unfortunately (nor does Wiesner), just when this occurred. Another familiar spot where "liberty" is shouted on stage is in the vaudeville at the end of Gluck's *Orfeo*, whose message on its face embraces willing servitude: "the bonds of love are preferable to liberty." What this has to do with the Orpheus story is not immediately apparent. But neither is the revised French text at this point merely a literal translation of the Italian original: it has been reshaped to allow these words to be heard again and again. This functions rather like the words of Max Ophuls's Contesse Louise in *The Earrings of Madame de . . .* when, her authoritarian husband lurking in the next room, she escorts her Italian lover to the door, whispering to him over and over: "Je n'aime tu pas."

69. For a fuller picture, see Otto Biba, "Da Ponte in New York, Mozart in New York," *Current Musicology* 81 (2006): 109–21.

70. Indeed, Metternich himself tied up the publication of a book on Austrian marriage law for seven years until it appeared, without permission, in Leipzig. Ogris, "Die Österreichische Zensur in der Ära Metternichs," 246.

71. Leandro Fernàndez de Moratín's 1801 play *The Maidens' Consent (El sí de las niñas)* put the subject center stage. See Moratín, *The Maiden's Consent*, trans. Harriet de Onís (Great Neck, N.Y.: Barron's Educational Series, 1962). We can recognize echoes of this usage, too, in the plays-within-the-play in Tieck's *World Upside-Down*.

Artemis of Versailles, "Diana Huntress, accompanied by a hind," 2nd half of 4th cen. BCE, marble, Louvre, Paris; Photo: Hervé Lewandowski; Réunion des Musées Nationaux / Art Resource, NY; By kind permission.

Eugene Delacroix (1798–1863), "Liberty Leading the People," [1830], oil on canvas, Louvre, Paris; Photo: Hervé Lewandowski; Réunion des Musées Nationaux / Art Resource, NY; By kind permission.

FIGURE 1.1 Everyone has a different picture of Estrella: Diana, Liberty on the Battlefield, Cloud Maiden, Sweet Snake.

Diego Rodriguez Velázquez (1599–1660), "The Immaculate Conception" (The Madonna of Seville), 1618–1619, oil on canvas, National Gallery, London; Photo: © National Gallery, London / Art Resource, NY; By kind permission.

Pierre Thomas Le Clerc (ca. 1740–?), "Liberty," 1794, etching on blue background, Musée de la Ville de Paris, Musée Carnavalet, Paris; Photo: Erich Lessing / Art Resource, NY. By kind permission.

This takes us back to Beethoven's canon. Several commentators have felt its presence behind Schubert's elaborate canon complex in the first-act finale.[72] That is interesting because the two canons do not sound alike at all, although memorable features of Beethoven's quartet enter into Schubert's canon too. Prominent solo viola and cello lines are used in Estrella's lead-in to the canon, along with horn fifths, a conventional way of stirring memory (Beethoven drew us in with divisi violas and celli, we will recall). When Mauregato begins the three-part canon "Was werd ich nun beginnen, wie schrecklich ist die Wahl (was wird er nun beginnen, wie lenkt er seine Wahl)," the texture thins to pizzicato strings, as the contemplative moment unfolds. Everyone sings similar words whose end rhymes "Wahl/Qual" are close in sound to Beethoven's rhymes "Gefahr/wunderbar/klar." One voice (Mauregato's) is made to leap out of the texture: "wie schrecklich ist die Wahl" (how dreadful is the choice)! A bit of this is shown in ex. 1.4. Released from the plot, these words —like Jaquino's "Mir fällt kein Mittel ein, der Vater willigt ein"—easily could be heard as an indictment of the 1820s political scene: Metternich or the emperor, it really was not much of a choice (although, absent Metternich, a constitutional

72. Among others, see Lühning, "Schubert als Dramatiker," 41–42, and Walther Dürr, "Schuberts romantisch-heroische Oper Alfonso und Estrella im Kontext französischer und italienischer Tradition," in *Der vergessene Schubert: Franz Schubert auf der Bühne*, exhibition catalog, ed. Erich Wolfgang Partsch and Oskar Pausch (Vienna: Böhlau Verlag, 1997), 94–95. (Dürr is reminded of the canon in *Così fan tutte* too, which is a three-part canon with an added obbligato voice that asserts itself by a rhythmic patter.)

EXAMPLE 1.4 *(continued)*.

monarchy might still have seemed a viable possibility). Schubert's richly hewn circular melody begins in F, turns to F minor, and returns to the parallel major at the close, after the bass has staked out root motions through A♭ and D♭, allowing a smooth glide back onto V/F. A Gluckian chorus joins in twice to shudder at the "grauenvolle Wahl" before Mauregato comes up with a way to evade Adolfo's claim, remembering the old prophecy: "Ein Mittel noch!" (Indeed, if Estrella were nothing more than Mauregato's daughter, why should there ever have existed a prophecy about whom she would marry?) Within the first-act finale, the canon melody comes three times (sinking by half step at its second appearance, then, after further interruptions, returning in faster tempo in A major, accompanied by new obbligato lines), whereby it becomes slowly engraved in memory. When, late in act 3 (no. 31), Froila then takes up this reminiscence motif once more (back in its original key, but with triplets and scoring that call up his tale of the elusive cloud maiden), it is to words that echo Beethoven's wondrous canon more closely:

Nun wird mir alles *klar,*	Now all becomes clear to me,
der Himmel tauet Segen,	Heaven thaws a blessing,
o Herr, auf deinen Wegen	O Lord, what paths you have found
wie bist du *wunderbar!*	And how wondrous you are!

Coincidence? Or deliberate invocation of a piece, and a composer, that everybody knew? Where the delight in *Mehrdeutigkeit* was a regular part of theatrical experience it hardly would have mattered. Associations were drawn between familiar pieces in the repertory just as connections were sought to the world beyond the theater. The Sevillian operas *Fidelio, Don Giovanni,* and *Le nozze di Figaro* all were a fixed presence in the 1820s, and they remain so today. And with *Alfonso und Estrella* more visible on the firmament now than ever before, we can perhaps make out a new constellation in the skies above Seville.

Playing out on stages and in drawing rooms across Europe was a lively conversation about the nature and limits of liberty, whose many facets Schubert systematically probed, undeterred by the ban on naming Liberty. She is the object of yearning in the Ernst Schulze song "Um Mitternacht"—the star that shines through darkest night and still into the dawn. Liberty as release in death or suicide is a focus in many of his songs, especially those on poems of Mayrhofer.[73] At the outer fringes of the conversation is the riveting tale of consensual murder found in the song "Der Zwerg" (1822), on a poem of Matthäus von Collin, one of the most frequently performed songs at the Gesellschaft der Musikfreunde. "Muth" from *Winterreise* captures the liberating madness of blasphemy—the greatest offense of all to Catholic authority. A strophic song with a pounding dance refrain, "Irdisches Glück," written late in life, is a free spirit's definition of earthly happiness and of a life well lived: if, when your time to leave this world has come, your friends gaze long into your eyes and press your hand, then you will have struck a good balance with liberty (meanwhile, advises the third stanza, lay low, enjoy life's quiet pleasures, and you need not fear for your neck). From 1817, we have a male partsong "La Pastorella al Prato," taken from Carlo Goldoni's libretto *Il filosofo di campagna,* which is a little demonstration: say it in Italian and say it in the pastorale mode, and Liberty's flag will wave still centuries later for all who know how to listen (as we hear in the final cadence in ex. 1.5).[74]

---

73. See Blake Howe's penetrating study of the four last Mayrhofer songs, "The Allure of Dissolution: Bodies, Forces, and Cyclicity in Schubert's Final Mayrhofer Settings," *Journal of the American Musicological Society* 62 (2009): 271–322.

74. Carlo Goldoni, *Il filosofo di campagna. A comic Opera; As performed in the King's Theater in the Hay-Market* (London: W. Griffin, 1768). As in so many works from this period, the theme of marital consent plays a role in this libretto. Schubert made a second setting for solo soprano, the perfect embodiment of Liberty.

EXAMPLE 1.5 Franz Schubert, "La pastorella" (Carlo Goldoni), D 513, 28–48.

EXAMPLE I.5 *(continued).*

La pastorella al prato	The little shepherdess on the pasture
Contenta se ne va	Is content when going to him,
Coll'agnellino a lato	With the lambkin at her side
Cantando in libertà	She sings in liberty.
Se l'innocente amore	When she receives the
Gradisce il suo pastore	Innocent love from her shepherd,
La bella pastorella	The beautiful shepherdess
Contenta agnar sarà	Is always content.

In his last, unfinished opera Schubert returned once more to the question of consent, painting a harmonious vision of a consensual three-way marriage: the libretto was banned. This is the subject of the following study. The numerous failed projects in Schubert's oeuvre especially deserve our imaginative engagement, for although their reception history proper must remain forever slim, they have as much to tell about the spirit of the age as do history's great successes.

Leit' alles, Gott, zum frohen Ende,
Wir geben uns in deine Hände!

—*DER GRAF VON GLEICHEN*, act 1, finale

2

The Matrimonial Anomaly (Schubert's Opera for Posterity)

I

The story of the Crusader Count Ernst ("Earnest") von Gleichen, who was granted a special dispensation from Rome to take two wives, has been repeated dozens, perhaps even hundreds, of times in German literature in accounts reaching back to the thirteenth century. Yet at no time before the late eighteenth century is there any indication that the traditional close, a three-way marriage sanctioned by the pope, was considered troublesome. Franz Schubert and Eduard von Bauernfeld's opera on the subject, as we shall see, posed a challenge to the Viennese court and the social engineers around Metternich (who employed an army of censors, some of them reluctant), precisely because it kept the medieval legend intact. The old legend became troubling in an age when the authorities expected that everything, including history, should conform to their modern social constructs; the city's stages were not to be used to present alternative visions of society or family.

In earlier times the story had appeared in every conceivable literary genre: as folktale or legend; as fairy tale; in poetry; in plays (for reading and for staging); as a dramatic work with incidental music; and in several operas. The Age of Sensibility witnessed a tremendous surge of interest in the story, which found its way by the later eighteenth century to French and English stages as well.[1] A tradition of visual representation flourished simultaneously, helping to feed and sustain the legend. Grimm's *Deutsche Sagen*

---

1. The most comprehensive survey of the legend's history is in a 1911 doctoral dissertation by Eberhard Sauer, *Die Sage vom Grafen von Gleichen in der deutschen Literatur* (University of Strassburg: Druck von M. DuMont Schauberg, 1911); documents important to the transmission of the story are collected in Wilhelm Johann Albert Freiherr von Tettau [1804–94], *Über die Quellen, die ursprüngliche Gestalt und die Allmählige*

of 1816 relates the story in a brief, unembellished account, only incorporating references to the most important place-names and artifacts that have fed its transmission. We learn of a tombstone in the churchyard at Saint Peter's monastery in Erfurt that depicts the Count with his two wives, the German countess, and the young sultan's daughter who rescued him from years of captivity in the Orient. The life-size monument, dated approximately 1250, still exists, having been moved to safety inside the Erfurt Mariendom when Napoleon's troops ransacked the town in 1813 (the events themselves are said to have taken place a century earlier, during the reign of Pope Gregory IX):[2] that same year an essay in a Weimar journal devoted to "curiosities in the physical, literary, artistic and historical worlds" rehearsed widespread contemporary debates over the historical foundation of the story—was the Count really a bigamist? did the pope really give his consent?—and printed engraved depictions of the tale. The most impressive is a meticulously colored portrait copied from the Erfurt grave monument by a Professor Wendel (shown in fig. 2.1).[3]

By the time the Viennese censors banned the libretto for Franz Schubert's opera on the same subject in October 1826, the story of *Der Graf von Gleichen* was already well known in that city, having circulated, been published, and even performed in nearly every one of the genres enumerated earlier. A laconic notation in the diary of Schubert's librettist and friend Eduard von Bauernfeld records the news: "The libretto banned by the censors. Schubert wants to compose it anyhow."[4] In a letter to Ferdinand von Mayerhofer on 13

Umbildung der Erzählung von der Doppelehe eines Grafen von Gleichen: Ein kritischer Versuch (Erfurt: Verlag von Carl Villaret, 1867). The *Neue Schubert Ausgabe*'s edition of Schubert's unfinished opera recently has appeared, with a detailed introduction to the legend's sources by Manuela Jahrmärker. Jahrmärker, ed., *Der Graf von Gleichen, Franz Schubert: Neue Ausgabe Sämtlicher Werke*, ed. Walther Dürr, Michael Kube, and Walburga Litschauer, ser. 2, vol. 17 (Kassel: Bärenreiter Verlag, 2006), ix–xxxii. I discuss only some of the same sources here.

2. On this point see Jahrmärker, *Der Graf von Gleichen*, xii.

3. "Der zweibeweibte Graf von Gleichen und seine Gemahlinnen," in *Curiositäten der physisch- literarisch- artistisch- historischen Vor- und Mitwelt: zur angenehmen Unterhaltung für gebildete Leser,* ed. A. Vulpius, vol. 3 (Weimar: im Verlage des Landes-Industrie-Comptoirs, 1813), 6–17 (plates at the back of the volume). Numerous engravings of the grave monument circulated from the middle of the eighteenth century; the earliest one I have located was published together with a disputation of the legend: Johann Heinrichs von Falckenstein, *Analecta Thuringo-Nordgaviensia* (Worinnen vor diesesmahl vorgestellet wird . . . Klarer Beweis, daß Graf Ernst von Gleichen nicht zwey Weiber zu gleichen Zeit gehabt, mithin kein *Bigamus* gewesen . . .), vol. 10 (Schwabach: Christoph Conrad Zell, 1744).

4. "Der Operntext von der Censur verboten. Schubert will sie trotzdem componieren." The diary entry is dated October 1826; Bauernfeld only prepared excerpts from his voluminous diaries for publication in the 1870s, however. This manuscript, which has never been printed in its entirety, is housed in the Handschriftensammlung of the Wienbibliothek. Select portions were published in the *Grillparzer Jahrbuch* in 1894 and issued separately under the title *Aus Bauernfelds Tagebüchern,* ed. Carl Glossy (Vienna, 1895). Because the pagination varies between editions, I shall cite entries by their date. Bauernfeld records first mentioning the idea of a libretto on the *Graf von Gleichen* material to Schubert in March 1825. The plan was brought to realization in May 1826, and the completed libretto handed over to Schubert in July of that year.

FIGURE 2.1 Wendel, "Grabmal des Grafen von Gleichen auf dem Petersberg zu Erfurt" from "Der zweibeweibte Graf von Gleichen und seine Gemahlinnen," in *Curiositäten der physisch- literarisch-artistisch- historischen Vor- und Mitwelt: zur angenehmen Unterhaltung für gebildete Leser* [ed. A. Vulpius], vol. 3 (Weimar: im Verlage des Landes-Industrie-Comptoirs, 1813), unnumbered Plate. Yale Collection of German Literature, Beinecke Rare Book and Manuscript Library. By kind permission.

October 1826, Bauernfeld had more to say: *"My opera is forbidden.* But it is causing a furor, and the censor himself condemned it to death with tears in his eyes. You wouldn't recognize it, there are so many alterations and embellishments. It won't do for Vienna—but steps are being taken toward foreign stages. Hofrath Mosel likely will make efforts on its behalf."[5] At just what point did the story told by Bauernfeld and Schubert cross the line of acceptability? The officially submitted copy of the libretto and the attendant censor's files have not survived, having presumably gone up in flames in the 1927 fire that consumed the Vienna Justizpalast. This leaves us only to reason from the text—the libretto and its musical realization—and from a consideration of its sources and precedents on the stage in Vienna and elsewhere.

5. *"Meine Oper ist verbothen.* Sie macht aber Furore, u. der Censor selbst hat sie mit Thränen in den Augen zum Tode verdammt. Du würdest sie nicht kennen, so verändert u. ausgeführst ist sie. Für Wien ist's nichts—indeß werden für das Ausland Schritte gethan. Hofrath Mosel wird sich wahrscheinlich thätig annehmen." Walburga Litschauer, *Neue Dokumente zum Schubert-Kreis: Aus Briefen und Tagebüchern seiner Freunde* (Vienna: Musikwissenschaftlicher Verlag, 1986), 57.

In his documentary biography of Schubert Otto Erich Deutsch relates that Bauernfeld had been impressed by Franz Volkert's heroic-comic opera *Ernst, Graf von Gleichen*, performed at the theaters in the Leopoldstadt and Josefstadt in 1815 when Bauernfeld would have been just thirteen years old.[6] These performances, we should note, took place under the heightened censorship restrictions imposed in 1813, just as Metternich was coming to power. Unfortunately, nothing of Volkert's opera is known to have survived, except the reviews, which at least provide brief hints of the plot. Bäuerle's *Theaterzeitung* reports that the second act moved inexorably toward a tragic close—a striking departure from the folktale and Schubert's opera both. The same reviewer remarks that the story is a familiar one, having only recently appeared before the public in another version.[7] The generic designation can perhaps tell us something more about this lost opera. According to a study by Helen Geyer-Kiefl, a *heroisch-komische Oper*, especially popular in Vienna in the suburban Leopoldstadt and Josefstadt theaters in the early decades of the nineteenth century, meant either a parody of a historical heroic subject (making the hero look ridiculous) or a story, like *The Magic Flute*, in which the hero only gradually learns to behave like one. (She discusses numerous librettos that conform to these patterns.)[8] Apparently, distancing the story through parody and cutting away the happy end overcame the censors' objections.

Our attention must also be directed to the city of Weimar because of the far-reaching influence of Goethe's treatments of the Graf von Gleichen material, extending from the first publication of his play *Stella* in 1776 (not coincidentally, one suspects, right at the time of the American Revolution), where the traditional tale is told at the climax of a modern eighteenth-century story about a man caught between two wives (more about this later), to his association with an opera by Carl Eberwein, a student of Carl Friedrich Zelter, bearing the same title as Schubert's, also in two acts, which premiered in May 1824 and made sporadic appearances in the repertory over the next eleven years. This opera (advertised, like the designation on Bauernfeld's libretto, as a "romantische Oper") reportedly was discussed and rehearsed in Goethe's home as it took shape.[9] Like

6. Otto Erich Deutsch, *Schubert: Die Dokumente seines Lebens*, Franz Schubert, *Neue Ausgabe sämtlicher Werke*, ser. 8, suppl., vol. 5 (Kassel: Bärenreiter Verlag, 1964), 356–57.

7. *Wiener Theaterzeitung*, ed. Adolf Bäuerle (Vienna: Keck Verlag), 28 November 1815, 350–51. According to the review, the opera premiered in the Theater in der Leopoldstadt on 28 October 1815: this means either that there was a change in venue or that the production moved soon after the first performance, for it shows up on a roster of operas performed at the Josephstadt in November. According to the *Theater-Journal und Verzeichniß der im Jahre 1815 auf dem k.k. privil. Theater in der Josephstadt und Meidling aufgeführten Trauer-Schau-Lust-und Singspiele*, ed. Carl Schmidt (Vienna: Felix Stöckholzer von Hirschfeld, 1816), the opera was performed at the Theater in der Josephstadt on 18, 19, 20, 22, and 27 November 1815. *Die Teufelsmühle* evidently played on 28 October 1815 in that theater.

8. Helen Geyer-Kiefl, *Die heroisch-komische Oper: ca. 1770–1820* (Tutzing: Hans Schneider, 1987).

9. Wilhelm Bode, *Goethes Schauspieler und Musiker: Erinnerungen von Eberwein und Lobe* (Berlin: Ernst Siegfried Mittler u. Sohn, 1912), 17. Bode reports that the opera found a friendly reception in other cities as well.

Schubert's draft, the first act takes place in the Orient, the second in the Occident. That will have been merely a function of genre, not direct influence: the five-act plays on the subject nearly all begin with the Count's departure for the Crusades from his home in Thuringia, a prehistory only implied in the operas. A lengthy review in the *Allgemeine musikalische Zeitung* in June 1824 painted an intriguing picture of Eberwein's opera, complete with a summary of its surprising twists to the inherited plot material. There is high praise for its dramaturgy, and for many of the individual numbers, including a striking four-voiced canon in the first act, and an overture, in E♭, plainly modeled on *The Magic Flute*.[10] Eberwein's penchant for unusual enharmonic modulation and his rich orchestration are given special notice. Much admiration also falls to the librettist, only cryptically identified in the review (his name is absent from the playbill for the premiere, shown in fig. 2.2).[11] Would Schubert have known of the existence of Eberwein's opera as

---

And on 14 July 1824 Zelter wrote to Goethe with the news that Eberwein had arrived in Berlin to offer his opera. Johann Wolfgang Goethe, *Briefwechsel zwischen Goethe und Zelter in den Jahren 1799 bis 1832*, ed. Edith Zehm et al., *Sämtliche Werke nach Epochen seines Schaffens: Münchner Ausgabe, Text 1799–1827*, (Munich: Carl Hanser Verlag, 1991), 20.1:810. An article on music in Berlin in the *Allgemeine musikalische Zeitung*, 10 May 1826, reported that a recitative and aria from the opera had been given in concert the previous month (318).

10. *Allgemeine musikalische Zeitung*, no. 26 (June 1824): 423–28. A full score and numerous parts for Eberwein's opera belonging to the Deutsches Nationaltheater (Sign. 160) are now housed at the Thüringisches Landesmusikarchiv in Weimar. The prompter's part contains indications that the opera was later arranged into four acts.

11. There is some confusion about the authorship of the libretto. The *Allgemeine musikalische Zeitung* reviewer identifies the librettist as Herr Regierungsrat S———, better known by his pseudonym Janus a costa, and remarks on the uncommon suitability of his text for music—a happy consequence of the librettist's own extensive musical background. Bode identifies the author as Friedrich Schmidt, an accomplished pianist and a great admirer of Beethoven, as does the critical commentary to the Goethe-Zelter correspondence in the recent Munich edition of Goethe's works. Johann Wolfgang Goethe, *Briefwechsel zwischen Goethe und Zelter in den Jahren 1799 bis 1832*, ed. Edith Zehm et al., *Sämtliche Werke nach Epochen seines Schaffens*, (Munich: Carl Hanser Verlag, 1998), 20.3:638. Some libretto catalogs give both Schmidt and Friedrich Peucer, a minor author and government official in Weimar. For reasons not specified, Peter Larsen's article on Eberwein in *Die Musik in Geschichte und Gegenwart: allgemeine Enzyklopädie der Musik*, founding editor Friedrich Blume, 2nd ed., ed. Ludwig Finscher (Kassel: Bärenreiter; Stuttgart: Metzler, 1994–2008), attributes the libretto solely to Heinrich Carl Friedrich Peucer. A charming volume of reminiscences of theatrical life in Weimar and Vienna by Heinrich Schmidt, a Weimar actor who moved to Vienna and eventually became director of the theaters at the Esterházy court, recalls the excellent pianism of his former schoolmate Geheimer Regierungsrat Friedrich Schmidt, who frequently played for Goethe and championed Beethoven's music. Peucer, too, was his classmate. In 1807 Goethe prepared copies and arrangements of several of his plays, including *Stella*, for Vienna. He sent them to Heinrich Schmidt, who hoped to arrange for their performance. Heinrich Schmidt, *Erinnerungen eines weimarischen Veteranen aus dem geselligen, literarischen und Theater=Leben* (Leipzig: Brockhaus, 1856). Incidentally, there is much else pertaining to music in this volume, including reports of the author's experiences with Haydn at Esterházy and accounts of performances by the castrati Marchesi and Crescentini in Vienna early in the century. A digital archive of Weimar theater programs and other associated materials in the Thüringisches Hauptstaatsarchiv is available at http://archive.thulb.uni-jena.de/ThHStAW/content/below/index.xml (accessed 16 August 2010).

Weimar.

Sonnabend, den 1. Mai 1824.

Zum Erstenmale:

Bei aufgehobenem Abonnement.

Der Graf von Gleichen

Romantische Oper in zwei Akten. Musik von C. Eberwein.

Noradin, Sultan von Syrien und Aegypten,	La Roche.
Chadija, dessen Tochter,	Jagemann.
Fatime, deren Vertraute,	L. Müller.
Ernst, Graf von Gleichen,	Stromeier.
Silvio, ein junger edler Venezianer, dessen Gefährte,	Eberwein.
Bruno, ein fränkischer Ritter,	Moltke.
Walther, Gleichens Vasall,	Franke.
Ein Mohr,	Engelmann.
Erscheinung der Irmengard, Gemahlin des Grafen von Gleichen,	Lorzing.

Kreutzfahrer,

Erwin,
Albert, } Gleichens Söhne.

Saracenische Krieger, Sclaven und Sclavinnen.

Thüringische Ritter, Reisige und Landleute.

Gefolge.

Chor von Klosterfrauen.

Der erste Act spielt im Morgenlande, der zweite in Thüringen.

Die Handlung fällt in die erste Hälfte des dreizehnten Jahrhunderts.

Der Text zu dieser Oper ist an der Casse für 3 gr. zu haben.

Preise der Plätze.

Balkon und Logen	—	—	—	16 Gr.
Parket	—	—	—	12 Gr.
Parterre	—	—	—	8 Gr.
Gallerie	—	—	—	4 Gr.

Anfang um 6 Uhr.　　　　　Ende gegen 9 Uhr.

Die Billets gelten nur am Tage der Vorstellung, wo sie gelößt worden.

Die freien Entreen sind heute ungültig.

FIGURE 2.2　Playbill for Carl Eberwein, *Der Graf von Gleichen*, Weimar, 1824. ThHStA Weimar, Generalintendanz des Deutschen Nationaltheaters und der Staatskapelle Weimar 2033, Bl. 116. By kind permission.

he contemplated his own? As it happens, the very next item on the same page of the *Allgemeine musikalische Zeitung* is a lengthy essay dedicated to Schubert's own music, a review of the song opuses 21 through 24, for which we have compelling circumstantial evidence that Schubert was familiar with its content.[12] A more attractive challenge could hardly have presented itself.

Weimar was also the home of Johann Karl August Musäus (1735–87), whose story "Melechsala," contained in the fifth volume of the *Volksmärchen der Deutschen* (1786; reprinted in Vienna in 1815–16), is the most direct literary source for Bauernfeld's libretto. Most obvious is the retention of the names for the Count's loyal companion, Kurt; for Fatime, who captures the free-spirited Kurt's heart; and for the countess Ottilia (whose name does double duty for Schubert in conjuring the world of Goethe's *Elective Affinities* of 1809).[13] The name of the title character, Melechsala, is changed to Suleika, infusing the story with the even more distinctive Goethean perfume of the *West-östlicher Divan*, but she retains the affectionate nickname given her by Musäus: "Die Blume der Welt."[14] Far more significant than the obvious borrowings from "Melechsala," however, are the thoroughgoing reworkings of many of its elements in Bauernfeld's libretto. Whereas Musäus's text bursts with the author's satiric commentary even as the story unfolds (in effect providing a script for a reader's or listener's response), the Bauernfeld-Schubert story maintains a naively sentimental posture from start to finish. We shall return to several crucial scenes presently.

A reading of Musäus's "Melechsala" almost certainly took place in the literary gatherings that Schubert and his friends regularly held, for Bauernfeld and Schubert were not the only ones to engage with the legend: in 1826 Moritz von Schwind sketched the homecoming of the Count von Gleichen, a scene of central importance in the architecture of Schubert's opera as well (it is shown in fig. 2.3). Additional drawings survive from the 1840s, and the story continued to hold Schwind's interest for many years thereafter. When, some thirty-five years after the initial sketched drawing was made, Schwind finally realized the scene as a full-scale painting, he again etched his own youthful self-portrait

---

12. The reviewer complains at length about Schubert's modulations and his "fantastic way of designating tones (which can hardly be called orthography)." Many of his suggestions for enharmonic respelling are drawn from the first of the Platen songs, "Die Liebe hat gelogen." The Wienbibliothek im Rathaus houses an autograph of the second Platen song, "Du liebst mich nicht," composed soon after, in which Schubert has crossed out one of the most complex passages and renotated it enharmonically (the manuscript, MH1862/c, is shown in plate 6.2). For its publication in op. 26, he returned to his original spelling. The song is taken up at length in chapter 6.

13. Bauernfeld follows Goethe's spelling of the name: Ottili*e*.

14. Melechsala is a name transmitted in earlier eighteenth-century accounts of the story such as Falckenstein. Coincidentally, most likely, in Carl Eberwein's opera the sultan's daughter, Chadija, identifies with the legendary Suleika. As she falls in love with the Count, whose image she first sees in a dream, she observes that he is every bit as handsome as the beautiful youth that Suleika chose for herself. "And what if I should wish to be Suleika?" she asks (act 1, fol. 74v; in the recitative preceding Silvio's Romanze, no. 5).

FIGURE 2.3   Moritz von Schwind (1804–1871), "Rückkehr des Grafen von Gleichen," 1826, study, pencil on paper, Angermuseum, Erfurt, Inv. Nr. 3477; Photo: Dirk Urban, Erfurt, 2007 © Angermuseum, Erfurt. By kind permission.

onto the figure of Kurt, the angelic page behind the Count who coyly solicits the viewer's gaze, competing for our attention with the shapely eastern Beauty on the horse (shown in fig. 2.4).[15] Traditionally, the Count's companion was an older man or his comrade-in-arms. In both Schubert's and Eberwein's operas the character becomes a charming youth, a *buffa* character along the lines of Mozart's Pedrillo in *The Abduction from the Seraglio*. Schwind (whom Schubert liked to call his Beloved) had both good looks and a lovely tenor voice; he might well have served as inspiration for Schubert's Kurt. The parallel character in Eberwein's opera is the young Silvio, a Shakespearean trouser role that was written for the composer's wife: a touch of gender ambiguity evidently was a traditional feature of this character's identity on the operatic stage.

A final constellation of influential sources emanating from Goethe's Weimar come from Musäus's famous nephew and student the professor August von Kotzebue (1761–1819, murdered by Karl Ludwig Sand), to whom Schubert had turned twice earlier in his

---

15. The identification of Schwind's self-portrait in the figure of Kurt in the painting is made by Friedrich Gross, "Zum Nutzen oder Nachteil der Gegenwart? Geschichte in Bildern Schwinds," in *Moritz von Schwind, Meister der Spätromantik*, ed. Siegmar Holsten et al., Staatliche Kunsthalle, Karlsruhe (Ostfildern-Ruit: Verlag Gerd Hatje, 1996), 204. The face depicted in the 1826 sketch appears to represent the same likeness.

FIGURE 2.4 Moritz von Schwind (1804–1871), "Die Rückkehr des Grafen von Gleichen,"
1863–1864, oil on canvas. Schack-Galerie, Bayerische Staatsgemäldesammlungen, Munich.
Photo: Bildarchiv Preussischer Kulturbesitz / Art Resource, NY. By kind permission.

youth for libretti (*Der Spiegelritter* [1811]; *Des Teufels Lustschloß* [1814]). Kotzebue produced
two separate plays on the Gleichen story, both replies to Goethe's *Stella*. In his play *La Peyrouse* (1797), the tale of a twelfth-century Crusader is brought into the present—as in
Stella—and displaced into an exotic South Sea island, where it doubled as an explanation of
the fate of the French explorer Jean-François Galaup, Comte de La Pérouse, who disappeared
after a shipwreck in 1788 and possibly was left stranded on a distant shore. The story was then
very much a current affair: La Pérouse had sent home his journals describing his voyage
around the world before embarking on the final leg of his journey, and these were published
in 1797. Kotzebue returned to the Gleichen story a second time in a mean-spirited parody of
the legend for "live marionettes" (*Der Graf von Gleichen, ein Spiel für lebendige Marionetten*
[1808]). Once again we meet the tendency to satirize the story. Goethe's annoyance over
this travesty of the legend and of his own recently revised *Stella* is well documented.[16]

16. Johann Wolfgang Goethe, *Dramen 1765–1775*, ed. Dieter Borchmeyer and Peter Huber, *Sämtliche Werke:
Briefe, Tagebücher und Gespräche 1*, vol. 4 (Frankfurt: Deutscher Klassiker Verlag, 1985), 988–89.

While *La Peyrouse* was immediately translated into English for performances at the Theater Royal on Drury Lane and traveled to the Parisian stage in 1810, early performances
in Vienna were blocked by censorship. The play was permitted, however, to be printed in
a Viennese edition of Kotzebue's works[17]—in 1825, the same year Bauernfeld and
Schubert first began to consider their own *Graf von Gleichen*. Nevertheless, even if Bauernfeld and Schubert encountered Kotzebue's treatments of the subject, there is evidence
to suggest that the censors treated potentially objectionable material more stringently
when it was to be put on stage than when merely buried in an edition of collected works.[18]
Moreover, as Kotzebue was murdered because of his suspected alliance with the Restoration cause, the censors perhaps felt it inappropriate to exclude even this play from the
complete edition of his works.

In early 1825 librettist and composer may have had entirely other grounds for optimism: news of the emperor's overturn of a ban on Franz Grillparzer's play *König Ottokars
Glück und Ende* had shot like wildfire through the city.[19] Joseph Schreyvogel, the chief
dramaturg of the Burgtheater and a part-time censor, had hoped to produce the play.
Grillparzer once maintained, as I have noted, that Schreyvogel became a censor only to
help worthy works come to performance—and this was not the first time he had placed
his reputation on the line for the poet. Schreyvogel submitted the manuscript to the
Bücherrevisionsamt with a strong letter of endorsement, preemptively warding off any
parallels an audience might draw between the figure of Ottokar, the thirteenth-century
Bohemian king (whose eventual downfall led to the rise of the Habsburgs), and Napoleon. Privately, Grillparzer admitted that Napoleon was very much on his mind as he
wrote the part, and he recalled in his autobiography that he had been intrigued by the
challenge of writing about historically remote subjects so as to bring to mind the present.
The play was immediately banned (in January 1824). After many months of frustrated
lobbying by Grillparzer and Schreyvogel both, an overturn was cleverly engineered by
Matthäus von Collin, whose historical dramas on the Babenberg dynasty are closely

17. August v. Kotzebue, *Erheiterungsbibliothek für Freunde romantischer Lectüre*, neue Folge, Theater, vol. 11
    (Vienna: bey Kaulfuß und Krammer, Buchhändler, 1825), 183–238.
18. See Walter Obermaier's discussion of the censorship battles over the Schiller song "Der Kampf" in Walter
    Obermeier, "Schubert und die Zensur," in *Schubert-Kongreß Wien 1978: Bericht*, ed. Otto Brusatti (Akade-
    mische Druck- u. Verlagsanstalt: Graz, 1979), 117–26. Briefly: the publisher Czerny sought approval to pub-
    lish Schubert's song in 1829: before purchasing the manuscript he had compared the text to five Viennese
    editions of Schiller's works and one from Graz. His petition was nonetheless denied. Obermaier's essay pro-
    vides a helpful account of the mechanism of Viennese censorship, as well as a valuable overview of all
    Schubert's encounters with censorship restrictions.
19. Anton Schindler filled Beethoven in on Grillparzer's history with the censors shortly before the two artists
    met in the spring of 1823. They discussed plans to collaborate on an opera soon after, and the conversation
    books from 1823 and 1824 vividly record Grillparzer's frustration over this latest episode. Ludwig van
    Beethoven, *Ludwig van Beethovens Konversationshefte*, issued by the Deutsche Staatsbibliothek Berlin, ed.
    Karl-Heinz Köhler and Dagmar Beck, with the help of Günter Brosche (Leipzig: VEB Deutscher Verlag für
    Musik, 1983), vols. 3–4.

intertwined with Grillparzer's story, and, what is more, who also hosted Schubertiades during these months: he persuaded a bedridden empress that the only good reading matter to be had was this one play, which the censorship office had unreasonably suppressed. As Karoline Auguste found in the play only the most loyal sentiments toward the state, she exerted pressure on her husband, the emperor Franz, to lift the ban. (That "Hail! Habsburg forever!" in the final scene must have done the trick.) This finally occurred just in the nick of time for the premiere in February 1825, with the popular actor Heinrich Anschütz in the title role—the same man whose Christmas Eve party in 1821 had been disrupted by police and Schubert reprimanded for playing dance music (as discussed in chapter 1).[20]

Bauernfeld's proposal to Schubert of an opera on the Graf von Gleichen story—another historically remote subject—came only weeks after the ban on *Ottokar* was lifted. If ever there was a promising moment to test the waters, this was it. A generation earlier Mozart's *Marriage of Figaro* had been given the green light by another emperor, even though the play of Beaumarchais upon which it was based was banned in Vienna. This overturn by appeal to a higher authority was a major victory for Grillparzer—and doubly noteworthy for the empress's role in the process. (It was a tested strategy: when *Fidelio* ran into trouble with the censors, Joseph von Sonnleithner had also appealed to the reigning empress, Marie Therese, who happily was partial to rescue operas.)[21]

---

20. My summary of these events draws on two sources. Heinrich Houbert Houben, *Verbotene Literatur von der klassischen Zeit bis zur Gegenwart*, vol. 1 (Berlin: Ernst Rowohlt Verlag, 1924; reprint, Hildesheim: Georg Olms Verlag, 1992), 221–35. Although Houben's magisterial study identifies sources only sparingly, it remains largely reliable. The chapter on Bauernfeld has not been superseded. A more recent volume supplies bibliographic material for Grillparzer's plays *König Ottokars Glück und Ende* and *Ein Treuer Diener Seines Herrn* and prints relevant passages from Grillparzer's diary, letters, and autobiography. Franz Grillparzer, *Dramen 1817–1828*, ed. Helmut Bachmaier, *Werke in sechs Bänden*, vol. 2 (Frankfurt: Deutscher Klassiker Verlag, 1986), 391–598 (texts); 830–911 (commentary). It was Heinrich Anschütz, incidentally, who delivered Grillparzer's funeral oration for Beethoven in 1827—yet another indicator of how closely interwoven these circles were.

21. Helga Lühning, ed., *Leonore. Oper in zwei Aufzügen von Ludwig van Beethoven: Das Libretto der Aufführung von 1806* (Bonn: Beethovenhaus, 1996), 8. Just a few years later it would be the emperor who sought to suppress a play that the censorship bureau had permitted: attending the first performance of Grillparzer's *Ein Treuer Diener Seines Herrn* (A Faithful Servant of His Master), the emperor grew suspicious over the enthusiastic and far too distended applause that broke out after Grillparzer declined to take a bow after the second act. The author was summoned to appear before the chief of police, Joseph Sedlinitzky, who informed him that His Imperial Majesty had so enjoyed the play that he wished to be its sole owner. Grillparzer was not to be shy about naming a price to compensate him for the suppression of his work. The poet replied that he would hate to see the emperor pay out a large sum to no avail: His Majesty was surely aware that there was an active underground market for plays? He knew for a fact that several copies of his latest work were already circulating. That put a quick end to the discussions. Grillparzer relates the story in his autobiography. The relevant portions are also quoted by Houben, *Verbotene Literatur*, 229–31. In the 1830s and 1840s, Bauernfeld became an even more outspoken opponent of censorship than Grillparzer, coming to near blows with the authorities on several occasions. Houben characterizes him as a master of tone, whose friends marveled at the lines the censors struck from his plays and delighted in the far more subversive ones left standing, which frequently were only realized in live performance through accent, gesture, or timing. Houben, *Verbotene Literatur*, 45–58.

Bearing in mind this immediate literary and social history, we must also consider the opera's relation to Bauernfeld's most direct source for the Gleichen story, Musäus's "Melechsala." To convey the distinctiveness of the opera's telling of the story, it is helpful to highlight the most significant adaptations of Musäus's *Märchen*. We should note from the outset, however, that "Melechsala" is essentially a satire upon the legend, whereas Bauernfeld and Schubert treat the legend with respect. Nevertheless, an element of parody is not missing from *Der Graf von Gleichen*: the old story is filtered through numerous familiar literary works and conventions of the operatic stage, with the result that the focus of the critique is completely redirected.

II

The opera opens in the Orient, where the Count has been held captive by the sultan of Cairo for seven years, put to work as a gardener. We encounter him in a moment of solitude, yearning for the wife and young son he has left behind. In a 1990 essay reviewing the publication of a facsimile edition of Schubert's draft, Richard Kramer drew out the striking parallels between this *scena* and the dungeon scene at the beginning of act 2 in Beethoven's *Fidelio*, which extend from the unhinged harmonies of their respective introductions well into the structure of the cavatina and final *stretta di tempo* (Florestan's "Und spür ich nicht linde, sanft säuselnde Luft"; the Count's "O sehnendes Verlangen").[22] It is the first of a series of fascinating correspondences between Schubert's opera and Beethoven's monumental story of marital devotion. Kramer also finds parallels in Schubert's treatment of the two female leads and Mozart's Donna Anna (Suleika) and Countess Almaviva (Ottilie). We know that Schubert attended performances of *Fidelio* both in 1814 and in 1822, and Schindler has an account of Schubert poring over the manuscripts for the opera in the months following Beethoven's death; Kramer deems this story of Schindler's to be credible.[23] Schubert's gestural language is muted, of course, matching the far more humane conditions of the Count's enslavement. (Musäus's story is actually closer than Schubert's to the scene of Florestan's "Gott, welch dunkel hier!" since

22. Richard Kramer, "Posthumous Schubert," *19th Century Music* 14 (1990): 197–216, esp. 204–5. The edition reviewed is *Franz Schubert: Der Graf von Gleichen; Oper in zwei Akten (D 918); Erstveröffentlichung der Handschrift des Komponisten aus dem Besitz der Wiener- Stadt und Landesbibliothek*, text by Eduard von Bauernfeld, ed. Ernst Hilmar, with an essay by Erich W. Partsch, vol. 2 of *Veröffentlichungen des Internationalen Franz Schubert Instituts* (Tutzing: Hans Schneider, 1988).

23. Kramer, "Posthumous Schubert," 204. Stephen Meyer has shown that the structure of Beethoven's act 2 opening belongs to a tradition of operatic dungeon "soundscapes." Nevertheless, the sheer number of parallels with *Fidelio* in Schubert's opera, some unmistakably close, point to an intensive engagement with that particular work. Stephen Meyer, "Terror and Transcendence in the Operatic Prison, 1790–1815," *Journal of the American Musicological Society* 55 (2002): 477–523.

his Count is held in chains in a dark prison for many years before his elevation to gardener puts the escape plot into action.)

We are introduced to Schubert's Graf von Gleichen on a special day, the fifteenth
birthday of the sultan's daughter, Suleika, to whom the Count has grown fondly attached.
He has tended a special purple rose (*purpur Rose*) to present to her, which she accepts in
stunned silence (the music breaks off midphrase) moments before her father's birthday

EXAMPLE 2.1   Franz Schubert, *Der Graf von Gleichen*, D 918, act one, no. 8 (no. 8), "Himmel was
mußt ich hören!" draft; based on *Neue Schubert Ausgabe*, BA 5540a. By kind permission.

EXAMPLE 2.1 (*continued*).

gift is announced: she is to select a bridegroom from among the three princes who have come to woo her (*star*light radiates from her eyes, they sing, invoking, among other things, Goethe's *Stella*), and her long-held wish to see the European captives freed is granted. Only when she is alone is Suleika able to give vent to the depth of her horror at her father's pronouncement that she is to belong to one of the three princes (think back to Estrella's defiant "Nimmer! nimmer!"). Schubert gives her the most impassioned accompanied recitative in the entire opera (shown in ex. 2.1), with a vehemence akin to Donna Anna's "Don Ottavio, son morta!" Unlike Mozart's Donna Anna, however, Suleika's display of *seria* histrionics has no witness on stage. It is under the pressure of his imminent departure that the Count and Suleika first begin to confront their feelings for each other, and Suleika's earlier shock is explained: in her culture, when a man presents this flower to a young woman, it is a declaration of his love.

Bauernfeld assures that his audience will not believe the Count when he protests his ignorance of this tradition by converting Musäus's hyacinth into a purplish rose (if anything, the Count is shocked to have the secret gesture grasped so unexpectedly). The shade of red may be slightly off from the quintessential western red rose, but not so far that the presentation could have been without significance to him or to the opera's audience. They might have remembered, too, the words of Bauernfeld's opening chorus in act 1, which makes striking reference to a flood of royal purple rising in the east: "Es hebt sich im Osten die purpurne Flut."[24] Bauernfeld's change is worth pausing over. In characteristically roundabout fashion, Musäus has identified the special flower that the Count has tended as the *Hyacinthus muscati*, explaining that its Arabic name, "Muschirumi" (a suspiciously macaronic construction), rhymes with a coarse term for "love's reward" and that its presentation is a decidedly "unplatonic" declaration. Musäus assures his readers that any Arab lover could have expected the mistress of his heart to arrive at the intended meaning as it is the only rhyme possible in the language ("Ydskerumi"). How was the Count to know? Never mind that the Latin name Musäus supplies already sounds like a euphemism and that the Count has modestly arranged his purple hyacinth atop a fig leaf on a silver platter! In the story of Melechsala, the scene unfolds as an outrageous spoof, designed to provoke winks and chuckles from its readers. The author's pose here as elsewhere is clear: only a fool would believe this ancient yarn.

Bauernfeld's reconfiguration of the scene, by contrast, draws our sincere sympathy for his character's bind. It takes just a shade of misunderstanding over the rose for him to portray the state of the Count's sentimental attachment. Literally only minutes earlier in the opera we have learned of the Count's allegiance to his absent wife. The flirtation with Suleika begins as a displaced expression of his longing for Ottilie, an innocent game of pretense turned self-conscious by the only half-intended act of communication. The escalation of feeling in the moments before the Count hands Suleika the rose is independently signaled by Schubert: the two flatter each other in a duet (shown in ex. 2.2a) transparently modeled on one of Mozart's, also an A-major andante in 2/4 in the form of a dialogue, and similarly with a striking ♯4 in the bass progression. By the coda, their vocal lines have become inextricably intertwined. The parallels with Mozart's "Là ci darem la mano" (shown in ex. 2.2b) would surely have struck many listeners fairly immediately, but today we may also note that both the bass line and melody of the duet resemble the song "Im Frühling" (composed in 1826; only published in 1828), whose picture of a heavenly beloved resonates with the iconography of celestial bodies that often accompanied the Gleichen story after *Stella*. The melody is wonderfully distributed across the piano right-hand and vocal line, as we can see from even the brief excerpt shown in example 2.2c. The poet believes to have seen reflected in the dark mirror of a mountain spring an image of his beloved *in the heavens*, an illusory double exposure on the water's surface.

---

24. The libretto is printed in Franz Schubert, *Bühnenwerke: Kritische Gesamtausgabe der Texte*, ed. Christian Pollack, Veröffentlichungen des Internationalen Franz Schubert Instituts, vol. 3 (Tutzing: Hans Schneider, 1988), 561–615. One interpretation of early nineteenth-century associations with the color purple and their possible origin in the myth of Hyacinth is offered by Robert Tobin in *Warm Brothers: Queer Theory and the Age of Goethe* (Philadelphia: University of Pennsylvania Press, 2000), 40.

EXAMPLE 2.2a Franz Schubert, *Der Graf von Gleichen*, D 918, act one, sc. 4 (no. 5c) duet, "Ich wünscht um dich zu schmücken," draft; based on *Neue Schubert Ausgabe*, BA 5540a. By kind permission.

EXAMPLE 2.2b Wolfgang Amadeus Mozart, "Là ci darem la mano," 1–12.

EXAMPLE 2.2C   Franz Schubert, "Im Frühling" D 882, 10–16.

Still sitz ich an des Hügels Hang,	So still I sit on the hilltop
der Himmel ist so klar,	The heavens are so clear,
das Lüftchen spielt im grünen Thal,	A breeze plays in the green valley
wo ich beim ersten Frühlingsstrahl	Where, at the first rays of spring
einst, ach, so glücklich war;	I once was, ah, so happy;
wo ich an ihrer Seite ging	Where I walked at her side,
so traulich und so nah,	In intimacy and so near,
und tief im dunkeln Felsenquell	And in the depths of the mountain spring
den schönen Himmel blau und hell,	Saw the fair heavens blue and bright,
und sie im Himmel sah.	And her in the heavens too.

TABLE 2.1

left: Schubert, *Der Graf von Gleichen*, act one, no. 4, duet

A ship has appeared. The Count's hesitation to ask Suleika to plead with the Sultan, her father, for their freedom leads Kurt to suspect the Count is in love. The two sing a duet: a courageous heart and warm blood are necessary above all; where there is hope and a cheerful disposition success is bound to follow.

KURT:	Sie bittet, und es ist getan.
GRAF (*beiseite*):	Suleika sollte—? Nein unmöglich!
	Sie ahndet uns're Trennung nicht.
KURT (*beiseite*):	Dies Zögern ist doch unerträglich,
	Doch gibt's mir in der Sache Licht.
GRAF (*beiseite*):	Das holde Kind ist mir ergeben—
KURT (*beiseite*):	Die Trennung macht ihn so betrübt!
GRAF (*beiseite*):	Ich weiß, sie liebt mich wie ihr Leben—
KURT (*beiseite*):	Kein Zweifel! Ja er ist verliebt.
GRAF:	Sei ruhig, Kurt, und hoffe mit mir,
	Vielleicht ist Rettung nicht ferne;
	Es leuchten uns am Ende noch hier
	Helle und freundliche Sterne.
KURT:	Wenn ihr nur hoffet, mich ficht es nicht an.
	Ich kann die Fesseln wohl tragen,
	Ich bin ein fröhlicher Reitersmann,
	Und will wohl nimmer verzagen.
BEIDE:	**Ein mutiges Herz, ein <u>warmes</u> Blut**
	Ist nötig vor allen Dingen;
	Wo Hoffnung bleibt und fröhlicher Mut,
	Da muß ja alles gelingen.

(continued)

Melodic resemblances between works, especially those composed in near proximity, are rarely in themselves revealing (most any composer's oeuvre is replete with them), but it is noteworthy how many in this opera are cued to texts that are readily brought into association with the Gleichen story.

A far more provocative variety of parody has shaped another crucial moment shortly before this number when the Count and Kurt first discuss an avenue of escape and Kurt realizes that the Count is in love. This intertextual connection has the potential to inflect our perception of the entire story—and, even more surprisingly, to shine a colorful spotlight back upon its source. Bauernfeld and Schubert both reinforce the bond with *Fidelio*

TABLE 2.1 (*continued*)

right: Beethoven, *Fidelio*, act one, no. 5, trio

To gain access to the dungeon where she suspects her husband is held, Leonore, in the guise of Fidelio, proclaims her courage. Marzelline hopes to marry Fidelio, and Rocco takes this sign of courage in his chosen son-in-law as a good omen: yes, yes, we/ I/ you shall find happiness they proclaim. The source of Leonore's hoped-for happiness must remain hidden.

ROCCO:	**Gut, Söhnchen, gut, hab**
	immer Mut,
	Dann wird's dir auch gelingen;
	Das Herz wird Hart durch Gegenwart
	Bei fürchterlichen Dingen.
LEONORE:	**Ich habe Mut!**
	Mit <u>kaltem</u> Blut
	Will ich hinab mich wagen;
	Für hohen Lohn
	Kann Liebe schon
	Auch hohe Leiden tragen.
MARZELLINE:	Dein gutes Herz
	Wird manchen Schmerz
	In diesen Grüften leiden;
	Dann kehrt zurück
	Der Liebe Glück
	Und unnennbare Freuden.
ROCCO:	Du wirst dein Glück ganz sicher bauen.
LEONORE:	Ich hab' auf Gott und Recht vertrauen.
MARZELLINE:	Du darfst mir auch in's Auge schauen;
	Der Liebe Macht ist auch nicht klein.
	Ja, ja, wir werden glücklich sein.
LEONORE:	Ja, ja, ich kann noch glücklich sein.
ROCCO:	Ja, ja, ihr werdet glücklich sein . . .

already staked out in the Count's opening soliloquy, permitting a sidelong (we might say camp) meaning to emerge, especially for anyone in touch with contemporary gender slang (please refer to table 2.1). The duet sung between the Count and Kurt in Schubert's act 1, number 4, parallels the plot structure, language, and military topic of Beethoven's deliciously oblique act 1 trio between a bass and two sopranos (one dressed as a man) who sing of their hopes for future happiness: Marzelline hopes to marry Fidelio, and Rocco is delighted in this show of courage in his chosen son-in-law; the source of Leonore's hoped-for happiness, as the audience well knows, must remain hidden. "Ich habe Mut! Mit kaltem Blut will ich hinab mich wagen" Fidelio proclaims while Beethoven's registrally displaced military wind band lends poignant ironic support to this ostentatious display of masculine courage.[25] The language of the duet between Kurt and the Count, likewise a show of courage, solidarity, and hope, appears to have been cribbed from this trio, even to the point of retaining the rhymes: Mut and Blut, gelingen and Dingen. But Fidelio's gender-defining "kaltem Blut" is replaced with "*warmes Blut*": in place of cold-blooded stoicism (sangfroid) in the face of political tyranny we have steadfast courage in the arena of passion. To be sure, the two pieces do not *sound* alike at all; it is only that both are powerful declarations (credos, even) directed at their audiences as much as at the characters on stage. The message of Schubert's opera, unsurprisingly, was shaped in relation to wider conversations taking place on contemporary stages.

"Warmes Blut": allowed to resonate in the ear for a moment a seasoned theatergoer might have remembered a young girl's famous speech about her forbidden fascination with her seducer in Lessing's *Emilia Galotti*: "Was Gewalt heißt, ist nichts: Verführung ist die wahre Gewalt—*Ich habe Blut, mein Vater, so jugendliches, so warmes Blut als eine. Auch meine Sinne sind Sinne. Ich stehe für nichts. Ich bin für nichts gut.*" (What's called force is nothing: seduction is the truest form of force—I have blood, my father, as youthful, as warm blood as any woman. My senses too are senses. I stand for nothing, represent nothing any longer.) This speech of Emilia confessing her powerlessness to resist the Don Juanish seducer whose passion has led to the murder of her fiancé comes at the close of Lessing's 1772 play.[26] To our great shock, this admission calls for her death: come to defend his daughter's honor, her father instead stabs her (after she goads him by comparing her own predicament to the "Virginia" story that Lessing's play is based upon—she literally "asks for it"). By this pact between father and daughter he has his assurance that the "rose's petals never will be ravaged by the storm," and she is spared the added shame of suicide. But whereas Emilia's admission of fear that she could cave in to the Prince's will brings about tragedy, Schubert's Count and his young page champion the prospect of a *lieto fine* for forbidden passion.[27] And to anyone acquainted with the

---

25. The association of cold-bloodedness with manhood is further reinforced in Pizarro and Rocco's duet, "Jetzt, Alter": "Du bist von kaltem Blute, von unverzagtem Muthe . . . *morden* . . . bist du ein Mann, bist du ein Mann?" (The theme also recurs, more subtly, in the play upon cold and warm in the melodrama.)

26. Gotthold Ephraim Lessing, *Emilia Galotti* in *Werke* II, ed. Gerd Hillen (Munich: Carl Hanser Verlag, 1971), 127–204. An English translation by Benjamin Thompson, Es. (London, 1800) is available in David Thomas, ed., *Four Georgian and Pre-revolutionary Plays* (New York: St. Martin's Press, 1998), 244–89.

27. The play was influential. During Mozart's time, Schikaneder's troupe had *Emilia Galotti* in its repertoire, as noted by Paolo Gallarati, "Mozart and Eighteenth-Century Comedy," in *Opera Buffa in Mozart's Vienna*, ed. Mary Hunter and James Webster (Cambridge: Cambridge University Press, 1997), 101n. We might reflect that Mozart's Donna Anna only recognizes Don Giovanni when, in a whisper, he offers his aid and invites her

then already current slang term "warm" connoting same-sex eros, the ever more fervent calls by two mens' voices for "ein mutiges Herz" "ein warmes Blut" ("warmes" always the accented, high note) will have sounded a still more radical manifesto than the one seeming to be proclaimed in the story unfolding before the spectator's eyes.[28] Schubert plays into a tradition here. Like the exaggerated rhetorical emphasis Mozart gave the words "viva la libertà" in *Don Giovanni*'s first-act finale, these political meanings (however we construe the politics) are calculated with an ear to live performance.[29]

Refracted through the *Graf von Gleichen*[30] threesome the emphatic closing lines of Beethoven's trio too communicate an unexpected message of hope: "Wir werden glücklich sein!" Indeed, the most surprising result of parodying a scene that already involves disguise is that it invites a transformed hearing of its source. (Listen again to Leonore's "Komm, Hoffnung" in this light, in which she clings to the star of hope for faith that love will conquer all.) None of this is to argue for the *necessity* of an oblique hearing of either opera, of course, but such meanings are easily released in juxtaposition: just imagine the

---

to his castle—this is precisely the situation into which Lessing's prince has lured Emilia. Donna Anna's narration to Don Ottavio, too, has a parallel in *Emilia Galotti*. Nearer Schubert, Franz von Hartmann reported to Anna von Revertera in May 1825 that he had seen wonderful plays at the Burgtheater: "*Lear, Emilia Galotti*, die *Ahnfrau* [. . .] *Ottocar*." Walburga Litschauer, *Neue Dokumente zum Schubert-Kreis 2* (Vienna: Musikwissenschaftlicher Verlag, 1993), 56.

28. As one contemporary definition had it: "Herren die sich mit der Päderastie amüsieren werden warme genennt." This usage comes from the *Briefe über die Galanterien von Berlin auf einer Reise gesammelt von einem österreichischen Offizier* (1782), attributed to Johann Friedel in an edition edited by Sonja Schnitzler (Berlin: Eulenspiegel, 1987). There is also discussion of this volume in Tobin, *Warm Brothers*, chap. 2. It is worth noting that the word "warm" appears together with a scene of gender disguise in a Gleichen play by Ludwig Philip Hahn written in the wake of *Stella*: Ludwig Philip Hahn, *Siegfried, ein Singeschauspiel* (Strassburg: Joh. Friedrich Stein, 1779). It is not the sultan's daughter the Count falls in love with in Hahn's play but her servant, Philaide, a Greek freedom fighter also held in captivity. Philaide's determination to rescue the Count leads her self-consciously to abandon her accustomed gender role. She escapes with the Count in male attire but is recognized as a woman by the Count's wife, Mathilde, herself disguised as a cleric. The Count, who has not recognized his wife, is perplexed by the mysterious cleric's ability to see through Philaide's disguise. What gave them away? His warm gaze ("Dein warmer Blick, dein zärtliches Gewinsel").

29. We can trace such a tradition through Mozart's works alone: before *Don Giovanni* he had already tested his ability to summon prohibited things in a safely comic situation, with the rousing trio "Marsch, marsch, marsch!" closing act 1 in *Die Entführung aus dem Serail*, a work that is also a forerunner of Schubert's orientalist opera. Even as this plot celebrates female virginity as a sign of constancy, the composer brings out an artillery of devices such as pitch-accent, repetition, and tones that grow long to turn the C-minor/major battle music accompanying Belmonte and Pedrillo's charge to gain entry to the palace and its harem into bawdy poetry: little cries of "nein!" are released in the *forte-piano* accents at "wir geh'n h*inein*"; the two men in grating seconds, sotto voce, isolate the suggestive phoneme "ei, ei, ei, ei"; and a firework of popping plosives at "*platz* fort!" brings the forbidden scene to a climax. Likewise in C major, Figaro's mock-military "Non più andrai" closes that first act. The "viva la libertà" passage in *Don Giovanni*'s first-act finale puts C-major martial music under cover of a masked ball for a more earnest message.

30. A Thüringian family name, "von Gleichen" *means* "of alike or equals." This might refer to the social status of the two women, a German countess and a Persian princess, or to their gender. The name resonates, too, with a term in the revolutionary slogan: "Freiheit, Brüderlichkeit, Gleichheit."

two operas staged on consecutive nights, as was done regularly, for instance, with *The Magic Flute* and Peter Winter's sequel *Das Labyrinth*.

Not long after the "Là ci darem la mano" parody and the confusion over the rose, the Count screws up his courage to tell Suleika that he will soon take his freedom and divulges to her that he is married and has a son. Suleika is undeterred: in search of words to describe their bond, she rejects every ready option. Most emphatically, the Count is no father to her, no "Gebieter," no "Herr," no mere "Freund." A fast-paced scene of raw emotion between them passes through every shade of denial and dissembling before the sheer insistence of Suleika's question "Liebst du mich?" forces the magnitude of the predicament to the surface. This scene, mostly *seria*-style obbligato recitative, and a parallel one in the second act, catalyze the dramatic action, rendering the struggle between impulse and conscious understanding, forced apart by the whirlwind events. Against all better judgment, Suleika resolves to accompany the Count into the unknown homeland where his wife and child await him. Disguised in the Frankish attire that she has so often donned to meet him in the garden, she will flee with him in the understanding that their inclinations can never be realized.

This brings us to the first-act finale. At this same juncture in the story of Melechsala, Musäus's narrator believes to detect a Presence—invisible and therefore unprovable, he coyly asserts—of heavenly guardians bearing swords and shields who watch over the travelers' journey at sea. Ludwig Richter (1803–84), whose illustrations for "Melechsala" were widely reprinted, chose this as one of the key moments in the story to depict: note the glistening star on his angel's shield in figure 2.5. Eminent spirits lurk behind the first-act finale of Schubert's opera too. As the ship carrying Suleika and the Count prepares to set sail for the West, they are joined in hope-filled celebration by double male choruses of newly freed prisoners and sailors. Any prisoners' chorus celebrating freedom is likely to put one in mind of Beethoven's, with its unforgettable appeals to "Freiheit" appearing at a similar point in the structure of his story, even if Schubert's music does little more to press the point. Similarly hidden (because the two choruses alternate), but just as tangible once it has struck us, is the derivation of meter, images, and even complete lines of text for the sailors' chorus from Goethe's "Glückliche Fahrt" (Prosperous Voyage), a poem celebrating the return of propitious winds at sea after the deathly calm explored in its companion poem, "Meerestille" (Calm Sea). The pair of poems was well known in Beethoven's memorable setting for chorus and orchestra, published with a dedication to Goethe in 1822: indeed, if Bauernfeld or Schubert knew one of the later printings, they would have seen that Beethoven personalized the dedication, affixing as a motto several lines from Book 8 of Homer's *Odyssey* in which Ulysses expresses his reverence for the bard whose song has moved him to tears: it is of course Ulysses's own story the bard is telling.[31] Schubert would have had good reason to be interested in Beethoven's

---

31. Book 8, lines 479–81 in the translation of Voß (the motto appeared in editions after 1824): "Alle sterblichen Menschen der Erde nehmen die Sänger/ Billig mit Achtung auf und Ehrfurcht, selber die Muse/ Lehrt sie den hohen Gesang, und waltet über die Sänger." See Georg Kinsky, *Das Werk Beethovens:*

FIGURE 2.5 The Archangel Raphael watches over the Count von Gleichen's ship as it sails back
home to Europe. Woodcut after a drawing by Ludwig Richter (1803–1884) illustrating a scene from
"Melechsala." Johann Karl August Musäus, *Volksmährchen der Deutschen: Prachtausgabe in einem
Bande*, ed. Julius Ludwig Klee, mit Holzschnitten nach Originalzeichnungen von R. Jordan.
G. Osterwald, L. Richter, A. Schrödter (Leipzig: Mayer und Wiegand, 1842), 635. Yale Collection
of German Literature, Beinecke Rare Book and Manuscript Library. By kind permission.

treatment of these poems: he had made two attempts himself at setting "Meerestille"
some years earlier.

The final scene shares something more with the most overtly political moment in
Beethoven's first-act finale. As Rocco's prisoners savor a brief taste of freedom in the sunny
courtyard, one clear voice calls for renewed faith that God will rescue them from injustice
("Wir wollen mit vertrauen auf Gottes Hülfe bauen …"). The moving delivery of these words
by a solo tenor gives them a resonance much wider than the plot. Schubert's Count, Suleika,

---

Thematisch-bibliographisches Verzeichnis seiner sämtlichen vollendeten Kompositionen, completed by Hans
Halm (Munich-Duisberg: G. Henle, 1955), 321–24. (Here, in Pope's translation, is a fuller context for the
passage: "This, let the master of the lyre receive, / A pledge of love! 'Tis all a wretch can give. / Lives there
a man beneath the spacious skies / Who sacred honours to the bard denies? / The Muse the bard inspires,
exalts his mind; / The Muse indulgent loves the harmonious kind." When Ulysses starts up again after a
brief pause, the Muse is supplanted by a god (Apollo): "O more than man! Thy soul the Muse inspires, / Or
Phœbus animates with all his fire: / For who, by Phœbus uninform'd, could know / The woe of Greece, and
sing so well the woe? … The god himself inspires thy breast with flame; / And mine shall be the task henceforth to raise / In every land thy monument of praise." Homer, *The Odyssey of Homer: In the English Verse
Translation by Alexander Pope, Illustrated with the Classical Designs of John Flaxman* [New York: Heritage
Press, 1942], 119).

TABLE 2.2

left: Schubert, *Der Graf von Gleichen*, act one finale

SAILORS:	Hurra! Hurra! Die Segel gespannt! **Es locken die Wellen,** **Schon schwindet das Land!**
CHORUS OF FREED PRISONERS:	O Freiheit, o Freiheit, Du himmlische Lust
SAILORS:	**Es treiben die Winde** **Die schwellende Brust!**
GRAF, KURT, SULEIKA, FATIME: [*prayer*]	Leit', alles, Gott, zum frohen Ende: Wir geben uns in deine Hände.
SAILORS:	Hurra! Hurra! Die Segel gespannt!
CHORUS OF FREED PRISONERS:	Erwartet, erwartet die Brüder vom Land.
SAILORS:	**Wie eben die Wellen,** **Die turmhoch oft schwellen!** **Geschwinde, geschwinde,** **Das Meer ist so gleich.**
GRAF, KURT, SULEIKA, FATIME:	Ihr Wellen, ihr Winde, Nun trau'n wir auf euch!
ALL:	Auf! Zaudert nicht länger! Die Segel gespannt! **Es locken die Wellen.** **Bald schwindet das Land!** Auf! Auf!

(*continued*)

TABLE 2.2 (*continued*)

right: Beethoven, *Fidelio*, act one finale; and Goethe, "Glückliche Fahrt"

PRISONER'S CHORUS:	O welche Lust, in freier Luft den Atem leicht zu heben Nur hier ist Leben der Kerker eine Gruft.
SOLO TENORS: [*declaration of faith*]	Wir wollen mit Vertrauen auf Gottes Hülfe bauen, die Hoffnung flüstert sanft mir zu: Wir werden frei, wir finden Ruh O Himmel! Rettung! welch ein Glück! O Freiheit, o Freiheit, kehrst du zurück?
Glückliche Fahrt	**Die Nebel zerreißen,** **Der Himmel ist helle,** **Und Äolus löset** **Das ängstliche Band.** **Es säuseln die Winde,** **Es rührt sich der Schiffer.** **Geschwinde! Geschwinde!** **Es teilt sich die Welle,** **Es naht sich die Ferne;** **Schon seh' ich das Land.**

Kurt, and Fatime make a similar appeal to the Lord to steer their story to a happy end: "Leit' alles, Gott, zum frohen Ende: Wir geben uns in deine Hände." Sung (a capella?) by the four soloists, a baritone, tenor, and two sopranos, their prayer stands out starkly against the prevailing sonority of the male choruses (the textual correspondence is shown in table 2.2). Listeners familiar with the story's history on the nineteenth-century stage (more on this later) might have delighted in this forecast of a *lieto fine*, aware that it would take nothing less than divine inspiration to surmount the obstacles imposed by the censors' bureau. Backed by these providential hopes for Godspeed, the curtain falls on Schubert's act 1.[32]

---

32. At a different point in the story Musäus makes his own sidelong reference to the pressures of censorship: his Count trembles to think that the garden he has created must pass the "strenge Zensur" of the sultan.

To hope for a happy end means to suppress the possibility of all other outcomes: Bauernfeld's libretto holds the disquiet of "Meerestille" below the surface of consciousness; only the optimism of "Glückliche Fahrt" is put into direct play. But the central finale in opera inevitably is the point of highest tension. With a hazardous sea voyage still before them when the curtain falls, the heroes of Schubert's opera remain in danger of being hurled into another familiar plot archetype: the shipwreck that brings about a radical change of fortunes. Indeed, the threat of shipwreck looms far more palpably over the first-act finale in Carl Eberwein's *Der Graf von Gleichen*, where two male choruses represent the opposing forces in battle, one of many opportunities for clamorous "Turkish music" in his opera. There the Saracens' pursuit of the ship carrying the fleeing Christians comes to a climax with a tremendous storm at sea. Only the Christians take the ultimate risk, passing through unharmed. (Just how commonplace it was to have a shipwreck in an opera's central finale may be gleaned from its figurative invocation in Mozart's *Figaro*: at the point of highest tension in that finale, Figaro stammers out the excuse that will save the day—"it is usual to seal a commission"—while Susanna and the Countess, obviously still terrified that the Count will discover compromising evidence of Cherubino's presence in the Countess's bedchamber, direct an aside to the audience. "If I can just weather this storm," they sing, "I won't be shipwrecked after all.")[33]

In Schubert's opera, the real danger—the psychological storm—still lies ahead. Once the ship has safely reached European soil at the start of the second act, the consequences of Suleika's rash decision begin to unfold. Goethe's aid is enlisted once more for the introduction of the countess Ottilie: her lament, "Wonne der Wehmuth," is a reworking of Schubert's 1815 setting of Goethe's poem (D 260, pub. 1829). With Penelope-like resolve, the Countess has faithfully awaited the return of her husband, who, like Odysseus, appears before her in pauper's guise. The ensuing scene of recognition and reunion is celebrated in Schubert's score with an ecstatic duet whose words and music inescapably bring to mind another reunion—that of Leonore and Florestan, leaving no doubt in anyone's mind over the intensity of this conjugal love.[34] For Ottilie, as for Leonore, the certainty of recognition comes with the first sound of her husband's voice, and it is followed by an impassioned entwining of their names—in the recitative before the duet in Schubert's case.[35] Beethoven, we might recall, cut away the accompanied

---

33. The plot of Mozart's *Idomeneo* is set in motion by a deadly storm. Shipwreck is averted only by Idomeneo's terrible vow to Neptune to sacrifice the first person he meets on shore. In accordance with an operatic tradition of placing storms at the height of tension, the sea monster's full fury is unleashed only at the end of the second (middle) act. The venerable plot-archetype did not die away with Mozart's figurative usage in *Figaro*, as the storm in Eberwein's opera makes clear.

34. For detailed discussions of the connection between "Laß ab, laß ab" and Beethoven's duet and the refashioning of the song "Wonne der Wehmuth" into an aria, see Kramer, "Posthumous Schubert," 206–8. As Kramer observes of the duet, "Schubert's music does nothing to dispel the similarities" between the opening lines of Bauernfeld's duet and the text of "O namenlose Freude" (206).

35. The only full realization of Schubert's opera available on CD is the Cincinnati production from 1996 based on a freewheeling completion by Gunter Elsholz (Centaur CRC 2281/2282). Here, between the end of the recitative and the beginning of the duet, "Laß ab, laß ab, mir sprengts die Brust," Elsholz has wedged in a

recitative preceding "O namenlose Freude" in the 1814 revision of *Fidelio*. A small detail in the spoken dialogue replacing it (nearly always abridged today) must surely have caught Bauernfeld's eye: Florestan proclaims that Leonore is without equal—a "Frau ohne Gleichen."

The introduction of the story of Odysseus is prefigured in "Melechsala," where it served an altogether different purpose. Standing in chains while still in his dark prison in the Orient, Musäus's Count has a powerful vision of his absent wife. As his imagination fleshes out the picture, it melds with a story from his childhood: he sees himself in the role of Odysseus returning home just in the nick of time to slay the suitors in bloody battle. Similarly reworked in Bauernfeld's libretto is a subplot concerning Saint Elizabeth of Hungary, whose legendary generosity toward poor strangers is displaced onto Ottilie to lay the foundation for the Count's disguise as a pauper. In Schubert and Bauernfeld's refashioning of the story, text, stage scenery, and music all are enlisted to lend the homecoming of the Count von Gleichen support from two of the most powerful tales of marital devotion in Western culture.

Embracing Suleika as a sister and a daughter, the Countess soon senses the turmoil in her young heart, and the Count warns her of Suleika's childlike incapacity to grasp dissemblance (a lesson he learned all too well in the episode with the rose). In a scene recalling the intensity of the exchange between the Count and Suleika in act 1, Ottilie confronts the younger woman with her own persistent question: "Liebst du meinen Gemahl?" Suleika's efforts to deflect or dodge the question yield to ever more desperate pleas to stop the probing. As in the parallel scene, the answer speaks out all too loudly in the refusal to respond. For the Countess the just and enlightened solution to the predicament is self-evident. The remainder of the libretto is given over to the definition and formalization of the unique bonds that unite the three. Suleika, newly baptized, is symbolically renamed Angelika, the Count announces that the pope has sanctioned the three-way union, and the opera closes—like a hundred other comic operas—with a wedding tableau. As Wye Allanbrook has observed, the convention is self-consciously invoked in the second-act finale of *Figaro*: "To finish the farce happily and after the custom of the theater, let us perform for them a matrimonial tableau," Mozart's Figaro proposes, trying to hurry along the happy end.[36] That is one way of making conventionality leap out at us: another, even more startling, is to adapt the familiar convention to a novel set of circumstances.

---

rising triadic introduction that forges an even closer link to Beethoven (the horns he adds no doubt have bled in from "Komm Hoffnung")! As in many other places, the score for the 1997 Graz performance prepared by Richard Dünser is more faithful to Schubert's draft. Franz Schubert / Richard Dünser, *Franz Schubert: Der Graf von Gleichen* (D 918, completion), Oper in 2 Akten, Score (Bad Schwalbach: Edition Gravis, 1997). The recent Bregenz production based on Dünser's score has unfortunately cut "minor" figures—like Kurt— out of the plot (OEHMS Classics OC 903).

36. Wye J. Allanbrook, "Mozart's Happy Endings: A New Look at the 'Convention' of the 'lieto fine,'" in *Mozart Jahrbuch 1984/ 85* (Bärenreiter Verlag: Kassel, 1986), 1–5. The Count, of course, hopes to see Susanna replaced by Marcellina in this tableau. After Marcellina and Bartolo are revealed as Figaro's parents and Bartolo offers to marry Marcellina as soon as she pleases, she replies "Today, and it will be a double wedding."

III

We will note that Schubert's draft of the opera, bearing a starting date of 19 June 1827, breaks off just before this final scene (even before Suleika learns of the Countess's solution). Bauernfeld's diaries can help us to narrow down the compositional chronology further. On 31 August 1827, amid heavy sighs about other censorship matters, he noted in his diary, "Schubert componiert den 'Graf von Gleichen.'" Two months later, in October 1827, he observed, "Grillparzer will uns die Oper an das Königstädter Theater senden, nimmt sich auch meiner bei Schreyvogel an und beim Grafen Czernin."[37] While reports by Franz Lachner and Bauernfeld suggest that Schubert was still talking about completing the opera on his deathbed a little over a year later, work on this draft appears to have broken off in the early fall of 1827. Richard Kramer writes that "the draft, unique among the autograph documents in Schubert's *Nachlaß*, is nothing less than a concept of the entire opera; it lacks only two final numbers: a comic duet and a finale of pomp and ceremony, both afterbeats to the essential unfolding of the dramatic action."[38] If the trajectory of the story were a conventional happy end, this might be taken to imply that a completion would have been a fairly routine matter. With a story like this one, however, so much more was at stake. On 12 December 1865, shortly after Johann Herbeck premiered the first numbers from the opera in concert, the *Wiener Zeitung*'s correspondent speculated that Schubert may have held off on composing the final scene until he was sure it would be permitted by the authorities.[39] While we have no documentary evidence to support this idea, it has the virtue of reminding us of the force that censorship could exert on creative acts, and it squares with the new concerns and the renewed hopes that Grillparzer's promise will have raised.

There must in any case have been immense pressure to find a suitable tone for the events leading up to the happy end, for the legend's conclusion had posed the greatest challenge to the age. Two obstacles stood in the way of the story's credibility for contemporary audiences: the consent of the first wife, and the blessing of the pope, both of which Bauernfeld skates over swiftly. Musäus's approach to both incidents is to turn up the irony with the invention of elaborate escape clauses that counteract the folktale's conclusion.

His Countess does initially feel angry and betrayed. She has a change of heart only after Melechsala appears to her in a dream as the archangel Raphael, protector of

37. The Königstädter Theater in Berlin, which opened its doors in August 1824, had staged numerous comic operas by Viennese composers—Wenzel Müller, Franz Volkert, and others whose operas had first played in the theaters in the Josephstadt and Leopoldstadt. Schreyvogel had repeatedly exploited his ties to the censorship office on Grillparzer's behalf. Graf Johann Czernin ran the K. K. Hoftheater (at which Grillparzer's play *Ein Treuer Diener Seines Herrn* premiered after the imperial objections were overcome).

38. Kramer, "Posthumous Schubert," 202. The reports by Lachner and Bauernfeld are assembled on page 212.

39. The *Wiener Zeitung* account is reprinted in Ernst Hilmar, "Zur Schubert-Rezeption in den Jahren 1831 bis 1865—Eine kommentierte Auflistung der Quellen in der 'Wiener Zeitung,'" in *Schubert durch die Brille, Internationales Franz Schubert Institut Mitteilungen* 29 (Tutzing: Hans Schneider, 2002), 223–25.

travelers—and, according to Musäus, of lovers—bearing his lance and shield as does Schwind's angelic page in *Die Rückkehr des Grafen von Gleichen* (compare Richter's depictions of Raphael and Melchsala-Raphael in figs. 2.5 and 2.6 with Schwind's painting in fig. 2.4). The angel's gaze initiates the soul-searching that wins over her heart—but not without the reader first being subjected to a good dose of Musäus's cynicism. He takes us painstakingly through all of *his* Countess's less than noble calculations: Melechsala had the power to keep the Count to herself, yet she chose to shepherd him safely home. If after this show of generosity by the sultan's daughter the Countess were to insist on her original rights, she might risk losing her husband altogether—and so forth, and so on.

As it happens, this dream apparition Melechsala-Raphael, invented to explain how a wife might yield her right to marital exclusivity, quite unexpectedly sheds light on the appearance in Schubert's score of a phrase hauntingly shared by a song in *Winterreise*. Rueful over her first reaction to Melechsala, the embodiment of Raphael, Musäus's Countess has gradually come to lament her inability from the first to accept this "Nebensonne" on the horizon of her marriage ("Sie konnte es ihrem Herzen nicht vergeben, daß es über die

FIGURE 2.6 Melechsala appears in the Countess's dream as the angel Raphael shepherding her husband back home. Woodcut after a drawing by Ludwig Richter, illustrating a scene from "Melechsala." Johann Karl August Musäus, *Volksmährchen der Deutschen*, 639. Yale Collection of German Literature, Beinecke Rare Book and Manuscript Library. By kind permission.

EXAMPLE 2.3a Franz Schubert, *Der Graf von Gleichen* D 918, act two, sc. 9 (no. 20b), duet, "Wie herrlich ist's im Arm des Gatten," draft; based on *Neue Schubert Ausgabe*, BA 5540a. By kind permission.

Nebensonne, die an ihrem Ehehorizont glänzen sollte, gemurret hatte"). Schubert's Countess never undergoes a comparable process of persuasion: there is no hint of coercion behind the consent in the opera. On the contrary, if anyone hesitates to take the final step it is the Count, who cautiously probes his wife's conviction ("Bin ich wirklich deiner wert?" etc.). Finally, Count and Countess, united in their resolve, consort to the words and music shown in example 2.3a, notated in the key of three sharps: "Wie herrlich ist's, im Arm des Gatten, wie rein das Leben, klar und hell! Ja nur die Liebe, das Vertrauen ist aller Freuden reinster Quell" (How heavenly to be in the arms of a spouse, how pure is life, how clear and bright! Yes, only love, only trust, is the source of true joy).

For the modern listener, the resemblance to the far better known song from *Winterreise* fairly leaps off the page: "Drey Sonnen sah ich am Himmel stehen. Hab lang und fest sie angesehen" (I saw three suns in the heavens: gazed long and hard at them), the protagonist

EXAMPLE 2.3b "Die Nebensonnen" D 911/23, mm. 1–15.

of the song cycle poignantly declares as Schubert's pitches summon a music apparently only recently associated with a moment of rapturous unity (shown in ex. 2.3b). The melodic horizon remains fixed for the next words: "und sie auch standen da so stier, als wollten sie nicht weg von mir" (and they stood there so firmly, as if they did not wish to leave me). In combination with the full-throttle dynamics and the harmonic tilt to the relative minor this radiantly mimics the intensity of the phantom suns. It is tempting to read into the tone of resignation in the song an autobiographical impulse, a projection of Schubert's (at least momentary) sense of loss over the opera. (With *Alfonso und Estrella* and *Fierabras* this was the third opera to fail among his ambitious, mature operas.) His work on part 2 of *Winterreise* reached the stage of a *Reinschrift* in October 1827—very near the time he set aside the opera. The exact chronology of composition, however, remains uncertain: there is a separate autograph of "Die Nebensonnen," and one for "Muth" (the song of blasphemy and false cheer), on a paper type also used for the opera during the summer of 1827.[40] These two songs, strikingly, were carefully positioned in the expanded sequence of twenty-four songs. As is well known, the ordering of songs in part 2 of *Winterreise*, problematical because Schubert had already completed part 1 when he discovered the twelve new poems interleaved by Müller, was determined by a simple mechanical process with the exception that Schubert inserted "Die Nebensonnen" between "Muth" and the final song, "Der Leiermann."

Still another instance of the integration of material from an earlier song resonates suggestively with Schubert's evident association of "Die Nebensonnen" with the opera. Suleika's act 2 prayer ("Guter Gott, nimm aus dem Herzen dieses Sehnen, diese Schmerzen!") is reminiscent of the very early song "Die Betende," D 102, on a text of Matthisson (only published posthumously).[41] The poem contains a striking image: Laura at prayer resembles a picture of innocence as painted by Raphael. Naturally neither the opera nor the songs rely for their effectiveness on a listener's recognition of these musical resemblances (or of the verbal triggers that may have given rise to them). Unlike Schubert's conjuring of "Là ci darem la mano" or "O namenlose Freude," the reworking of material from his songs in the opera (or the inverse) is revealing primarily for what it may suggest to us about Schubert's own process of association with the story, and it can have been

40. Gesellschaft der Musikfreunde, A235 ("Muth" is in private hands, but a small facsimile is printed in Alexander Weinmann, "Zwei neue Schubert-Funde," *Österreichische Musikzeitschrift* 27, no. 2 [1972]: 76). Kramer reviews the evidence for the dating of "Die Nebensonnen." Both he and Richard Dünser were struck by the musical and textual resemblance between duet and song, even without knowing of Musäus's explicit reference to phantom suns. Kramer, "Posthumous Schubert," 209–11; Schubert / Dünser, *Der Graf von Gleichen*, v–vi. Schubert had encountered this striking image twice in a very short span. But could Müller himself have had in mind the Gleichen story? Hahn's play *Siegfried* (1779) ends with the three main characters singing a naive little song that distills a moral for the audience: Am Himmel stehn drey Sternelein / So fröhlich beysammen, und leuchten / so fein— / Sie haben im Herzen sich gern. / O laßt, wie diese Sternelein / Uns leben, lieben, glücklich seyn, / Von allem Unfriede fern. The Count's name—Siegfried—reflects the harmonious outcome that is at the heart of the legend. Perhaps the resemblance to Müller's "Drey Sonnen sah ich am Himmel steh'n" is merely coincidental; however, Müller was in close contact with Achim von Arnim, who also treated the story on numerous occasions. He even solicited a review of Arnim's play *Die Gleichen* (1819) for his journal *Askania* from Wilhelm Grimm. No review was submitted, as Arnim was stung by criticisms Wilhelm and Jacob Grimm had leveled against his play in private correspondence.

41. The resemblance is noted by Ulrich Schreiber in the entry on *Der Graf von Gleichen* in *Schubert Handbuch*, ed. Walther Dürr and Andreas Krause (Kassel: Bärenreiter, 1997), 342.

appreciated by only a select handful of friends who knew the songs, many of which remained unpublished.[42]

There remains one crucial scene that the libretto treats in a way radically different from Musäus's story: the matter of the pope's consent, an integral fixture of the legend. The reasoning behind his decision is never addressed by Bauernfeld; the pope's decree is merely reported to those assembled. Like the arrival of Beethoven's minister of justice, the message comes just in the nick of time to confer official sanction on the actions already well under way.

In contrast, Musäus pulls out all the stops to explain the papal blessing. The sultan's daughter has converted to Christianity, taking the name Angelika, as in Schubert's opera. Her audience with the pope is a protracted scene during which he tries desperately to persuade her to exchange her Persian veils for a nun's: when she bares her face, revealing her profound distress at this suggestion, even the pope is sufficiently moved to be at a loss. He convenes a council of Roman casuists, denying them food and water until they find a resolution to the matter. The eventual ruling in favor of the "matrimonial anomaly" is thus reached under duress, and it does not issue directly from the pope! In each of the episodes that challenge conventional morality—the scene of seduction with the sultan's daughter, the acquiescence of the first wife, the consent of the pope—Musäus resorts to heavy-handed irony to explain the events dictated by legend. This impulse to frame or distance the troublesome (or no longer credible) elements of the legend was shared by nearly all subsequent treatments of the story.

Kotzebue's play *La Peyrouse*, for example, delivers what amounts to just another form of compromise. While much closer to the legend than Goethe's loose retelling in *Stella*, both the setting (a sparsely inhabited South Sea island) and the time (the present) have been altered. After scenes of terrible jealousy and rage between the two women, both of whom have had a child by the Count, they finally consent to form a domestic arrangement à trois. It is evident to all that no such union would ever be tolerated on European soil, so the Count must accept his lasting banishment from his home, and the three partners renounce physical love, redefining themselves as a brother and two sisters. Even that was too much for the Viennese censors (who no doubt objected to the implied moral relativity: one need only escape papal rule to find a harmonious resolution to the crisis).

Carl Eberwein's 1824 opera, set in the traditional time and place, has a rival of the Count attempting to steal his lands and his wife. She escapes into a convent and dies before her husband and the sultan's daughter return to fight the fierce battle to regain

---

42. Curiously, the editors of the Deutscher Klassiker Verlag edition of Goethe's *Stella* are led to the painter Raphael by a different route: *The Knight's Dream* (1504–5) is a painting in which the head of a knight inclines toward Athena, his body toward Venus: "Ganz in diesem Sinn ist auch die ternäre Verbindung Stella-Fernando-Cezilie zu deuten, die aus gleichwertigen, aber nicht gleichartigen, einander in ihrer Substanz vermeintlich nicht störenden Beziehungen besteht" (The ternary union between Stella-Fernando-Cezilie is to be interpreted in just this sense. It is constituted of equal, but dissimilar, relationships that presumably do not interfere with each other in substance). Goethe, *Dramen 1765–1775*, 995.

his home. The spirit of the first wife enters the fray at a decisive moment, securing a happy outcome.

Even more surprising than these tortuous rationalizations of the folktale's conclusion in the early nineteenth century are the number of revised endings to appear following Goethe's change of heart over *Stella*. At the moment of decision in Goethe's 1776 play the first wife, Cezilie, passionately recounts the traditional tale. "Once upon a time there was a Count . . . ," she begins, and the story closes with the fairy-tale formula "and they lived happily ever after": "And God in Heaven delighted in their love, and his holy Emissary spoke his blessing. And their happiness and love embraced one home, one bed, and one grave." Barely able to comprehend his fortune, her husband, Fernando, cries out: "God in Heaven who sends us angels in our time of need, give us the fortitude to bear this mighty vision! My wife!" Moments later, Fernando, Stella, and Cezilie step into the roles outlined for them by the fable, exclaiming, "Mein! Mein!" "Ich bin dein!" "Wir sind dein!" (That language is adapted by Bauernfeld for the Count and Countess's duet of reunion.)[43]

Stella became one of Goethe's most controversial works, ardently championed and passionately decried. The first staging in Hamburg was shut down under clerical pressure after ten performances and an anonymous sixth act circulated in which Fernando is tried and convicted of bigamy. In 1806 Goethe revised the play to end in tragedy; it circulated widely in this form in Cotta's second edition of 1816. Cezilie still recounts the *Graf von Gleichen* story, but it comes too late: Stella has already swallowed poison, and Fernando shoots himself in despair. The fairy tale remained a poignant fantasy, not to be realized in this world.[44] Manuela Jahrmärker supposes that Goethe revised the play because he no longer found the ending believable. This assumes, of course, that he thought the revision improved, that his change was construed as a rejection of the earlier ending.[45] But the play was notorious: since the original close was so well known, surely some readers must have taken the revised ending instead to be a devastating commentary on their own changing times.

In 1818 Kotzebue's *La Peyrouse* followed suit with a new ending, a variant on the double suicide, made at least partly in response to his play's lack of success on the stage[46] (it

---

43. My translations. For the text of *Stella* I, see Johann Wolfgang Goethe, *Der Junge Goethe, 1757–1775,* 2, ed. Gerhard Sauder, *Sämtliche Werke nach Epochen seines Schaffens: Münchner Ausgabe* (Munich: Carl Hanser Verlag, 1987), 1.2:37–77; *Stella* II is contained in volume 6.1 of the same series, *Weimarer Klassik 1798–1806,* ed. Victor Lange (Munich: Hanser, 1986), 462–505. The Munich edition arranges Goethe's writings by significant chronological periods, permitting connections between works in different genres to emerge more readily. The Deutscher Klassiker Verlag edition is arranged more traditionally by genre (chronologically within each genre). Its commentary is sometimes more venturesome.

44. Goethe, *Dramen 1765–1775* (Deutscher Klassiker Verlag), 976–1000. For the events surrounding the first performance, see especially page 987. According to the commentary in the new Munich (Hanser) Goethe edition, it was only after the first (Hamburg) production traveled to Berlin that the performances were shut down. Goethe, *Der Junge Goethe, 1757–1775,* 1.2:713.

45. Jahrmärker, *Der Graf von Gleichen,* xv.

46. Goethe, *Stella* (Deutscher Klassiker Verlag), 989.

was, however, the original ending that was printed in the 1825 Viennese edition of Kotzebue's works). His earlier response to Goethe's revised play, the 1808 parody for live marionettes, had ended with a triple suicide.[47] Achim von Arnim's *Die Gleichen* (1819) even
circulated with three different outcomes, one tragic, one happy, one supernatural, an
emblem of the difficulty the story's conclusion had come to pose for the age. Like all good
comedies, the happy end culminated in multiple weddings. Arnim's Count and Countess,
having married only out of familial duty, are separated even before their wedding night.
In the end, his Countess is allowed to marry her true love, and the sultan's daughter is wed
to the Countess's brother. The Count is left out in the cold.[48] The legend's triangular
marriage is again made to conform to the mores of an emerging bourgeois society and
anything taken to reflect aristocratic marital custom (and privilege) is rebuked.

The theater had long been the most important forum for airing social arguments
before a public, but not all positions could be openly represented. In retelling only the
naive ancient story at the heart of Goethe's *Stella* ("Es war einmal ein Graf...") Schubert's
opera runs counter to every tendency of his age, steering a course directly into the barrier
reefs of censorship. Did he continue to hold out hope that the gods (or an empress?)
might intervene to save his opera from creative shipwreck? Without making recourse to
any of the evasive strategies marshaled by his contemporaries, Schubert, a humble com-
moner, asks us rather to take on faith the mysteries of the inherited tale. His concern is to
flesh out the psychology of the lovers to make the magical conclusion both plausible and
desired: whatever the story's relation to the world beyond the theater, its narrative structure had to be brought effortlessly to a happy end. The drama that unfolds on stage offers
a vivid account of how a puzzling historical record came to be, enacting a time-honored
function of the fairy tale. "Let us hold together tightly," sings the Count just moments

---

47. This tendency was lampooned by Thomas Love Peacock in *Nightmare Abbey* (1818). Torn between a woman
who calls herself Stella (her real name is Celinda) and his love for Marionetta (!), Scythrop, waving a pistol
(and drinking port like Goethe's Werther), proposes that the only way out is to shoot himself: he wants both
women ("Both! That may do very well in a German tragedy; and the Great Mogul might have found it very
feasible in his lodgings at Kensington; but it will not do in Lincolnshire"). Thomas Love Peacock, *Nightmare
Abbey and Crotchet Castle*, with an introduction by J. B. Priestley, The Novel Library (London: Hamish
Hamilton, 1947), 90. Following the happy end of a 1798 English translation of *Stella* we find this note: "This
conclusion may be less supportable to the English than to the Germans, who are accustomed to the *lefthand*
wife of their princes. The protestant reformers were so far obliged to accomodate themselves to German
manners, as to grant a like permission to the Landgrave of Hesse—and a recent instance of the kind appears
in Mirabeau's Mem. Secretes de la Cour de Berlin, with regard to the late King of Prussia and Mademoiselle
de Vosse." Johann Wolfgang Goethe, *Stella*, translated from the German of M. Goethe, Author of *The Sorrows of Young Werther* &c. &c. Absolvent Amantes. (London: Printed for Mookham and Carpenter, No. 14,
Old Bond Street, 1798), 113.

48. Reinhold Steig, ed., *Achim von Arnim und Jacob und Wilhelm Grimm*; *Achim von Arnim und die ihm nahe
standen*, ed. Reinhold Steig and Herman Frierich Grimm, vol. 3 (Stuttgart: J. G. Cotta, 1904), 448–50. Unfortunately, as of this writing, the projected volume on *Die Gleichen* in the new critical edition of Arnim's
works (Tübingen: Niemeyer) is not yet available.

after announcing the pope's blessing of their special union, "the world will age, long before our love shall; let posterity gaze in wonder at this picture of the Count von Gleichen and his two wives."[49] The magic spell is unbroken even as the entire cast turns to face the audience with a hymn to the sanctity of the bonds of marriage.

IV

Before the nineteenth century, it was taken for granted that any treatment of the Gleichen story should adhere to the basic facts of the legend. That was true even for Musäus, who simply went to greater lengths than anyone before to explain those events. The eighteenth-century taste for happy endings in comedy and in opera may have contributed to the continued appearance of the traditional close, even as writers become increasingly fascinated to explore the psychological and social ramifications of the story, a propensity that only highlighted the rift between the legend's conclusion and institutionalized moral norms. By century's end the line between retelling the legend and using the story to make a social statement had become increasingly blurred, and this quite predictably frequently aroused the concern of a censor.

A five-act play by Julius Reichsgrafen von Soden published in Berlin in 1791 interpreted the story along passionately freethinking lines.[50] The Count's loyal companion (a far more sober fellow than Schubert's flirtatious Kurt) is so appalled to see the Count in the grips of passion that he is ready to abandon their friendship. He takes pity only after recognizing the Count's genuine anguish at the thought of having to tell either woman he must leave her. The Count's eloquent, if mostly specious, argument for the ethical basis of his plan ultimately wins the day—and Soden himself went on to write a polemical essay in defense of bigamy.[51] Indeed, more reactionary readers (like the author of that anonymous sixth act for *Stella*) had already detected a similar vein in Goethe's play. A more measured criticism leveled against *Stella* was that in the removal of the historical circumstances—the Crusades and the Count's captivity—the heroic basis for the crisis had been lost. Fernando is merely restless, bored with ordinary domestic life. No further justification for his wandering affections is ever put forth.[52]

---

49. "Laßt uns fest zusammenhalten, / Eh' soll die Welt, als uns're Lieb veralten; / Die späte Nachwelt mag verwundert schauen / Des Grafen Gleichen Bild und seiner beiden Frauen!" Franz Schubert, *Bühnenwerke*, 614. The vision of marriage presented here, an uncoerced and flexible consensual agreement, would surely have fanned contemporary debates on the subject.

50. Julius Reichsgrafen von Soden, *Ernst, Graf von Gleichen, Gatte zweyer Weiber* (Berlin, 1791).

51. Otto Hachtmann, "*Graf Julius Heinrich von Soden als Dramatiker*" (Ph.D. diss., University of Göttingen: Druck der Univ.- Buchdruckerei von W. Fr. Kaestner, 1902), 53. Soden's Count acts first, justifies his actions later. Schubert's opera proposes something quite different: his Count contains his feelings until he has confided in his wife and reached a consensual arrangement with her.

52. Goethe, *Stella* (Deutscher Klassiker Verlag), 983. While Goethe carefully distinguished the personalities of all the female characters, Fernando was left intentionally blank: he is "everyman."

In the 1770s Goethe's fascination with unorthodox (triangular) relationships was fueled by literary models as well as by personal relations within his own circle of acquaintances. Goethe scholarship has long recognized in the title of the play a reference to Jonathan Swift's *Journal to Stella* (published only in the late 1760s). Stella was the fictional name Swift gave to one of the two women in his life. More immediately, Goethe followed with warm interest the relationship between Friedrich Heinrich Jacobi, his wife, and Jacobi's intimate friend Johanna Fahlmer. Goethe corresponded with both Jacobi and Fahlmer as he wrote *Stella*.[53] One letter in particular, to Fahlmer in March 1775, brings his involvement with their circumstances into direct contact with the play. The letter begins:

> Dear Aunt, I knew what Stella would mean to your heart. I am weary of complaining about the fate of *our kind* of people, but I wanted to depict it; you shall recognize yourself in it, as I have recognized you I trust; may you be, if not consoled, then yet stronger in your unrest.
>
> (Liebe Tante, ich wußte was Stella ihrem Herzen sein würde. Ich bin müde über das Schicksal *unsres Geschlechts* von Menschen zu klagen, aber ich will sie darstellen, sie sollen sich erkennen, wo möglich wie ich sie erkannt habe, und sollen wo nicht beruhigter, doch stärker in der Unruhe sein [emphasis in Goethe's original]).[54]

Much had changed on the aesthetic landscape in the three decades since Goethe first conceived the play. By the early nineteenth century, Shakespearean tragedies no longer were being mounted with newly crafted happy endings, productions of Mozart's *Don Giovanni* regularly left off the conciliatory *scena ultima*, and the shockingly tragic close to Rossini's *Otello* was just a few years away. Once the door had been opened to a tragic close for the events of the Gleichen story, it came quickly to be accepted as the only natural outcome. Surely Goethe's work on *Elective Affinities* (published in 1809)—in which the introduction of two new members into a peaceful marital household invites a disastrous realignment of affections—will have inflected his own thinking about the play, and vice versa. Goethe's claim that the novel's tragic end assured morality's triumph was met with skepticism by Walter Benjamin, who viewed the novel as Goethe's protest against the conventions of a world to which he himself had recently succumbed with his late marriage.[55]

---

53. Goethe, *Stella* (Deutscher Klassiker Verlag), 984–985.
54. Goethe, *Stella* (Deutscher Klassiker Verlag), 979.
55. For a more practical explanation of Goethe's decision finally to marry, see Peter J. Schwartz, "Why Did Goethe Marry When He Did?" *Goethe Yearbook* 15 (2008): 115–30. Schwartz has an illuminating account of the various grades—or degrees—of marriage recognized under rapidly evolving Weimar marriage law. This resonates in fascinating ways with Kwame Anthony Appiah's discussion of modern American marriage law, its European heritage, and debates over gay marriage in "The Marrying Kind," *New York Review of Books*, 20 June 1996.

For Benjamin, one line holds the key to the mystery of *Elective Affinities*. It comes as the first pair of illicit lovers declare their passion and agree to a new union if only the second pair will agree to the same: at that moment, Goethe observes, "Hope shot across the sky above their heads like a falling star."[56] My purpose here, however, is not to speculate at length on the reasons for Goethe's change to *Stella* but merely to emphasize the surprising nature of the revision. It is remarkable that Goethe felt compelled so radically to alter the trajectory of a story written decades earlier. The new ending is attached with surgical precision, leaving the main body of the play intact. At the climactic point of crisis—roughly the same point at which Schubert's opera draft breaks off—a newly crafted hinge negotiates the shift from comedy to tragedy.

We gain a sense of the immense inward distance Goethe had traveled since the play first appeared by the impressions Carl Friedrich Zelter shared with his longtime friend on 5 September 1821 after attending a production of *Stella* with the tragic close. Zelter expressed his satisfaction that the events still fed smoothly into the newly crafted final scene but observed that the play had not entirely left behind its former affront to morality. The suicides still give offense, he confided to Goethe, as this (no less than the impulsive ternary union of 1776) remains an act entered into from a state of despair. Zelter wondered further if there might not have been a way to bring about the accidental deaths of the guilty parties, so that nature would be avenged, the culpable ones punished, and the innocent survivors, Cezilie and her daughter, left to face a world still wide open to them.[57] It is hard to imagine the Goethe of the 1770s having shown patience for a proposal couched in these upright, even righteous, moral terms—even if it was made only half earnestly—yet Zelter clearly writes with the expectation that his suggestion will be met with approval, or at least bemusement, by Goethe ("you never imagined that I could be so clever, did you?" a beaming Zelter closes).

Comparably rich documents in reception for Schubert's last opera project never will be forthcoming. Nevertheless, clear tendencies emerge from a consideration of

---

56. Walter Benjamin, "Goethes Wahlverwandtschaften," in *Illuminationen: Ausgewählte Schriften*, ed. Siegfried Unseld, 2nd ed. (Frankfurt: Suhrkamp Verlag, 1980), especially p. 134. The essay is translated in *Selected Writings*, vol. 1, *1913–1926*, ed. Marcus Bullock and Michael W. Jennings (Cambridge, Mass.: Belknap Press of Harvard University Press, 1996), 297–360. This passage in Benjamin has lately attracted critical notice. Richard Kramer probes Benjamin's speculation that mysteries analogous to Goethe's falling star reside in music's "mute world from which its reverberations will never sound forth." Richard Kramer, *Unfinished Music* (Oxford: Oxford University Press, 2008), 370–72. And Berthold Hoeckner, in a meditation on the same passage, reminds us that "only at the moment of its fall does a star shine at its brightest. Only then does it become a source of hope." Berthold Hoeckner, *Programming the Absolute: Nineteenth-Century German Music and the Hermeneutics of the Moment* (Princeton.N.J.: Princeton University Press, 2002), 23.

57. Goethe, *Briefwechsel zwischen Goethe und Zelter in den Jahren 1799 bis 1832*, 20.1:666–67.

the opera from this wider vantage point. It is evident that by the nineteenth century no staging of this story could escape taking a stand on institutional forms of morality: one either had to reinforce traditional values or to challenge some aspects of them, and the challenges had grown fewer and fewer in the decades before Bauernfeld and Schubert set to work on their story. The threat of censorship, especially in Vienna, loomed over any provocative (faithfully naive) treatment of the legend, and this one walked a very fine line. That is not to say that a sympathetic censor could not have found arguments to permit the opera to come to performance (in widely Protestant Berlin or Dresden or Weimar, much nearer the legend's source, perhaps more readily than in Catholic Vienna). The opera does not, like Soden's play, seize upon the traditional story to advocate bigamy. It only uses the legend as a vehicle to promote a sentimentally charged message of tolerance, respect for unusual personal circumstances, informed consent, domestic and social harmony. While realized in an unconventional way, the values espoused are explicitly likened to long-standing Western values— hence the parallels with *Fidelio*, with Mozartian characters, and with the *Odyssey*. We are invited to embrace the unfamiliar, to have faith in the integrity of these unorthodox personal ties, however strange they may seem. When the mysterious ancient portrait by which the legend has been transmitted is brought to life on the stage, it tells a surprisingly familiar story: that is the marvel the opera's final *Bühnenbild* (the Count flanked by the two women in festive attire, backed by a chorus of well-wishers) leaves its audience—posterity—to ponder. The marital happy end remains intact, but it is transformed.[58]

There are signs that Bauernfeld and Schubert were not alone in their rejection of the widespread propensity to bring the facts of the legend into line with the moral structure of contemporary society. An extensive correspondence between Achim von Arnim and Wilhelm and Jacob Grimm takes up this very issue. All three of Arnim's variants of the play *Die Gleichen* alter significant features of the legend, including, in all three versions, the ending and, evidently only by careless oversight, the original location of the story.

---

58. Schubert's handling of another stage convention, the story-within-the-story, likewise turns a theatrical commonplace on its head: after the Crusaders have returned home, Kurt entertains a captive onstage audience with a narrative ballad about the heathen Muslims. The townsfolk egg him on, while the real audience knows his story is nothing more than a tall tale: they are shamed into confronting their usual enjoyment of such sport. Traditionally, the story-within-the-story draws the spectator into a confidence, hinting at a relation between what is happening on the stage and the world beyond the theater. Think of Pedrillo's romance in the *Abduction from the Seraglio*: his song of a medieval rescue tale sends a secret message to the characters within the fictional world ("midnight, the hour to act, has come") and simultaneously invites the audience to think about its own relation to the fiction. An enumeration of other precedents in opera might include Antonio's recurring *chanson* "Un pauvre petit savoyard," in Cherubini's *Les deux journées*, where the opera's seventeenth-century plot is gradually assimilated into the story memorialized in the song—or, indeed, Schubert's own "Ballad of the cloud maiden" in *Alfonso und Estrella*.

Wilhelm and Jacob Grimm both objected that Arnim's convoluted play had grown too distant from the legend. Jacob is adamant:

> I maintain that for as long as the legend or story is known and recalled it is inviolable. The poet may clarify, flesh out, elevate, or bring the story home anew, but the given facts must be held sacrosanct. It is a huge miscalculation on your part (or if you did not think of it, an error that has cost you) to have confused the Thuringian Gleichen family with the one from Hannover, and to have altered entirely the ending of the fable known to all. As Wilhelm rightly observes, in so doing you undermine our belief that the events truly unfold as depicted—because the reader's or listener's recollection of the truth, or of what is held to be the truth, is unshakeable.[59]

Legends (like biblical stories) lose their attraction if they are bent to conform to our everyday lives. In the end, any effort to update such well-known stories will merely cast a spotlight on the political offices that structure present society, whether *Polizeihofstelle* or house of worship or city hall: Goethe's revised ending to *Stella* effectively assured that his original play would never be forgotten. And against the mainstream of their age, Schubert and Bauernfeld understood that legends persist not because they hold an exact mirror to the modern world but because they transmit articles of belief, speaking in ever-changing ways to the circumstances of the present.

---

59. "So weit die Sage und Geschichte bekannt und erinnerlich ist, behaupte ich, ist sie unverletzlich, der Dichter darf sie nur erklären, ausfüllen, höher heben und wieder nahe rücken, aber das gegebene factische muß er heilig halten. Es ist ein Hauptversehen, oder wenn du nicht daran dachtest, ein Dir schädlich gewordener Irrthum, daß du die thüringischen Gleichen mit den hannöverischen vertauschest und den allbekannten Ausgang der Fabel total veränderst; damit benimmst Du, wie Wilhelm recht bemerkt, unvermeidlich den heimlichen Glauben, daß sich die Sache wirklich so verhalte, denn dem Leser oder Hörer ist die Erinnerung an das wahre und für wahr geltende unabwendlich." Steig, *Achim von Arnim und Jacob und Wilhelm Grimm*, 457–58.

FIGURE 2.7   A mirror-image ("verkehrt") of the Gleichen family tombstone. Woodcut after a drawing by Ludwig Richter for "Melechsala." Johann Karl August Musäus, *Volksmährchen der Deutschen*, 651. Yale Collection of German Literature, Beinecke Rare Book and Manuscript Library. By kind permission.

3

Frauenliebe und Leben *Now and Then*

Rarely has the reputation of a poet come to be yoked so closely to a musical setting as is the case with Adelbert von Chamisso (1781–1838) and Robert Schumann's song cycle *Frauenliebe und Leben*. Celebrated as a German poet the equal of Heine or Eichendorff during the nineteenth century (doubly remarkable as he was a French émigré who reportedly retained a heavy French accent), Chamisso was read widely and set to music on dozens of occasions, mostly by composers who have since vanished from our historical horizon. But it is the prestige of Schumann's setting that has continually rekindled reactions to a collection of poems that many critics feel would likely have dropped out of sight if not for the fact that we are brought face-to-face with them each time we encounter Schumann's cycle. Thanks in no small measure to the attention Schumann paid to them, the now negative reputation of the *Frauenliebe* poems has come to dominate discussions of this poet—who was also a renowned author of stories and of a celebrated travel account of his journey around the world—in literary histories, especially those from the last decades of the twentieth century.

A recent (1998) social history cautiously calls for a reevaluation of the poet's eroded reputation from a wider perspective, arguing that Chamisso's oeuvre gives expression to polar extremes, including decidedly unpatriarchal sentiments.[1] Paul Reimann's 1963 history of literary tendencies, while not addressing matters of gender, had gone further in this direction, placing Chamisso at the forefront of an emerging literary realism driven by the poet's progressive (democratic, anticolonial, and antiracist) politics. *Frauenliebe und*

---

1. Gert Sautermeister, "Lyrik und literarisches Leben," in *Hansers Sozialgeschichte der deutschen Literatur*, vol. 5, *Zwischen Revolution und Restauration, 1815–1848*, ed. Gert Sautermeister and Ulrich Schmid (Munich: Hanser Verlag, 1998), 459–84 (regarding Chamisso: 470–77).

Leben (1831) receives only passing mention as part of a larger project to portray neglected segments of culture and to champion the lives of the ordinary people within them.[2] Chamisso's work and his political ideals earned him the admiration and friendship of Mme de Staël, E. T. A. Hoffmann, the Varnhagens, and Heinrich Heine, among many others.

Much more characteristic of writing about this poet in our time, however, is the wholesale dismissal we encounter in Gerhard Kaiser's *Geschichte der deutschen Lyrik von Goethe bis Heine* (1988). Calling the poems representative love lyrics of their time (why, then, are they always singled out?), he mentions Schumann's setting briefly, then continues:

> Here daughters of the citizenry could find their womanly role in life sketched out for them, from first love, through wedding, motherhood, and widowhood, to old age and death. Like Gretchen's song at the spinning wheel, these poems too involve role-playing. They portray a man's wishful image of woman, prescribing to the point of embarrassment her path to exemplary status through subjugation to man. She finds fulfillment in self-sacrificing service to him and in glorifying him.
>
> (Hier haben Töchter des Bürgertums ihre Lebensrolle als Frau vorgezeichnet finden können von der ersten Liebe über Hochzeit, Mutterschaft, Verwitwung zu Alter und Tod. Wie Gretchens Lied am Spinnrad sind auch diese Gedichte Rollengedichte. Sie entwerfen ein männliches Wunschbild der Frau, das sie bis zur Peinlichkeit darauf festlegt, vorbildlich durch Unterordnung unter den Mann zu sein. Sie erfüllt sich, indem sie ihm entsagungsvoll dient und ihn verherrlicht.)[3]

Kaiser goes on to characterize "Er, der Herrlichste von allen" as *Devotionskitsch*, mocking its language to draw a clear line of demarcation between himself and his readers and this embarrassment from another age: "And yet the Virgin Mary was still fortunate, for she at least was recognized by her Lord—indeed, was known by him in the biblical sense—whereas in Chamisso one must ask oneself why such an exalted star should need a lowly maid at all" (Dabei hat die Jungfrau Maria noch Glück gehabt, denn sie ist wenigstens angesehen, ja, sogar—im biblischen Sinne—von ihrem hohen Herrn "erkannt" worden, während man sich bei Chamisso fragen muß, wofür ein hoher Stern eigentlich eine niedre Magd braucht).[4]

Kaiser's sarcastic wit entertains, and many modern readers will understand his discomfort with the idolizing posture Chamisso's woman assumes toward her husband. (Asking to be viewed in this way today would be a display of vulnerability in the man.) But this

---

2. Paul Reimann, *Hauptströmungen der deutschen Literatur, 1750–1848: Beiträge zu ihrer Geschichte und Kritik* (Berlin: Dietz Verlag, 1963), 639–54.

3. Gerhard Kaiser, *Geschichte der deutschen Lyrik von Goethe bis Heine*, 3 vols. (Frankfurt: Surkamp Verlag, 1988), 1:238.

4. Kaiser, *Geschichte der deutschen Lyrik*, 240.

poetic history does not reach far beyond asserting the superiority of modern social values. Kaiser's closing remarks cut off further inquiry by declaring the poems trivial: "So much on the subject of Trivial Poetry. It is unintentionally parodistic—whereas Heine employs trivial tropes to parody an already declining concept of love and marriage" (Soviel zum Thema Triviallyrik. Sie ist unfreiwillig parodistisch, wo Heine triviale Muster zur Parodierung einer heruntergekommenen Konzeption von Liebe und Ehe anwendet).[5]

This points to an interesting difference in the respective uses to which the two poets put familiar tropes of love and marriage. Heine's irony was always recognized, however, and I have found no evidence that Chamisso's poems were understood as parody in their own time: Heine himself had rare praise for Chamisso's poetic manner.[6] Does the "unintentional parody" Kaiser detects reveal itself only across a historical and ideological divide? And can this, properly speaking, be parody?

Appearing within an ostensibly impartial history (*Geschichte der deutschen Lyrik von Goethe bis Heine*), Kaiser's sharp tongue-lashing is representative of a by now familiar stage in the reception history of overtly gendered texts from the past: an unapologetically modern reaction to the poems, it makes no effort to recover what might once have appealed in them. Of course it is true that this portrayal of "A Woman's Love and Life" is limited in scope. Only scenes of emotional intensity or crisis in a woman's relation to her husband are presented. Yet in his exclusive focus on the story line and the exaggerated gender stereotypes, Kaiser leads us to conclude that what we find most alienating today is precisely what appealed most to Chamisso's contemporaries. We might consider the alternative—namely, that what alienates today, because it was taken for granted then, would have passed unnoticed in many a reader, allowing other elements to speak. No doubt there is truth in both perspectives, but the latter view more readily encourages us

---

5. Kaiser, *Geschichte der deutschen Lyrik*, 241.

6. "I may not properly speak of Adelbert von Chamisso here. Although a contemporary of the Romantic school, in whose movements he participated, the heart of this man has of late been so wondrously rejuvenated that he has moved into entirely new tonalities, and has come to be recognized as one of the most original and important modern poets, belonging far more to the young Germany than to the old. But coursing through the songs of his early period is the same current that wafts toward us from the poems of Uhland—the same tone, the same color, the same scent, the same melancholy, the same tears.... Chamisso's tears are perhaps even more touching because, like a spring erupting through a boulder, they burst forth from a far stronger heart."

(Von Adelbert von Chamisso darf ich hier eigentlich nicht reden; obgleich Zeitgenosse der romantischen Schule, an deren Bewegungen er Theil nam, hat doch das Herz dieses Mannes sich in der letzten Zeit so wunderbar verjüngt, daß er in ganz neue Tonarten überging, sich als einen der eigenthümlichsten bedeutendsten modernen Dichter geltend machte, und weit mehr dem jungen als dem alten Deutschland angehört. Aber in den Liedern seiner früheren Periode weht derselbe Odem, der uns auch aus den Uhlandschen Gedichten entgegenströmt; derselbe Klang, dieselbe Farbe, derselbe Duft, dieselbe Wehmuth, dieselbe Thräne.... Chamissos Thränen sind vielleicht rührender weil sie, gleich einem Quell der aus einem Felsen springt, aus einem weit stärkeren Herzen hervorbrechen.) Heinrich Heine, "Die Romantische Schule" [1835], in *Historisch-kritische Gesamtausgabe der Werke*, ed. Manfred Windfuhr, vol. 8/1 (Düsseldorf: Hoffmann und Campe, 1979), 238.

to look beyond the obstacled surface of the poems, to consider what else might have been going on in—and around—them.

With the modern revaluation has also come a tendency to remark on the poems' defective construction: the dull couplets, the trite images, the simple rhymes. Thomas Mann's 1911 Chamisso essay, an anomaly in twentieth-century criticism, stands as an elegantly understated reminder of an earlier sensibility. Forgoing the self-conscious disclaimers characteristic of nearly all writing about these poems in our time, he quietly expressed his admiration for the masterful play of voices ("Sang und Gegengesang") and the epic-dramatic construction of even these most "blumenhaft Lyrische" of Chamisso's works, *Frauenliebe und Leben* and the *Lebenslieder und Bilder*.[7] ("Florid lyricism": the description itself exudes a whiff of the deep sentiment enshrouding the bygone era for Mann.)

Schumann's song cycle has kept these texts alive in the present, but our appreciation of the songs has also been tempered by a sensitivity to the outmoded social values reflected in Schumann's (and, residually, Chamisso's) portrayal of the life of an abstract figure of woman. Ruth Solie speaks to the heart of the objection in a spirited critique of the social politics underlying what she describes as "the *impersonation* of a woman by the voices of male culture, a spurious autobiographical act."[8] The story of the cycle, in this view, is more an effort to impose an ideology than to document one already in place; poet and composer (the greater culprit here) have placed words into the mouth of the singer, whose task it is to project them as her own experience, conveying someone else's message as if it were her own. (Just which thought causes the greater consternation today: being asked to assume the self-effacing posture of "Er, der Herrlichste von allen" in performance, or the idea that the composer we admire has exposed a wish to have sentiments at odds with our own egalitarian ideals addressed to him?) To judge by the remarkable number of new recordings over the last decades, however, singers' interest in the songs has not diminished with the feminist critique—even if this viewpoint has dominated the accompanying program notes. Performers have evidently found it possible to draw from these songs something that continues to appeal to them and to put it forth persuasively.[9]

---

7. Thomas Mann, "Chamisso," in *Aufsätze, Reden, Essays* (1911; reprint, Berlin: Aufbau Verlag, 1983), 1:230–53 (quotation on 240).

8. Ruth Solie, "Whose Life? The Gendered Self in Schumann's *Frauenliebe* Songs," in *Music and Text: Critical Inquiries*, ed. Steven Paul Scher (Cambridge: Cambridge University Press, 1992), 219–40, (quotation on 220); reprinted in *Das Andere: Eine Spurensuche in der Musikgeschichte des 19. und 20. Jahrhunderts*, Hamburger Jahrbuch für Musikwissenschaft, vol. 15, ed. Annette Kreutziger-Herr (Frankfurt: Peter Lang, 1998), 247–70.

9. As a strategy for keeping the cycle in the repertory, Suzanne Cusick has advocated a "resisting" performance, on the model of something she detects in Jessye Norman's recording. Cusick finds Norman "ill at ease with her own voice," observing that "in her choice of exaggeratedly clear diction Norman performs in a way that forces our attention to the words. . . . [She] invites us to hear the Frau's voice struggling with the enforced discipline of enunciating someone else's seemingly uncongenial words" (106–7). I know what Cusick is talking about but recognize in it a familiar disappointment with many of this singer's performances of

Although it is tempting to dismiss Chamisso's poems (following the lead of many modern histories) as the wishful thinking of nineteenth-century "male culture" (better: "male-dominated culture"), this would be an ungenerously exclusionary reply to the past, an effort to block, rather than to contend with their continued effectiveness in the present through the power of Schumann's songs. Recognizing those elements that are treated as cultural "givens" within a text is a crucial step in any effort at historical understanding; but the longevity Schumann's cycle has enjoyed is not explained by the pronounced, even exaggerated, gender ideology etched into its poetry (or its music). On the contrary, the songs have survived into the present despite this stumbling block. We cannot filter out the ideology from the rest of the work, of course, but to sing these songs today is not to advocate a return to the social conditions that gave rise to them. (Here it matters little whether we understand poet or composer to have been actively promoting or primarily reflecting the conditions of his time.) Rather, aside from the purely musical attractions that Schumann's work offers us, a performance stands as a valuable living document of a past ideology and its former sway. It serves as one of our most immediate modes of access to this past—in all its complexity.

While the social ideals preserved in Chamisso's story have lost their once widespread appeal, his poetic enterprise never was *merely* an articulation of commonplace views. It must have taken a special kind of ambition for a male poet to have made public an act of imagination so intimate as to include a woman's invocation of erotic bliss (song 3: "O lass im Traume mich sterben, gewieget an seiner Brust, den seligsten Tod mich schlürfen in Thränen unendlicher Lust" [O let me expire in my dream, lulled upon his breast! Let me relish the most heavenly death in tears of eternal delight]).[10] Even Goethe, who could render characteristic patterns of thought and speech with uncanny precision, shied away from assuming so personal a woman's perspective in a lyric cycle, deferring instead (tacitly, it is true) to the poems of Marianne von Willemer in his *Westöstlicher Divan*.[11] Novels or plays, because they speak through specific, well-developed characters, allow, and even

German Lieder. If there are aspects of these songs that no longer speak to us, do we really need a singer's stiffness to bring this home? I should think a truly fabulous performance would suffice. Suzanne G. Cusick, "Gender and the Cultural Work of a Classical Music Performance," *Repercussions* 3 (1994): 77–110.

10. The pairings of *Tod* and *Thränen* with *seligsten* and *Lust* bring common metaphors for erotic passion right to the surface. Beyond this, the substitution of one image of emotional release for another was so widespread a poetic device that it would not easily have been misunderstood. In a remarkable little volume on the relation of dream images to poetic language, Gotthilf Heinrich Schubert comments on the inversion of affects in dreams. He observes: "So bedeutet Weinen und Betrübtseyn im Traume öfters nahe (sinnliche) Freude" (And so in dreams, tears and melancholy often signify the close proximity of sensual happiness). *Die Symbolik des Traumes* (Bamberg: Kunz, 1814), 8. Richard Kramer identifies numerous instances of this trope in familiar Lieder texts in his *Distant Cycles: Schubert and the Conceiving of Song* (Chicago: University of Chicago Press, 1994), 127n5.

11. Whatever all Goethe may have hoped to achieve by the inclusion of her poems, this became something of a social experiment, for it was Willemer's Suleika poems that composers flocked to. Their uncommon perspective leapt out at contemporary readers, as Goethe must have known they would. Experiments to nourish talent

invite, greater freedom in this respect. Goethe's most extraordinary representation of a woman's passionate fantasy, Gretchen's song in *Faust*, does not appear as an impersonation because it is understood to be performed by the character we have come to know through the play (or at least know to come from a play). The unmediated "lyric I" in a collection of poems is a different matter: we assume a close correlation, if not an exact identity, between the author's poetic persona and the first-person speaker in the poem. A male poet who undertakes to write *as a woman*, not merely to portray a female character, confounds this assumption, sustaining the illusion that he has shed his own identity in adopting her point of view. Only the title page and the author's signature stand to remind us that this is an exercise in role-playing.

Does the added mediation of a musical performer obscure the difference between these two modes, turning even the most confessional first-person lyric into a character portrayal? (The major song cycles of Schubert and Schumann are in fact based on poetry that falls between these two extremes, presenting neither an abstract lyric subject nor a specific fictional individual, but rather archetypal protagonists: a miller, a wanderer, a poet, a woman.) We know the singer who lends her voice to Schumann's woman is performing a role, not speaking directly to us in her own words. Indeed, the performer's illusion is successful only if our awareness of the singer's person recedes, allowing her character to step forward.

The scene from *Faust* may cast light on Chamisso's cycle from yet another angle; for it is paradoxically the very specificity with which Franz Schubert paints the picture—the sustained mimesis of the action of Gretchen's spinning wheel—that allows his "Gretchen am Spinnrade" to move beyond the particulars of its gender-marked circumstance, opening the door to a broader psychological insight into the relationship between monotonous menial activity and passionate fantasy. The song invites our empathy because it represents an experience familiar to us all, no matter whether we have ever sat before a spinning wheel. To suppose of every work whose effect depends on a closely wrought picture of contemporary life first and foremost an ideological investment in the situations depicted surely is too sweeping a judgment. We must try to distinguish whether the scene is the substance or merely the vehicle of the message, or at least to gauge the balance between these forces.[12]

---

flourished among paternal figures influenced by Enlightenment thought, as we can see from the actions of Mozart's and Clara Wieck's fathers. The emperor Franz likewise was protective of those young men (like Franz Schubert) who had won a spot at the elect Stadtkonvikt by virtue of their talent, not as a birthright of class.

12. In contrast to his reading of Chamisso, Kaiser admires Goethe's portrayal of Gretchen: "But Goethe's lover approaches her beloved with a desire that breaks all convention, indeed, which has forgotten all conventions, as if she had never heard of them" (So geht auch Goethes Liebende in einem Verlangen auf ihn zu, das alle Konventionen sprengt, ja alle Konventionen so sehr vergessen hat, als hätte sie nie von ihnen gehört) (Kaiser, *Geschichte der deutschen Lyrik*, 239). Situating Gretchen at her monotonous domestic task above all provides a convenient foil for the representation of her passion.

Although the emphasis in her essay falls elsewhere, Solie's focus on the role of impersonation in Chamisso's poems opens an important question about the peculiar tensions between empathetic portrayal of another and veridical self-expression in early nineteenth-century literary culture. By the later eighteenth century a distinct woman's voice had come to be missed in poetry—perhaps even more keenly by some broad-minded male critics than by female authors whose more pressing concern was to gain recognition within the literary mainstream.

The marvelously witty Georg Lichtenberg, an astute commentator on all aspects of eighteenth-century culture, once wrote that he always welcomed the news of a new poetess. If only women would not merely school themselves in the writings of male authors, he mused, much could be learned from what they might have to say (especially about men). Characteristically tongue-in-cheek, the opening sentence of his aphorism invites a range of divergent—although not actually incompatible—meanings: "Indisputably, male beauty has not yet been drawn abundantly enough by the only hand which truly could portray it: a woman's" (Unstreitig ist die männliche Schönheit noch nicht genug von den Händen gezeichnet worden, die sie allein zeichnen könnten: von weiblichen).[13] Is this a sincere wish? An ironic provocation to women? Or a sly condemnation of self-admiration in the writings of men?

Occupied with the relationship between social convention and nature, Lichtenberg was fascinated by the insights a woman's perspective might bring. He had speculated sometime earlier that the drive to procreation underlies the ideals of women that men construct in poetry. It is a pity, he commented, that women are not permitted—as they surely could—to write with similar passion about the young men (die schönen Jünglinge) whom they admire, for "it is likely that the spirit glimpsed by a pair of enchanted eyes in a body that has enchanted them reveals itself in a very different way to a maiden gazing upon the male body than to a youth finding it in the female form."[14] An influential man of letters (and, incidentally, a good friend of Goethe) Lichtenberg showed remarkable insight into the workings of his own culture. His observations are distinguished by a rare capacity to step outside his time, to imagine the consequences of a different set of circumstances. (On another occasion he wondered what would happen to the world of love if one could not distinguish the sexes according to their attire—if, indeed, one had to puzzle out the other's sex.)[15]

As we may infer from Lichtenberg's remarks—and to the disappointment of more than one of his male colleagues—ambitious female authors aspiring to reach beyond the

---

13. "Heft F," par. 1086 (1776–79) of the so-called *Sudelbücher*. Georg Christoph Lichtenberg, *Schriften und Briefe*, 2 vols. (Munich: Carl Hanser Verlag, 1968), 1:615.

14. "Es ist wahrscheinlich, daß das Geistiche, was ein Paar bezauberte Augen in einem Körper erblicken, der sie bezaubert hat, ganz von einer andern Art sich den Mädchen im männlichen Körpern zeigt, als es sich dem Jüngling in weiblichen Körpern entdeckt." Lichtenberg, *Schriften und Briefe*, 1:40, "Heft A," par. 139.

15. Lichtenberg, *Schriften und Briefe*, 1:505, "Heft F," par. 320.

restricted realm of so-called *Frauenliteratur* frequently chose to invent male protagonists or to adopt an apparently masculine narrative voice instead of writing openly from a woman's perspective. (Some, like Karoline von Günderrode—writing under the ambiguous pseudonym Tian—sought instead to obscure their own identities.) In a bemused letter to his brother August, for example, Friedrich Schlegel describes his impressions of Sophie Mereau's first novel *Das Blüthenalter der Empfindung* (1794). He is struck by her failure to construct a convincing male persona: the young person who appears at the opening of the novel and in whom "all manner of feelings swim together in a purplish flood" (alle möglichen Gefühle Purpurisch durcheinanderfluthen) appeared to him to be a girl, although it was supposed to be a boy. If she were in fact capable of depicting, he concludes, then she would do so like the painter Angelika Kaufmann, "from whose hands breasts and hips also inevitably flow as if by a will of their own [wie von selbst]."[16]

In a richly nuanced study, cultural historian Daniel Purdy contends that these apparent failures in gendered character portrayal are deliberate. Both Schlegel and recent feminist studies of Mereau maintaining that "the vaguely masculine narrator . . . is nothing more than a mask forced upon a woman writing in a masculine literary society" fail to appreciate the nature of her masquerades. Purdy argues that

> even when Mereau writes about female figures in her novels and her historical essays, she posits them as possible configurations of female identity rather than as mimetic representations of her own true self. . . . In Mereau's "feminist" prose the contingency of her characters' relation to real historical conditions is used to doubly and deliberately mark as ideal inventions these literary figures who in their irrationality cast a critical gaze upon existing historical conditions. Her fictional characters are often deliberately implausible representations of their own era.[17]

Thus the boy, Albert (whom Schlegel insists is an "it," not a "he"), expresses his desire with uncommon passivity and "makes overt statements against patriarchal marriage and inheritance laws that strip women of their property and personal freedom."[18] Purdy's sympathetic revisionist insight paints a compelling picture of Mereau's project. Nevertheless, it remains a striking facet of literary reception history that authorial voices such

---

16. Letter of 27 May 1796, Friedrich Schlegel, *Kritische Friedrich-Schlegel-Ausgabe*, ed. Ernst Behler, vol. 23 (Paderborn: Verlag Ferdinand Schöningh, 1987), 305.

17. Daniel Purdy, "Sophie Mereau's Authorial Masquerades and the Subversion of Romantic *Poesie*," in *Women in German, Yearbook 13: Feminist Studies in German Literature and Culture*, ed. Sara Friedrichsmeyer and Patricia Herminghouse (Lincoln: University of Nebraska Press, 1997), 29–48, (quotation on 33).

18. Purdy, "Sophie Mereau's Authorial Maquerades," 35. Her literary stance is illuminated by a passage from the letters of Ninon de Lenclos (1620–1705), which Mereau translated into German: "I see that the emptiest and most hollow expectations are set before us; and that men reserve the right to strive for the highest and most dignified goals, so that from this moment on I declare myself a man." Contemplating the role her activity as a translator played in Mereau's effort to situate herself within a broader tradition of women's literature, Purdy

as Mereau's have been felt to be inauthentic, or at least strained, by Romantic critics and recent feminist literary historians alike.

Neither Schlegel's suspicion that women were by nature inadept at depicting male characters (he seems not to have called into question the reverse) nor Lichtenberg's related, but much more generous, assessment that women were not *permitted* to express their feelings for men with genuine passion remained isolated views. Caricatured echoes of both perceptions sound half a century later in Joseph von Eichendorff's hopelessly obdurate—and anonymously published—essay "Die Deutsche Salon-Poesie der Frauen," from 1847. Identifying women's restricted sphere of experience as the cause of their literary deficiencies (a circumstance he adamantly insists must not change—presumably because he feels it is rooted in nature), he rehearses a litany of symptoms marring women's writing: it lacks clarity, is fantastical, merely lyrical, conventional, minute, decorative, intellectually insignificant, too sentimental, boring, and, once again—lacking in passion. While, on the one hand, the essay documents the persistence of suspicions about women writers at midcentury—in fact, it acts as a magnet for such attitudes—its defensive posturing sets in relief quite another tendency. Already forced to give up the aristocratic benefits to which he had grown accustomed in his youth because of his family's bankruptcy, Eichendorff displayed a transparent anxiety over the loss of the only form of privilege remaining to him. His essay was clearly a reactionary effort to turn back the advancing tide of social opinion, which increasingly encouraged women—and the dreaded masses overall—in their literary ambitions.[19]

---

shows how easily her work is misunderstood when read against prevailing gender norms (30–31). It would be interesting to compare her writing to other contemporary visions of utopian worlds. Perhaps it is only because the hero of Heinse's notorious *Ardinghello* (1787) is himself so aggressively defiant of any existing social reality that none of the dozens of reactions to the novel reproduced in the generous commentary in the Reclam critical edition have paused to consider the utter irreality of the blank female characters who populate this hedonistic and grandiosely male-chauvinist utopian fantasy. The only character of any depth is the male narrator, who is both dazzled by Ardinghello and unendingly devoted to him.

19. Eichendorff acknowledges this tendency at the outset of his essay. But for him writerly genius remains a function of phallic aggressiveness, from which women are constitutionally barred. The medieval knight's sword, recently replaced by the aristocratic poet's quill ("you know what I mean," he writes with a wink), are outward symbols of the medium by which worthy men achieve greatness, engaging in heated battle with each other over distant idealized women. Even those who have been overpowered in bloody battle, like Heinse and Hölderlin, are to be celebrated as fallen heroes in a courageously waged fight. A defense of "natural" male privilege, the essay is a rousing call to arms against female authors, whose increasing presence on the sidelines of the battlefield is seen as posing a threat to the very source of male creative power. Anticipating an objection, Eichendorff briefly puts forth Bettina Brentano as the female exception proving the rule, only to assure his readers that on closer inspection, she too will be shown to have failed like all the rest. Obstinate and shortsighted, his arguments suppose that male creativity can flourish only under extremely limited conditions. Ironically, although Eichendorff is no doubt right in identifying the competitiveness among contemporary male authors as a tremendous source of creative stimulus, his absolute lack of faith in men's ability to adapt to a changing playing field undermines the very essentialist theory he propounds. The essay is reprinted in Joseph von Eichendorff, *Werke*, vol. 3, Schriften zur Literatur (Munich: Winkler Verlag,

While evaluation of the merits and goals of female authors' works differed widely, there does seem to have been general agreement on one point. Like her male colleagues, whether sympathetic or antagonistic, Mereau recognized that women's writing (in particular, she is speaking of love letters) was generally "less fiery and enthusiastic" than that of men. Explaining this as a consequence of women's dependence on their husbands, she nevertheless championed the difference in a manifesto defining "feminine epistolary style."[20]

I have sought to map out a landscape of attitudes toward women's literary voices over the first half of the nineteenth century, calling up strong pronouncements by prominent historical figures to fix crucial focal points within a complex and rapidly shifting cultural discourse. The convergence of two tendencies is particularly striking: a fermenting uneasiness with male domination of literary culture, and a disinclination of prominent female authors to step into the literary roles their male colleagues fancied for them. This can be no more than a partial picture, of course, an effort to trace the dynamics of the intellectual space within which Chamisso's cycle made its appearance. Yet I think we can glean from even this brief sketch of contemporary views that these singular circumstances provided Chamisso with both a challenge and an opportunity to give poetic voice to an underrepresented, passionate "woman's perspective." While this surely was not the solution that Lichtenberg had envisioned, *Frauenliebe und Leben* may be understood as a shrewd— and a fascinating—response to the widely perceived male-centrism of the poetic market. It was an attempt to fill an imagined void in literary production—"Das Gedichtete behauptet sein Recht wie das Geschehene" (Things invented have their rights as much as things that happen), as Goethe once put it.[21]

The effort was welcomed by a large segment of the reading public, women and men alike. If even at its publication in 1831 the mere story line of Chamisso's cycle will have seemed old-fashioned to some—the Schillerian ideal of womanhood echoed in these poems had already been dismissed as outdated in some Romantic critical circles[22]—the

---

n.d.), 87–101. For an assessment of the very different effect of Eichendorff's loss of social status on his early poetry and on his later career as a conservative essayist, see Alexander von Bormann, "Romantische Erzählprosa," in *Deutsche Literatur: Eine Sozialgeschichte*, vol. 5, *Zwischen Revolution und Restauration: Klassik, Romantik, 1786–1815*, ed. Horst Albert Glaser (Hamburg: Rowohlt Verlag, 1980), 181–84.

20. Found exclusively in her translation of Lenclos's letters, the letter putting forth these arguments is likely Mereau's own invention. See Purdy, "Sophie Mereau's Authorial Masquerades," 38–39. The famously promiscuous Lenclos would probably have argued the case somewhat differently.

21. Quoted in Walter Benjamin's essay on *Elective Affinities*. Reprinted, among other places, in Johann Wolfgang von Goethe, *Wahlverwandschaften*, ed. Hans-J. Weitz (Frankfurt: Insel Verlag, 1978), 276–77. Noteworthy in this regard is that the Suleika poems contributed to the *West-östlicher Divan* by Marianne von Willemer were seized upon by contemporary composers: one way of bringing about change in the world was to lend an authoritative voice to a woman's perspective.

22. In a letter of 14 October 1799 to Auguste Böhmer, for example, Caroline Schlegel reported that on hearing Schiller's "Das Lied von der Glocke" (a poem famous for its didactic crystallization of gender roles) at table, the entire company nearly fell off their chairs with laughter. Her letter represents one of three radically

passionate language and vivid engagement with a woman's inner thoughts in a lyric cycle were novel and fresh. Despite the commonplace gender hierarchies that leap out at us today, *Frauenliebe und Leben* effected a surprising reversal of a familiar trope of chivalrous poetry. Instead of a woman appearing as the distant, abstract idol of a male lover, Chamisso undertook to imagine a woman's impassioned fixation on her (equally abstract) idealized lover and eventual husband. The celebration of marriage as a choice born of passion, not merely the fulfillment of a duty imposed by patriarchal authority, must have been especially attractive to couples (like Robert Schumann and Clara Wieck) whose desire for each other was at odds with parental wishes. New laws were making it possible to challenge patriarchal authority in the courts, of course, but only with proof of sufficient income. (Robert had even dared suggest to Clara that perhaps her substantial earnings might be factored into the household budget, which he knew full well would antagonize her father.) The ideal of marriage for love and the right to marry by a woman's own consent remained a rallying cry of the women's emancipation movement in the 1850s and 1860s.[23]

The cycle continued to be extremely popular throughout the nineteenth century, and Chamisso could report proudly in an 1832 letter to his wife that a lady from Hamburg had praised his poetry's special attractiveness to women:

> I've received a long and loving letter from S. from Hamburg. Here is an excerpt: "If only I could send you greetings from all the gentle women who not only hearken the singer with highest pleasure and delight as do men, but who extol in

---

different reactions at the center of a probing study in reception history by Rainer Noltenius. Whereas Caroline immediately contextualizes Schiller's poem, situating it in the company of perceived literary relatives, a reader in 1859 found the poem merely "a rich picture of German life." (As the poem is distanced from its own literary environment, it is seen as preserving elements of the past, yet inevitably this view is filtered through the ideological concerns of a later age; in the latter reading, even the term "German" is brought to the poem from outside, as Noltenius astutely points out.) Rainer Noltenius, *Dichterfeiern in Deutschland: Rezeptionsgeschichte als Sozialgeschichte am Beispiel der Schiller- und Freiligrath-Feiern* (Munich: Wilhelm Fink, 1984), esp. 9–59.

23. By midcentury the growing insistence on self-determination (the right to divorce as well as marry) was for conservative critics a sign that women's emancipation had gotten out of hand. See Peter Gay *The Bourgeois Experience. Victoria to Freud*, vol. 2, *The Tender Passion* (New York: Oxford University Press, 1986), 98–100. In her discussion of the situation in France in 1848 after men were granted the vote ("in a move too long known as 'suffrage universal'—without the qualifier 'masculin'") Karen Offen explores the analogy of marriage with slavery. "How (and Why) the Analogy of Marriage with Slavery Provided the Springboard for Women's Rights Demands in France, 1640–1848." She traces the analogy back to seventeenth- and eighteenth-century authors (including Jean le Rond d'Alembert and other "male feminists"). Her essay appears in *Women's Rights and Transatlantic Antislavery in the Era of Emancipation*, ed. Kathryn Kish Sklar and James Brewer Stewart (New Haven, Conn.: Yale University Press, 2007), 57–81, which grew out of an international conference at Yale University's Gilder Lehrman Center (25–28 October 2001). In the same volume, see also Bonnie S. Anderson's "*Frauenemancipation* and Beyond: The Use of the Concept of Emancipation by Early European Feminists," 82–97.

you especially the poet of women, of their loves and of their lives. If only I could tell you of the shiny tear droplets glistening from radiant eyes that I have spied when we read aloud your *Lebenslieder und Bilder* [published shortly after *Frauen-Liebe und Leben*]—oh, dearest Herr v. Ch., what a marvelous thing it is to be a poet beloved by Germans and by women.

(Ich habe von S. aus Hamburg einen langen und liebevollen Brief;—hier eine Probe daraus: "Wollte ich ihnen alle Grüße lieber Frauen zuschicken, die nicht nur, wie die Männer, mit hohem Genuß und Entzücken dem Sänger lauschen, sondern in Ihnen ganz besonders den Dichter der Frauen, ihrer Liebe und ihres Lebens preisen; wollte ich Ihnen von den hellen Thränen reden, die ich aus frischem, strahlenden Auge perlen sah beim Vorlesen Ihrer Lebenslieder und Bilder—o liebster Herr v. Ch., es ist etwas herrliches, ein Dichter zu sein, den Deutsche und Frauen lieben.)[24]

If Chamisso's poems spoke to the experience of these women, it must have been in part because he took pains to catch the echoes of real, and distinctive, women's voices, lending the poems an aura of familiarity: "Das ist der erste Schmerz, den Du mir gemacht hast, aber der trifft," he jotted in one of his Latin exercise notebooks. Next to this (as if the remark had surprised him) is the annotation: "authentic words of Karl Müller's widow upon his death." The line is taken over nearly verbatim at the opening of the penultimate poem: "Nun hast du mir den ersten Schmerz getan, der aber traf" (Now, for the first time you have inflicted pain on me—and it struck its mark). An acquaintance of Chamisso, Müller had died just a year and a half into his marriage.[25] Confronted with the permanence of this loss, all previous injuries—and there must have been others, even in a marriage so brief—fall into perspective for the surviving spouse. It is a sentiment of remarkable power in any age. There are other lines that depart from the overriding tone of poetry album maxims ("Das Glück ist die Liebe, die Lieb' ist das Glück" [Happiness is love, and love is happiness]) and ring rather of attitudes overheard: "O wie bedaur' ich doch den Mann, der Mutterglück nicht fühlen kann!" (O how I pity man, who cannot feel the happiness of motherhood!). This proud championing of maternal happiness gains its force by reversing a commonplace of patriarchal rhetoric: it is she who pities the limitation of man.

In a review of Julius Eduard Hitzig's 1839 biography of Chamisso, Friedrich Hebbel characterized Chamisso as the kind of poet who used his talent as a medium to absorb all that was foreign and even opposed to his own nature.[26] Whatever the mix of social

---

24. Adelbert von Chamisso, *Adelbert von Chamissos Werke*, ed. Julius Eduard Hitzig, 5th expanded (Berlin: Weidmann'sche Buchhandlung, 1864), 6:122. I am grateful to Leon Plantinga for directing me to this letter.

25. Adelbert von Chamisso, *Sämtliche Werke*, 2 vols. (Munich: Winkler Verlag, 1975), 1:798–99.

26. Friedrich Hebbel's sämmtliche Werke, vol. 12 (Hamburg: Hoffmann und Campe, 1867), 258–60. "Aber es gibt Dichter, in denen die Poesie eher ein Einsaugen, als ein Ausströmen ist, und die das Talent, das sie in sich finden, als Medium benutzen, das ihrem Wesen Fremde, oft sogar entgegengesetzte, sich einzuverleiben, oder

realism and popular *Wunschtraum* in the portrayal of his subject, Chamisso had a sensitive ear for tone. The interior posturing of the widow's reproach to her departed husband in the penultimate poem is worlds removed from the young girl's worshipful infatuation at the opening of the cycle.

A serious endeavor to situate Chamisso's poems—and later Schumann's songs—within the conflicting currents of thought and action defining mid-nineteenth-century gender relations will likely bring some surprises. The movements of culture are rarely unilateral. Social tendencies that appear to us "progressive" or "retrogressive" may mingle in the past in combinations unfamiliar and even alienating today. Attitudes that once coexisted comfortably within a single personality will appear as contradictions in a present whose trajectories of thought have been realigned or rebalanced. While I do not imagine that a Mereau would have championed Chamisso's poems had she lived to see them (or perhaps she would have?), I am not at all certain that the appearance of Schumann's song cycle, despite the sentimental domestic ideal it carries, was utterly at odds with the concerns of many aspiring professional women. However removed we may feel from aspects of its emotional content today, we should recognize that Schumann's work took a step in the direction of filling a sizable gap, providing women singers with a remarkable cycle of songs that did not require *them* to impersonate a male persona. (At the very least, the pronouns fit: women may have grown accustomed to finding themselves addressed under the male pronoun, but the trouble with such honorary manhood was always that it was indirect—and that it could be withdrawn at any time. Nor was exploiting the expressive power of gender dissonance a true option for performers as long as it was imposed by a limited repertoire, not assumed as a matter of personal artistic choice.)

There are also biographical circumstances to consider. About to marry a virtuoso pianist when he composed these songs, Schumann's personal message to Clara Wieck can have been effective only if taken as a touching declaration of his wish to remain with her always, certainly not as a literal-minded (if subversive, because so beautiful) effort to rein in her future activity. If some hint of the latter wish reached her as well, it is one to which Clara, whose extraordinary career continued after marriage, chose to pay no heed. In a remarkably forthright correspondence spanning the years of their engagement, both Clara and Robert in turn aired their worries that economic constraints in their marriage might put pressure on them to amend their chosen paths (for a time, Robert considered opening up a bookshop to support them). Both sought to reassure each other that the fulfillment of their musical pursuits was a necessary component of their mutual domestic bliss.[27]

---

sich näher zu bringen." Although as a Frenchman Chamisso never entirely lost his accent, many of his contemporaries marveled at his ability so completely to absorb German culture.

27. *Clara und Robert Schumann: Briefwechsel: Kritische Gesamtausgabe*, ed. Eva Weissweiler, 2 vols. (Frankfurt: Stroemfeld/Roter Stern, 1984–87); available in English as *The Complete Correspondence of Clara and Robert Schumann*, trans. Hildegard Fritsch and Ronald L. Crawford, 2 vols. (New York: Peter Lang, 1994–96). While they both agreed that her travel should be scaled back, Clara's pianism was never in question. She did

One might well imagine that at least for these two musicians, the *Frauenliebe* songs provided a happy escape fantasy from the inevitable strains and isolation of professional travel. Frequently apart during their secret engagement, Clara and Robert had exchanged blissful visions of domestic union, especially during her lengthy stay in Paris in the spring of 1839. Absence inspired the creation of lively internalized images of each other. Robert gave characteristically vivid expression to this process in his letter of 17 March 1839, in which florid images of intimacy and longing in the body of the letter spill over into the formulaic cadential endearments at the close, delaying the moment of separation. The feeling of intimacy is sustained through a playful blending of identities, whereby the inner voices of letter writer and letter recipient are joined contrapuntally in a single persona:

But now I must end, just one more stolen kiss underneath the veil, and then I pull the veil over my gentle maiden and gaze after him with melancholy. Adieu. You depart but you do not leave me—

Adieu, my heart of hearts, beloved brother of my heart, dearest husband-to-be, adieu, I love you with all my heart; give my best to your dear friends; to Emilie I'll write with the next letter. And now we must part. Robert Wieck.

(Nun aber muß geendet sein, nur noch einen verstohlenen Kuß unter den Schleier, und nun zieh ich den Schleier über mein holdes Mädchen und seh ihm wehmüthig nach. Adieu. Du gehst aber Du verläßt mich nicht—

Adieu lieber Herzensmensch, lieber Herzensbruder, mein lieber Ehegemahl, adieu, ich liebe Dich von ganzem Herzen; grüße auch die lieben Freundinnen— an Emilien schreib ich mit nächstem Brief. Nun muß geschieden sein. Robert Wieck.)

---

harbor terrible anxieties about her ability to compose, but this was always a secondary occupation for her, and there is no reason to suppose her anxiety was imposed entirely—or even largely—by Robert. Seeking rather to broaden her musical ambitions (perhaps partly in the hope of enticing her to remain closer to home), Robert tried to encourage Clara's composition, sought out publishers for her work, and painted idyllic pictures of the future works they would create together. Whatever disappointments may later have emerged, they began their marriage on a solid ground of goodwill and deep affection. By way of contrast, the correspondence between Robert and Clara appears positively emancipatory next to the partronizing tone with which Heinrich von Kleist, some decades earlier, had labored to persuade his bride to embrace a vision of domestic happiness built entirely on feminine subjugation, sacrifice, and acceptance of the innate limitations of her sex. Attitudes had changed considerably in the intervening forty years, but the difference goes far beyond this. Kleist does not merely give voice to prevailing ideas about differences between the sexes; he goes to great lengths to derive and justify them. (See especially the letters of 15 September, 10–11 October, and 13 November 1800). His rigid need to control his bride may have had a deeper ambivalence at cause. When his sister Ulrike confided her disinterest in marriage, he deemed her decision criminal, adding: "for if you should have the right not to marry, why not also I?" (May 1799). Not long after Wilhelmine von Zenge—finally!— rejected his suit, Kleist began practicing a very different style of amorous letter writing on a young soldier, Ernst von Pfuel. Heinrich von Kleist, *Sämtliche Werke und Briefe*, vol. 2 (Munich: Hanser Verlag, 1965).

The shift to the masculine pronoun arrives almost imperceptibly, in midsentence.[28] By giving voice to Clara's style of closing in his own letter (hers are actually only rarely quite so effusive), he communicates among other things his pleasure in hearing her address similar endearments to him.[29] Above all, though, adopting the perspective of the other was a gift of intimacy. Quibbling over the verisimilitude of the representation surely would have been beside the point. Of course such private communications will have had little bearing on the contemporary public reception of Schumann's cycle, but their affinity to his mode of expression in the songs grants us a wider outlook on the expressive intent behind such acts of identification.

To linger a moment longer in the private sphere—one can only wonder what effect the memories forecast in these songs will have had on Clara with the passage of years. During their extended courtship she had frequently written to Robert that his music brought him close to her:

> Last night I dreamt of you all night, and I must thank you for the immense pleasure your marvelous fantasizing brought me. The tones still hover before me; I wanted to hold onto them as I wakened. It was not without some squeezing of hands either—what a marvelous night! May the coming night again unite me with my beloved Robert.
>
> (Vergangene Nacht hab ich die ganze Nacht von Dir geträumt, und muß mich bei Dir bedanken für den großen Genuß den Du mir da durch Deine herrliche Fantasie [imagination] verschafft. Noch schweben mir die Töne vor, ich wollte sie noch immer fassen als ich bereits schon wachte. Auch einige Händedrücke blieben

---

28. Technically this is correct, of course, since diminutives take the masculine form (even for feminine subjects like Mädchen or Weiblein), but this rub was a common source of gender play in nineteenth-century writing. One familiar instance where this ambiguity is exploited, and even compounded, is the third stanza of Goethe's "Heidenröslein," where "ihm" may refer either to the "wilder Knabe" or to the "Röslein" (whose gender, moreover, is left to the reader's imagination): "Und der wilde Knabe brach / 's Röslein auf der Heiden; / Röslein wehrte sich und stach, / Half *ihm* doch kein Weh und Ach, / Mußt es eben leiden. / Röslein, Röslein, Röslein rot, /Röslein auf der Heiden."

29. *Briefwechsel,* 2:447. They regularly spelled out their private associations with terms like "Kind" (CW, *Briefwechsel,* 1:42; 12 November 1837): "Wenn Du mich *Kind nennst,* das klingt so lieb; *aber, aber,* wenn Du mich *Kind denkst,* dann tret' ich auf und sage '*Du irrst*'!" (When you call me Child, that sounds so lovely, but if you should think me a child, I'll rise up and say 'you're mistaken'!); "Clärchen" (RS, *Briefwechsel,* 1:73; 4 January 1838): he hated the diminutive form of her name until he read *Egmont;* or "Weib" (RS, *Briefwechsel,* 2:547; 3 June 1839). Robert especially delighted in finding their names unexpectedly joined: "Clara Schumann wie das schön aussieht—in Deinem Brief an mich steht's einmal" (Clara Schumann—how lovely that looks. It appears once in your letter to me) (RS, *Briefwechsel,* 1:69; 3 January 1838). Clara had reported of her father's threat to disown her if she married Schumann: "Wenn Clara Schumann heirathet, so sag ich es noch auf dem Todtenbett, sie ist nicht werth meine Tochter zu sein" (If Clara marries Schumann, I'll say it even upon my deathbed—she is not worthy of being my daughter!) (*Briefwechsel,* 1:61; 26 December 1837). Robert's most emancipatory sentiments (some perhaps even worthy of a Mereauian hero) would come to be expressed in opposition to Clara's overprotective and controlling father: this does not make them any the less genuine.

nicht aus—das war eine schöne Nacht! möchte mich die künftige Nacht wieder mit meinem lieben Robert zusammenführen.)[30]

In keeping with Lichtenberg's observation, her expressions of physical intimacy are extremely reserved—until they become blurred with her passion for Robert's music. On 24 March 1839, for example, she wrote of the *Kinderszenen*:

Is it really true that the poet who speaks in them is to be mine? Isn't that too great a happiness? I cannot grasp it! My delight increases every time I play them. How much lies in your tones; and so thoroughly I understand every one of your thoughts, and wish to expire in you and your tones.

(Ist es denn wahr daß der Dichter der da spricht Mein sein soll, ist denn das Glück nicht zu groß? ach ich kann's nicht fassen! Mein Entzücken steigert sich mit jedem Male, daß ich sie spiele. Wie viel liegt doch in Deinen Tönen, und so ganz versteh ich jeden Deiner Gedanken, und möchte in Dir und Deinen Tönen untergehen.)[31]

Clara herself accompanied singers in Robert's *Frauenliebe* songs and continued to do so for many years after his death. Apart from this personal connection, however, under what conditions were these songs performed in their own time—and by whom? Here I find myself at odds with the scenario outlined by Ruth Solie. The historian who collapses into one a composer's purpose and the performance conditions he might, even commonly, have found funnels our view of the past through the perspective of a single keyhole. Something entirely different may have been going on in the next room, not to speak of the next larger hall. Wishing to expose the mechanism by which Schumann's *Frauenliebe* songs might have accomplished "cultural work" through their performative meaning, Solie's commentary on this point erases any distinction between the work's conception and its realization in performance and further paints an exaggeratedly insular domestic scene that sets aside the growing importance of the professional singer:

Though actually conveying the sentiments of men, *they are of course to be performed by a woman*, in a small and intimate room in someone's home, before people who are known to her and some of whom might well be potential suitors; she is unlikely

---

30. *Briefwechsel*, 1:89; 29 January 1838. Clara's reference to Robert's "herrliche Fantasie" cannot mean the C-major Fantasy, although he was immersed in revising the work during that very week. Robert describes the piece to her for the first time in a letter dated 18 March 1838 in language strongly suggesting that she knew nothing of it before. She evidently still did not know it by the start of the following year, for on 26 January 1839 Robert wrote to her, "die Kinderscenen sind nun erschienen; auch die Phantasie (von der Du nichts kennst) die ich während unsrer unglücklichen Trennung schrieb erscheint nun bald" (The Kinderscenen have now appeared. And the Fantasy—which you don't yet know—that I wrote during our unhappy separation is soon to appear).
31. *Briefwechsel*, 2:458; 24 March 1839.

to be a professional singer but, rather, someone's daughter or niece or cousin—an ordinary woman, significantly enough—and she sings, in the native tongue and contemporary idiom of herself and her hearers, texts which seem already to have been popular favorites, no doubt to an audience of approvingly nodding heads.[32]

Perhaps the occasional performance did take place in circumstances resembling these; but when our analyses of the ideological underpinnings of a work proceed by hemming in (not just teasing out) the conditions by which meanings might have arisen, they run the risk of freezing into cartoonish clichés the very cultural manifestations they set out to critique. (And these images, like the words once put to famous symphonic melodies, prove annoyingly difficult to rid oneself of.)

Whereas in the eighteenth century the Lied was confined to amateur music making, the genre had gained considerably in both ambition and professional stature by the middle of the nineteenth century. Professional singers like Johann Michael Vogl, Anna Milder, and Karl Schönstein around Schubert and Wilhelmine Schröder-Devrient (the dedicatee of *Dichterliebe*)[33] and "the Swedish nightingale" Jenny Lind around Schumann widely performed Lieder not only in public but, even more important, at larger private concerts. I should think that what amateur singers strove to emulate—and what Schumann might have envisioned—would have been above all the captivating voices that had seized their imaginations. As one astute critic for the *Allgemeine musikalische Zeitung*, Johann Karl Friedrich Triest, had already recognized in 1802, it takes but one virtuoso public performance to transform the playing of hundreds of amateurs.[34] In any case, overstating the power of domestic performance rituals over the impressionable amateur singer's sensibility quickly leads to absurdity, for then a work like *Die schöne Müllerin* must have performed the equivalent, but dubious, cultural work of enticing masses of young men to suicide. The notorious example of Goethe's *Werther* notwithstanding, this blind an identification with a fictitious character was an aberrant reaction even

---

32. Solie, "The Gendered Self," 226 (my emphasis).

33. The Chamisso cycle was dedicated to Schumann's friend Oswald Lorenz, a passionate lover of song and a principal reviewer of Lieder in the *Neue Zeitschrift für Musik*. Schumann's autograph for the "20 Lieder und Gesänge," which later became *Dichterliebe*, bore a dedication to Felix Mendelssohn. The title pages of the first editions are reproduced and the dedication history reviewed in Helmut Loos, ed., *Robert Schumann: Interpretationen seiner Werke*, vol. 1 (Laaber: Laaber Verlag, 2005), 273–80, 309–18. Note the orthography *Frauenliebe und Leben* in the first edition, as it appears in Clara Schumann's edition too. (The meaning-restricting hyphen "-leben" that so often is inserted into the title is present in neither source. Chamisso's original is given as "Frauen-Liebe und Leben").

34. Triest's serialized articles on touring virtuosos were published in the *Allgemeine musikalische Zeitung* in 1802. ("Abhandlung: Ueber reisende Virtuosen," *Allgemeine musikalische Zeitung* 46–48 [1802]: 737–49, 753–60, 769–75.) His 1801 articles titled "Development of the Art of Music in Germany in the Eighteenth Century" are now available in English in *Haydn and His World*, ed. Elaine Sisman, trans. Susan Gillespie (Princeton, N.J.: Princeton University Press, 1997), 321–94.

within the cultivated excesses of the nineteenth century.[35] (Or would the Müller songs, too, beyond the composer's immediate circle, have been sung mainly by female amateurs in the home? The place of the amateur male so far has received little notice in studies of the sociology of private and public performance.)

To understand the wide range of impact Schumann's cycle may have had within musical culture in the nineteenth century, it is also important to recognize that the much-remarked unwillingness of male singers in our time to sing the *Frauenliebe* songs is an unreliable measure of their reception among Schumann's nearer contemporaries. There was at least one notable exception. The great baritone Julius Stockhausen (like Chamisso, a native Frenchman), who regularly performed the song cycles of Beethoven, Schubert, Schumann, and Brahms, often accompanied by Clara Schumann or Brahms, included *Frauenliebe und Leben* in his repertoire—and he taught his women students to sing the male cycles.[36] Stockhausen's diaries from 1862, the year he first performed the cycle (on at least one occasion with or in Clara Schumann's presence), are filled with unabashed efforts to project himself into the position of an admired married woman whose identity he is at pains to protect—"Wenn ich Frau wäre..." (If I were a woman...) is the recurring refrain in these eye-opening private musings. The singer's empathetic projections lead him to articulate often surprising generalized rules of conduct. Under the spell of his attachment to this mystery woman—and perhaps also of his association with Brahms and Clara Schumann—he reflects that the single man who falls in love with a married woman, and finds his feelings returned, must honor the bond between them by never marrying.[37]

Stockhausen's attitudes resonate with the view of manhood expressed nearly a century earlier in Adam Smith's *Theory of Moral Sentiments*: "Our sensibility to the feelings of

---

35. I am reminded here of the fearful predictions of some eighteenth-century clerics and pedagogues over the social ills that would follow from widespread literacy: how could ordinary citizens be expected to separate their own lives from the fantastic and constantly changing worlds presented to them in books? The abundance of readers, many of them women, who devoured sentimental novels, identifying first with one character, then the next, may have been a nuisance to authors who found the subtler points of their works ignored, but the very fact that readers gave themselves over so easily to new characters demonstrates how transitory—and essentially escapist—the identification. For a fascinating discussion of the interactions between identificatory reading, the controversies surrounding literacy, and the cultivation of empathy and sympathy as an intellectual exercise, see Daniel L. Purdy, *The Tyranny of Elegance: Consumer Cosmopolitanism in the Era of Goethe* (Baltimore: Johns Hopkins University Press, 1998), chap. 2.

36. Present standards can appear to be so entrenched that we cannot see how they reflect the aberrations of our own time even more deeply than those of the past. In a sympathetic review essay following the release of Christa Ludwig's *Winterreise*, for example, Will Crutchfield wrote that "in the 19th century, men did perform 'female' Lieder more than they do now, but it would always have been thought repulsive—and I don't sense a change in the air—for a man to interpret Schumann's dramatically explicit 'Frauenliebe und -leben' cycle. This double standard echoes all the other ways in which history and society suggest that while women may aspire to manliness, men are shamed and degraded by womanliness" (*New York Times*, 17 July 1988, Arts and Leisure, 27) ("... it would always have been thought repulsive ..."—we know this how?).

37. Julia Wirth, *Julius Stockhausen, Der Sänger des deutschen Liedes nach Dokumenten seiner Zeit dargestellt von Julia Wirth, geb. Stockhausen* (Frankfurt am Main: Englert und Schlosser, 1927), esp. 497 (list of Stockhausen's

others, so far from being inconsistent with the manhood of self-command, is the very principle upon which that manhood is founded."[38] Although the marriage between an empathetic ideal and the social hierarchy built into an eighteenth-century view of manhood was a manifestation of the times, this surely is not a necessary coupling. It would be a great loss if, in our enthusiasm to grant privileged status to self-representation, we were to insist on suppressing (or dismissing as inauthentic) all insight gained by empathy, the arbiter of mutual understanding.

No doubt Stockhausen was as much a maverick in this as in his radical insistence on performing song cycles in their entirety[39]—a practice that has since taken so firm a hold that we easily forget how dubious an "experiment" (Hanslick's term) *it* was once considered. In 1856 the reaction of the musical press to Stockhausen's performance of the whole of *Die schöne Müllerin* in Vienna was mixed at best. Many were impressed by the singer's stamina, but even those who found it moving warned that repeating the idea would quickly wear thin.[40] Stockhausen backed off, but only slightly. The singer's first complete performance of *Dichterliebe* took place with Brahms at the piano in 1861. They divided the cycle into two groups of eight songs—Brahms played two pieces from *Kreisleriana* between the two lyric halves.[41] A program of an 1866 concert featuring "k. k. Kammer-Virtuosin" Clara Schumann at the Gesellschaft der

concerts, including, according to Wirth, the entire *Frauenliebe und Leben* in Cologne in 1862) and 224–34. My thanks to Nicola Gess for calling my attention to his volume. Stockhausen did marry in 1864, however. Soon after, he again pressed the thought that extending empathy to women would be beneficial to men as well. The arrival of their first child prompted an outcry of fury against men's insistence on maintaining their ignorance of the excruciating realities of labor. Would not the joys of fatherhood be so much greater if men were witness to the birth pangs? (Wirth, *Julius Stockhausen*, 283). Renate Hofmann mentions a performance by Stockhausen of songs from *Frauenliebe und Leben* at a 24 February 1862 soirée at the Riggenbachs in Cologne at which Clara Schumann and Theodor Kirchner both also performed. Which of them accompanied Stockhausen is unclear. Renate Hofmann, *Clara Schumanns Briefe an Theodor Kirchner mit einer Lebensskizze des Komponisten* (Tutzing: Hans Schneider, 1996), 69–70n2.

38. Adam Smith, *The Theory of Moral Sentiments* [1759] (New Rochelle, N.Y.: Arlington House, 1969), 213. Smith's concern is only with a (gentle)man's relation to those around him. But I think it safe to infer that with regard to relations between the sexes (or, say, between a man and his servant) he would not have thought this empathy a two-way exercise.

39. He was not, however, entirely alone. Kazuko Ozawa discusses a letter from P. F. August Strackerjan to Schumann (16 February 1834) that reports his frequent delight in singing these songs. Kazuko Ozawa, "*Frauenliebe und Leben*: Acht Lieder nach Adelbert von Chamisso für eine Singstimme und Klavier op. 42," in *Robert Schumann: Interpretationen seiner Werke*, ed. Helmut Loos (Laaber: Laaber Verlag, 2005), 274–80.

40. See Edward F. Kravitt's interesting study of Stockhausen's critical reception in "The Lied in 19th-Century Concert Life," *Journal of the American Musicological Society* 18 (1965): 207–18. Perhaps the day will again come when we have performances dramatizing the man behind the woman: the vocal register of *Frauenliebe und Leben* is better suited to a male alto like Jochen Kowalski than *Dichterliebe*, which he sings in the notated ("woman's") octave in "medium-voice" transpositions.

41. And he evidently liked to preface performances of Beethoven's *An die ferne Geliebte* with the E♭ Sonata *quasi una fantasia*, op. 27, no. 1 (Wirth, *Julius Stockhausen*, 212).

Musikfreunde—a full decade after Robert's death—announced that *Frauenliebe und Leben*, sung by "k. k. Hofopernsängerin" Frln. Bettelheim, would be performed in two parts, separated by Beethoven's C-minor Variations, op. 36, and a piano duo by Ernst Rudorff.[42]

The striking independence of performance and publication history from a composer's compositional considerations is a familiar facet of much of the music of this time. We know that Schubert performed the whole of *Winterreise* for a small group of his friends, and yet *Die schöne Müllerin* was issued to the public in five volumes. Similarly, Clara Schumann recorded in her diary that at a soirée on 14 October 1848 Wilhelmine Schröder-Devrient (in the midst of her second divorce proceeding) performed *Frauenliebe und Leben*—"all eight songs, and wonderfully. It was for us a great pleasure, and again we had to cry out: 'there is but one Devrient'!" On the same occasion, Devrient also performed Schubert's "Am Meer" and "Trockne Blumen." Two weeks later at a concert sponsored by the Frauenverein für arme Familien, she sang two songs by Schumann. "I cannot imagine 'Du Ring an meinem Finger' more beautifully sung," wrote Clara.[43]

Given the reaction of the musical press to Stockhausen's performance "experiments," it is unlikely that audiences for amateur performances in a typical bourgeois domestic setting would in fact have heard more than a few isolated numbers from the Chamisso cycle on any one occasion. Even then, it is impossible to generalize about the kind of reception they might have had. The gap in understanding between merely polite—if that—listeners and more musically sophisticated audiences could be enormous. A concert at the court in Hannover on 23 November 1862 elicited this cranky entry in Julius Stockhausen's diary: "'Dichterliebe'; Frau Schumann at the piano. Beethoven's sonata in F. The women crochet and knit; at the momentous events they lift their heads." Two days later, in Hamburg: "'Dichterliebe.' Not one of the charming pieces failed to impress. Several were requested a second time."[44]

---

42. The program is reproduced in Edward F. Kravitt, *The Lied: Mirror of Late Romanticism* (New Haven, Conn.: Yale University Press, 1996), 19.

43. Berthold Litzmann, *Clara Schumann: Ein Künstlerleben: Nach Tagebüchern und Briefen*, 3 vols. (1925; reprint, New York: Georg Olms Verlag, 1971), 2:118–19.

44. Wirth, *Julius Stockhausen*, 233. For a detailed study of the early history of Stockhausen's performances of Schubert and Schumann song cycles, see Renate Hofmann, "Julius Stockhausen als Interpret der Liederzyklen Robert Schumanns," in *Schumann Forschungen*, vol. 9, *Robert und Clara Schumann und die nationalen Musikkulturen des 19. Jahrhunderts. Bericht über das 7. Internationale Schumann-Symposion am 20. Und 21. Juni 2000 des 7. Schumann-Festes, Düsseldorf*, ed. Matthias Wendt (Mainz: Schott, 2005), 34–46. The repertoire sandwiched between the two halves of *Dichterliebe* varied from performance to performance; we learn, too, that Stockhausen made it a practice to perform large torsos (nine or ten songs) of the Schubert cycles. There is no mention here of the circumstances in which he sang *Frauenliebe und Leben*; Wirth records that the cycle was performed in its entirety (497). Her study was based on only a selection of the documents in her possession (the Julius Stockhausen *Nachlass* is housed in the Universitätsbibliothek in Frankfurt am Main).

II

Schumann's *Frauenliebe und Leben* will cast a much longer critical shadow than has been possible in recent years if we recognize that implicit in any sincere impersonation is always also a sympathetic identification with one's subject. What can have made the abstract woman of Chamisso's poems an attractive subject specifically for a song cycle, a genre that by the 1820s had evolved into an ambitious medium for exploring the inner workings of the human psyche? Since this woman is as much the product of a male Romantic imagination as is the poet of *Dichterliebe* or the miller and wanderer of the Schubert cycles, perhaps we should consider that her appeal may have had to do with something she shares with her masculine counterparts even quite apart from the composer's—or, for that matter, the poet's—sentimental attachment to a cultural ideal romanticizing feminine subservience. Like poetic youths and millers, the woman of the *Frauenliebe* poems maintains an extremely active life of the imagination. For a historian of gender constructs it is of course significant that *in her* this tendency is held up as a virtue, a source of strength, not as the excess of melancholy it is when, say, a miller gazes too fixedly into the heavens reflected in the surface of a brook. A certain vividness and involvement in imagination are taken to be normal constituents of womanhood. It is easy to see how this aspect of the figure might have appealed to Schumann, whose own lively imagination could be a source of both inspiration and terror to him.

Many early nineteenth-century song cycles trace a character's psychological journey by presenting a series of "snapshots" into his consciousness. The chronological ordering of these images is more sharply delimited in some cycles than in others, but the fact that they generally fall within a limited time span—a few months, perhaps a year—helps to create a continuity of character. While *Frauenliebe und Leben* would seem to depart from this norm in depicting typically significant stations in the lifetime of *any* woman (in fact, we can easily imagine these events concentrated within only a two- or three-year span), this abstraction is projected through the perceptions and experience of an *individual* personal. The notion that the specific example presented in these poems stands for the unchanging experience of all womankind is made explicit only in Chamisso's final poem, in which the widow, many years later, passes on her accumulated experience to her granddaughter, herself now a bride. The eight preceding poems come retrospectively to be defined as flashbacks. As is well known, Schumann omitted setting this self-conscious shift in narrative perspective, replacing it with a piano postlude that continues the train of the present story, representing the young widow's just announced retreat into her world of memory. An autobiographical act thus becomes an explicit element in Chamisso's story, but not so in Schumann's, which sustains the pretense of interior dialogue and immediate experience to the end.[45]

---

45. For Solie, the returning music in the postlude represents not a brief moment of interiority, but rather it points to the "endless repeatability of the woman's experience, the 'all-encompassing and infinite' time that, as Julia

I would guess that Schumann's decision to omit a setting of the final poem arose mainly from a consideration of the strengths and constraints of the musical genre. Schubert, too, omitted setting Müller's prologue and epilogue to *Die schöne Müllerin*. Like Chamisso's epilogue, these poems stand apart from the prevailing experiential perspective of the other poems, introducing a reflective narrating voice that frames and comments on the intervening story. While a residue of the poet's universalizing message surely does speak through in Schumann's retention of Chamisso's title, his own compositional energy is turned to portraying the inner life of an archetypal female character, a special manifestation of a more general type of song cycle protagonist. And, while we surely have a greater variety of male archetypes (millers, poets, wanderers: their distinct personalities molded in significant part by their occupation), all protagonists of song cycles, including—and perhaps even especially—Schumann's woman, share a similarly introverted nature, prone to vivid *phantasieren*. All are somewhat tragic figures for whom fantasy provides a defense against the conditions of their environment. A pervasive image of inner visioning, the dream, turns up in five of Chamisso's nine poems, a clear measure of the priority that states of imagination, both fantasy and memory, are granted in the cycle. It is this aspect of the poetry that Robert Schumann responded to with the greatest invention.

"Seit ich ihn gesehen, glaub ich blind zu sein. Wo ich hin nur blicke, seh ich ihn allein" (Ever since I first saw him, I have felt myself blinded; wherever I gaze, I see only him). With this intimate admission, the woman in Schumann's *Frauenliebe und Leben* begins the inward narration of her love affair with her husband. The simple piano accompaniment first anticipates, then doubles, the vocal part: the singer's words issue forth from the hypnotic chord changes as if caught in a daydream. With the increasing passion of the vocal phrases at measures 9–15—as she marvels that her beloved's image rises up before

---

Kristeva has told us, represents the feminine in many cultures throughout history" ("The Gendered Self," 228). Whereas the cyclical replication of women's experience is indeed the message of Chamisso's epilogue, it strikes me that Schumann's postlude is about something nearer the opposite, the *impossibility* of actually repeating, the poignant irreality of an individual's memory. Solie does not take note of this distinction, explicitly rejecting the characterization of the postlude as a memory: "It seems to me both curious and misguided that musicians always refer to recurring musical material as 'reminiscences.' Such a notion gives undue interpretive privilege to the first occurrence of any 'recalled' music, whereas the recurrence itself may be much more to the point, as so often in life—many of the songs in this cycle suggest instead the appropriateness of the psychoanalytic notion of 'repetition compulsion.' In the present situation, the common assumption is that Schumann's postlude represents more or less happy memories for the solace of the new widow. But she does not speak of memories—indeed, in several texts including the first and fourth poems she has explicitly repudiated memory; rather, she speaks, dissociatively, of turning within herself, where he now is" (229n). I do not see how "turning within herself" differs from memory. In the first and fourth poems, the woman distances herself from specific elements of her childhood past in order to embrace her new life as a married woman: this does not amount to a repudiation of memory, which is never an evenly weighted chronicle of all past experience. When a woman entered into marriage in patriarchal culture, she relinquished a part of her identity and birth ties in favor of her newly accepted identity (the taking of her husband's name was the outward symbol of this shift in affiliation). Chamisso's poems astutely register the psychological effect of this momentous act.

EXAMPLE 3.1   Robert Schumann, "Seit ich ihn gesehen," Op. 42/1, mm. 1–17.

her as if in a waking dream—the piano's doubling of the vocal line retreats to an inner
voice, disappearing into the counterpoint in measures 11–13, and the bass descends into
the deepest octave. Left registrally isolated and exposed, the singer's voice soars free of the
accompaniment, the passionate independence of her phrase a musical analogue for the
intensity of her vision (ex. 3.1).

EXAMPLE 3.2A Robert Schumann, "Helft mir ihr Schwestern," Op. 42/5, mm. 1–10.

Although we learn little about the woman's exterior surroundings, the poems of *Frauenliebe und Leben* are saturated with metaphoric images of sight: a sequence of interior visions. By contrast—or, better, by extension—in the song depicting the central event of the cycle, the location of the scene is defined entirely through sound. The nervously excited vocal melody of song 5, "Helft mir ihr Schwestern," is grafted onto a background of pealing bells, suggested by the din of the hollow turning figures, which give way, at the close of the song, to a solemn wedding march as the bride begins her procession toward the altar (the opening page is shown in ex. 3.2a). The singer's melody anticipates the tune of the wedding march, but the piano is only gradually eased into a supporting, accompanimental role.[46] Over the first several measures, the singer's and

---

46. Charles Rosen points to the resemblance between Schumann's march and the wedding march in *Lohengrin*: Did Wagner borrow the tune from Schumann, or was there already a traditional wedding march at this time?

EXAMPLE 3.2B Franz Schubert, "Der Leiermann," D 911/24, mm. 1–5.

pianist's parts are indifferent to each other to the point of clashing. At the beginning of the song, and at the start of every subsequent stanza, the pianist plays a repetitive figure that consists in striking a tonic triad, voiced to sound a prominent open fifth in the left hand, on the downbeat of every measure, then arpeggiating the triad in bare octaves, first rising, then falling through the octave. All the while the sustaining pedal is depressed ("Immer mit Pedal"): when heavy bells are struck at regular intervals, we can isolate individual pitches within the sonorous din, and we hear the sound bend as its source swings forth, then back.

I would venture to speculate that Schumann drew inspiration for this representation from Franz Schubert's memorable portrayal of mechanically produced sound in *Winterreise*: like the hurdy-gurdy's drone that takes several cranks of the instrument's handle to come to pitch, the premature grace note initiating Schumann's chiming pattern captures the effect of a bell being struck before its full swinging momentum has been attained (ex. 3.2b). In both Schubert's and Schumann's songs, an experiential perspective is fixed by the representation of the precise moment at which the sound is initiated.

It is clear from the poem that the marriage ceremony is imminent, but there is no mention of bells or of a march—nor indeed any explicit indication of the space in which the scene unfolds—in Chamisso's text. It is Schumann who contributes an auditory dimension to the images that will surely become an indelible part of the bride's memory of this day. Chiming bells were evidently an integral aspect of Schumann's experience of weddings: "Früh wachte ich auf unter vielem innerlichen Glocken-geläute" (I awakened early to the din of inner bells), Robert had written to Clara on 9 June 1839 (the day after his birthday, and a Sunday, so the bells were likely only half dreamt). This is the opening sentence of a charming dream sequence that melds into a vision of his future wedding day.[47] Their wedding in fact took place on the day before Clara's birthday the following year.

---

47. *Briefwechsel*, 2:558; 9 June 1839.

Throughout the poems, selective, emotionally charged stimuli from the woman's world fix her attention and are later recalled, at first involuntarily, then by acts of will. At the start of the cycle, no matter where she turns, she "sees" only him: "seit ich ihn gesehen, glaub ich blind zu sein, wo ich hin nur blicke, seh' ich ihn allein." In the third song, "Ich kann's nicht fassen, nicht glauben," unable to believe her fantasy of union could actually be realized, even after he has proposed marriage ("mir war's—ich träume noch immer" [it seemed to me—I am dreaming still]), she resists awakening to face the present, preferring to cling to the vivid sensual scenes she has constructed around her beloved: "O lass im Traume mich sterben . . ." (O let me expire in my dream . . .). On the brink of attaining what she has longed for, the young woman exhibits a momentary reluctance to trade in passionate fantasy for lived experience, which is of a single mind with her effort, at the close of the cycle, to fend off grief with idealized memory. Indeed, what the postlude will recall is music associated not objectively with her beloved but with the woman's fixation on his image as it turns up wherever she rests her gaze.

Elaborating the trope of love's blindness, external seeing and interior vision are already closely intermingled in the opening lines "wo ich hin nur blicke, seh' ich ihn allein" (wherever I gaze I see only him) and "[es] schwebt sein Bild mir vor" (his image hovers before me): just as she professes blindness to all but him when he is present, she continues to be able to "see" him—in Schumann's transliteration: to sing passionate phrases—even when he is momentarily absent.

Used metaphorically here, blindness later became the theme of another poetic cycle, *Die Blinde*, in which Chamisso portrayed the interior visioning of a woman deprived of sight. The systematic study of perception through sensory deprivation had been a favorite topic of eighteenth-century French philosophy—one thinks of Diderot's *Lettre sur les aveugles* and *Lettre sur les sourdes et muets* or Condillac's *Traité des Sensations*, for example. A striking number of such studies in human perception proceed by projecting an abstract image of woman, perhaps to make the introspective exercise appear more objective. Reminiscent of the Pygmalion story, Condillac's treatise imagines a lifeless female statue gradually endowed with consciousness through a series of empathetic projections by the philosopher. He adds the senses to his statue one by one, beginning with smell, and pauses at each stage to reflect on the resulting gain in cognitive faculties. The final step in this sequence of exercises is signaled by a shift from third- to first-person prose, erasing all narrative distance between the fictive philosopher and his imagined woman. He becomes her.[48]

Dream and present reality are again juxtaposed in "Du Ring an meinem Finger," in which Chamisso's woman characterizes her childhood as a spent dream ("Ich hatt' ihn ausgeträumet, der Kindheit friedlich schönen Traum"). Later, as she awaits the birth of her own first child, she looks expectantly to the future, trying to picture what their

---

48. The publication of Condillac's book in 1754 led to charges of plagiarism. Diderot's 1751 letter on the deaf and mute had anticipated his ideas, and Georges-Louis Leclerc de Buffon claimed that he had stolen the idea of the statue from the third volume of his 1749 *Histoire naturelle*. Condillac's defense is remarkable: he owed many

offspring will look like: when the dream finally awakens it will be her husband's like-ness—"dein Bildniss"—that smiles up at her. Finally, betrayed by the death of her spouse, she indulges a painfully desolate projection, envisioning *herself* forlorn in an empty world—"es blicket die Verlass'ne vor sich hin: die Welt ist leer" (the forsaken one gazes before her: the world is a void)—and, declaring herself no longer alive (as if arresting external experience could preserve the past), she resolves to retreat into her inwardness: "da hab ich dich und mein verlornes Glück, du meine Welt" (there I have you and my lost happiness, you are my world).

In Chamisso's poetic cycle the surprising brief shift to third-person narration in the penultimate poem provides a transition to the epilogue; it comes to be explained as the emerging narrator's voice, the aging widow seeing an image of herself in the past. But Schumann chose to end his cycle of songs in the present, omitting the widow's nostalgic reflection on her story from a distant future. Relief from the extreme psychological dev-astation of "die Welt ist leer" comes not with the passage of time but by an act of will (harmonically as well as emotionally) in the remarkable voice leading that brings the toni-cized dominant of D minor, where the singer ends, back to the tonic, B♭ (as is shown in ex. 3.3). One tone is sustained across the barline after the fermata. Reaching across several octaves, the remaining tones of the required dominant minor ninth are re-collected, and the sustained A♮ turns from a root into a leading tone. As in *Dichterliebe*, consolation arrives through the agency of instrumental music: with the return of the accompaniment of the first song, the widow is transported back to the time she first allowed the image of her husband to rule her imagination, to the origin of her internally constructed world.[49]

of his ideas to his frequent conversations with the insightful Mademoiselle Ferrand, he said. This illuminates the complicated role that women played in the eighteenth-century commerce of ideas, for if the Pygmalion theme was in the air, then the thoughts Ferrand shared with Condillac almost certainly were not formed in a total void. Accustomed to giving her own ideas freely, she cannot have been overly concerned with proper authorial attri-bution in conversation. The story of the plagiarism charges is recounted, among other places, in Etienne Bonnot de Condillac, *Abhandlung über die Empfindungen*, ed. Lothar Kreimendahl, *Philosophische Bibliothek 25* (Ham-burg: Felix Meiner Verlag, 1983), xxiii–iv. Kreimendahl reports that a 1750 letter from Condillac to Gabriel Cramer, discovered in 1978, supports the contention that the inspiration came from Mademoiselle Ferrand.

49. Distinct varieties of remembering are suggested in the narration of *Frauenliebe und Leben*. The first eight poems are told in the first-person-present, seeming to unfold in the moment, except at two striking points. The brief lapses into past-tense narration in the third poem—"Mir war's, er habe gesprochen . . . mir war's, ich träume noch immer, es kann ja nimmer so sein" (It seemed to me, he spoke . . . it seemed to me 'I am dreaming still,' it cannot ever be so)—are the first hint that the woman might be reliving her wonder and confusion from a distance. At this point in the story, nothing yet indicates to the reader whether 'it seemed to me' took place yesterday or two decades ago. The far more wrenching appearance in the final poem of third-person-present speech—"Es blicket die Verlass'ne vor sich hin"—may be explained as what psychologists call an ob-server memory (more on this in chapter 4). Reliving her devastation and shock, the woman projects an image of herself into the mental scene. This view of events is supported by Chamisso's epilogue, where we learn that the narrating voice all the while belonged to the aging widow. In omitting it, Schumann's song cycle leaves ambiguous the identity of the voice that remarks upon the grieving widow's posture in the final song. Stark, disjointed harmonies underscore the surprising brief shift into third-person speech, magnifying the disloca-tion of the moment. Nothing in Schumann's setting demands the shift to old age that Chamisso's epilogue makes explicit in Chamisso's epilogue. That falls to the performer to decide.

EXAMPLE 3.3   Robert Schumann, *Frauenliebe und Leben*, Op. 42: the postlude.

Chamisso's epilogue reveals that the impetus for the widow's vivid reminiscences has been her identification with another bride, her granddaughter. This falls away in Schumann's postlude, only to be replaced with an even greater psychological insight: our earliest memories of those we have loved always retain a special intensity. Since the piano began by prompting and doubling the vocal line, the words of the opening stanza come easily to mind. But, as Charles Rosen has observed, at the climactic vocal phrase, "[es] schwebt sein Bild mir vor" (his image hovers before me), the piano's doubling of the melody retreats into an inner voice, the dynamics shift to *pianissimo*, and we are left to supply in our own minds not only the missing words but also the missing melody. As Rosen eloquently describes, the effort to do so becomes frustrating, especially at "taucht aus tiefstem Dunkel" (emerges from the darkest depths), where crucial melodic notes, and the most expressive leap in the song, vanish into the counterpoint. (The pitches are all in fact present, but the melody's registral and rhythmic contours are lost, its notes scrunched into the same octave as the accompanying inner voice.)[50] Schumann's music provides only the stimulus for a recollection, making the widow's loss all the more poignantly felt.

In allowing ourselves to be drawn into Schumann's imaginative construct (I want to say: *ihm nachzuempfinden*—to follow in his perceptual footsteps) and straining to supply words and melody, we discover that the postlude is not merely a rote transcription of the accompaniment of the first song. Tiny changes in detail subtly reflect the widow's altered perspective. Try to fit the words of the first stanza to the postlude, and you will falter at "seh ich ihn allein." Here the rhythms of the original vocal melody have been conflated with the right-hand accompaniment, and the phrase is compressed—the C♮ of "seh" is distended, the G♭ in the inner voices comes sooner, the final two quarter notes are squeezed into the space of two eighths, and the *ritard* falls away—creating a quickened rhythm that prompts a revised diction for this phrase. The only words that will now fit comfortably are "seh ich ihn," with the nostalgic sigh figure at "ihn," B♭–A, doubled in

---

50. Charles Rosen, *The Romantic Generation* (Cambridge, Mass.: Harvard University Press, 1995), 112–15. Some pages later, in a discussion of Romantic landscape description, Rosen again reminds us of this moment, drawing out an implication that is earlier left unstated: "In music, too, composers were often unsatisfied by the static representation of sentiment by simple musical analogy, but sought to portray the process of feeling and even, as we have seen with the end of Schumann's *Frauenliebe und Leben*, the actual functioning of memory" (159). There is none of this ambition in Carl Loewe's 1835 setting of the *Frauenliebe* poems (he composed all nine but published only the first seven). Loewe's sentimental songs use a wide array of musical styles and gendered tropes (battle song, lullaby, dances, funeral march, and lament, even a music box when the baby smiles) to paint a still tableau of each scene: see the girls dancing, see the women lament at the funeral etc. (Brigitte Fassbaender's imaginative recording draws out the gendered stereotypes by amplifying them. She hums the final refrain of the cradle song and speaks the widow's words of advice to her granddaughter over the piano accompaniment in the final song.) There is no effort to inhabit the perceptions of the character, to portray her emotional life. Schumann's *Frauenliebe und Leben*, by contrast (but in keeping with his other song cycles), projects a powerful persona precisely by a represention of her inner experience.

octaves (the only such doubling), resonating poignantly into the following quarter rest. The sum of all these alterations is to make the phrase jut out of its surroundings in a brief surge of—simulated vocal—expressiveness. This serves both to make the melody more prominent, in preparation for its withdrawal, and, at the same time, to distort it in a meaningful way. As she rehearses her past, the widow no longer marvels, as she once did, that she sees him at every turn; what impresses her in the present moment is that she is still able to envision him, however fleetingly, even as he is forever absent.

The following words similarly take on a new meaning after the husband's death. "Wie im wachen Traume, schwebt sein Bild mir vor" (As in a waking dream, his image hovers before me) are the words that echo silently, and in midphrase the melody descends into the deeper octave. This time, far from setting in relief the increased passion of the singer's character at the imagined sight of her beloved, as in the opening song, the retreat into an inner voice mimics a physiological manifestation of self-absorption, taking the melody into the register in which the widow might hum it consolingly to herself: sounding from within the texture, an octave below the original sung register, it becomes an emblem of her interiority.

But Schumann's effect goes beyond any such pictorial aspect, depending on the auditor's active participation in the construction of the memory. Because the vocal melody sounds in the piano accompaniment, we are easily prompted to imagine vocalizing along. If, at the point the piano drops into the deeper octave, we continue to imagine the melody in the now absent original register, we easily lose the thread, finding our interior voices isolated in the upper octave; if, instead, we match the melody at the piano's pitch, the expressive leap down a seventh at "taucht aus *tiefstem* Dunkel" will take us out of range, forcing a leap into the physical void. (Literally humming along with the piano—not that I would recommend this as a performance practice—will make the physical boundary vividly apparent.)[51] It is at just this point in the postlude that Schumann has made the melody vanish into the surrounding counterpoint, and the leap to the deep E♭ is evaded. On the following words, "heller, heller nur empor," the tune is regained (his image reemerging from "dem tiefstem Dunkel," as it were), and although the melodic line descends almost as far, it does so by stepwise motion. To have set the words "taucht aus tiefstem Dunkel" with a passionate downward leap in the opening song was an inspired, and counterintuitive, bit of word painting: his image *rises* from the depths. Here in the postlude, the suppression of the memorable phrase creates a momentary (and even very physical) void, which can only be filled in by our own shadowy recollection.

---

51. I am of course assuming a hummer whose natural voice falls within the vocal range of the cycle. Others will have to adjust the octave to replicate the same effect. To suggest that the songs have been calculated to a specific vocal range naturally indicates nothing about the composer's willingness to sanction performance transposed by register and/or octave. (The place that might lose most in performance by a male singer is perhaps "Nun hast du mir den ersten Schmerz getan," which begins with a stark midrange D-minor triad that mimics the resonance of a mature woman's voice. The bass octave pointedly is withheld.)

Schumann's postlude may be thought to represent a memory, not merely a symbolic or formal return, precisely because the past is brought back through the filter of present emotion and experience. The very inaccuracy of the repetition, its muted passion, imitates the perceptual mechanisms of a memory that has no hope of being revitalized by physical proximity.[52]

The postlude stands as one of the most innovative passages in Schumann's oeuvre, but many other moments in the cycle contribute to a portrayal of the character's immediate experience. Schumann's control of contrapuntal textures and fluid harmonic changes allowed him to suggest the movement between emotional states with remarkable specificity. In "Er, der Herrlichste von allen," the premature entries of the theme in the piano's interludes wonderfully capture the woman's excitement at seeing the man she will marry. Then, in "Ich kann's nicht fassen, nicht glauben," his magic words—as they resonate in her mind—are set to softly changing chords over a pedal point, the harmony tracking her every movement between reality and imagination. The song's coda brings back the opening words as the music choreographs her effort to hold on to the fantasy before it dissolves.

The sixth song is an intimate scene in which she discloses her pregnancy to her husband. It is the first time she has addressed him directly. The revelation itself is whispered, so we do not hear her words. (Schumann famously cut the poetic stanza that spells out her message.) Transported by the piano's expressive solo to a cathartic release in the subdominant, the lyrical passage that follows at "Bleib an meinem Herzen" (Stay at my heart) is reminiscent of Beethoven's *An die ferne Geliebte*—which had earlier served Schumann as a source for the C- major Fantasy. The appearance of this signature Schumannian melody, in the piano alone at first, momentarily obscures the boundary between the woman who is speaking and an implied addressee of her words. Coming immediately after "du geliebter, *geliebter* Mann" (the added emphasis is Schumann's), the heightened passion of the phrase suggests a gesture of reciprocity. Both Clara and Robert,

---

52. Schumann's approach to portraying the widow's immersion in memory bears a kinship with the ambitions of a visual artist from the turn of the next century. In a fascinating essay written for the catalog of an exhibit shown at the Tate Gallery, London, and the Museum of Modern Art, New York, curator John Elderfield examines the "adventures of the optic nerve" of Pierre Bonnard, a painter who famously preferred to work from memory, and whose paintings have long been thought to portray the perception or memory of objects as much as the objects themselves. Speculating that Bonnard exploits certain properties of visual perception (the fuzziness of peripheral vision, the effect of light that results from a juxtaposition of high-intensity oppositional colors) to guide the beholder's attention and the eye's scan path across the surface of a painting so as "to cause particular, intended, effects to be represented," Elderfield proposes that "this is, effectively, an idea of painting not as a representation given over to the beholder but, rather, as a stimulus for a representation to be created by the beholder." The kinds of things he has in mind involve above all the temporal dimension of visual perception: the effort to show what one sees and the order in which one sees it when entering a room suddenly, or the effort to recover and thereby retain an image lost to the memory. John Elderfield, "Seeing Bonnard," in *Bonnard*, exhibition catalog, ed. Sarah Whitfield (New York: Museum of Modern Art, 1998), 33–52 (the brief quotations are drawn from pp. 35 and 36). Like Bonnard's visual representations, Schumann's auditory constructions of memory exploit the observer's perceptual capacities and expectations to indicate a direction—but the representation is fully realized only with the active engagement of the auditor.

we might say, are present in the scene. Passions merge. Maybe it gave him pleasure to imagine Clara addressing him in this way. Or, perhaps, the recollection of *An die ferne Geliebte* let Schumann's inner voice sing those words to a man whom he revered as deeply as the woman in the poem does her husband. (*An die ferne Geliebte*, after all, was performed at the memorial concert for Beethoven in Vienna on Easter Monday 1827, and the C-major Fantasy was Schumann's contribution to a fund-raiser for the Bonn Beethoven monument.)

Frauenliebe und Leben is a paradox. Even as its more concrete subject matter has died out in the world, the intensity of Schumann's engagement with the figure of this woman remains deeply affecting. To my mind, it is precisely the uninhibited imagination of Schumann's act of empathy, his remarkable effort to portray his character's process of mind, that stands to account for the work's continued effectiveness in the present— against all shifting social odds. The vehemence of reaction against the poems today is perhaps an indication that the social injuries they have come to symbolize for some remain still too raw. But this—I should like to imagine—will recede, and with it, an understanding of what all the fuss in our century was about.

Postscript: There has been renewed interest in these songs of late, and I now have heard *Frauenliebe und Leben* sung (movingly) by a tenor, and performed as a trouser role. Baritone Matthias Goerne has performed it several times in prominent venues. (See especially the 6 November 2005 review by Matthew Gurewitsch in the *New York Times*, provocatively titled "Why Shouldn't Men Sing Romantic Drivel, Too?" which records Goerne's delight in the cycle's "timeless and wonderful" quality, its expression of "unconditional devotion, without mental reserve.") Soon after an earlier version of this essay appeared in 2001, Rufus Hallmark kindly shared with me his paper "Schumann and Other Frauenliebe Songs," delivered at Queens College in 2001, and he is completing a book-length study of *Frauenliebe und Leben* now. Elissa S. Guralnick looks to Chamisso's popular story *Peter Schlemihl's Wundersame Geschichte* (1813) for insight into the sensibilities behind the poems, in "'Ah Clara, I Am Not Worthy of Your Love': Re-reading 'Frauenliebe und Leben,' The Poetry and the Music," *Music and Letters* 87 (2006): 580–605; Robert Samuels draws a comparison with Dichterliebe in "Narratives of Masculinity and Femininity: Two Schumann Song Cycles," in *Phrase and Subject: Studies in Literature and Music* (Oxford: Legenda, 2006), 135–45; and Jonathan Dunsby wrestles with Ruth Solie's study of the cycle in "Why Sing? Lieder and Song Cycles," in *The Cambridge Companion to Schumann*, ed. Beate Perrey (Cambridge:Cambridge University Press, 2007), 109–14. I myself have turned to performances, especially older recorded performances, for insight into the ways that singers and pianists have grappled with this character. More directly than with other song cycles, the age of the singer can affect how we perceive the time span of the story: Is it told from the vantage point of a very young widow (as in Anne Sofie von Otter's 1995 record with Bengt Forsberg) or in the voice of the grandmother? Lotte Lehmann embraced the powerful role of Schumann's woman, and she sang *Dichterliebe* too (both recorded with Bruno Walter in 1942, when she was in her fifties). We may gain some perspective on her performance from her captivating film role in *Big City* (1948), where she plays the grandmother of an abandoned baby, discovered on New York's Lower East Side by the cantor, her son, who shares custody of the little girl with two other neighborhood men, a Protestant chaplain, and an Irish Catholic patrolman. Lehmann's performance there leaves little doubt that she knew the power of the voice to overcome uncongenial politics. The grandmother's authoritative moral presence calms wary neighbors' fears about the unconventional family: all eyes are transfixed when Lehmann's character spontaneously erupts into a vocalise on Schumann's "Träumerei" from the rocking chair where she has sat quietly embroidering as the three men play chamber music together. Lehmann directly addressed her approach to the cycle in *More Than Singing: The Interpretation of Songs*, first published by Boosey and Hawkes in New York in 1945. Just two sentences here: "You should begin the cycle with the kind of reverence and enchantment with which you might take from an old cabinet a rare piece of precious lace which had been the proud possession of your great grandmother. You would touch it very carefully and would be rather moved as you replaced it beside the little musical clock—another relic of a bygone day". In her detailed commentary on the individual songs, she brings in God whenever possible, even proposing that the words "Nun hast du mir den ersten Schmerz getan" be directed at him, not the deceased husband. And in a recording of *Frauenliebe und Leben* that Marian Anderson made with Franz Rupp in 1950, we find a fascinating performance decision. Rupp plays the postlude to "Helft mir ihr Schwestern" at a tempo so brisk that we cannot take it as a wedding march (the closing horn calls vanish too). It becomes, instead, an exhilarating dash to embrace the future. Her most memorable day may not have been her wedding, their performance lets us imagine. I do not presume to know what was on these performers' minds, but there is another day that might just as easily have fit the bill. Seated at one end of the long aisle where Anderson performed before a crowd of 75,000 (having been denied the use of Constitution Hall by the Daughters of the American Revolution) on Easter Sunday, 1939, a day when church bells were rung, there is a statue of "Er der herrlichste von Allen": the Lincoln Memorial. Meanings are not fixed; we shape them ourselves. The only other performance I have heard that approaches this tempo choice is the 1909 recording Julia Culp made with Otto Bake, where the fast tempo at the beginning of the wedding march—drastically slowed as it blends into the horn calls—strikes us less because there has been so much rubato throughout.

4

Music Recollected in Tranquillity: Postures of Memory in Beethoven

Schumann's portrayal in the postlude to *Frauenliebe und Leben* of a woman's effort to bring to mind the image of her departed spouse (discussed in the previous chapter) depicts a moment when emotions are still raw from the trauma, when the absence of the familiar presence is still more palpable than anything else in the rememberer's perception. There is consolation and frustration both in the intensive effort to grasp in the mind's eye images of a happiness that will not be renewed, to shore up the memory before it can decay.

Some years later, Marcel Proust would explore a different side of remembrance. In a famous passage near the close of the final volume of *Remembrance of Things Past*, Marcel, the narrator of Proust's novel, has grown disenchanted with his autobiographical project. His efforts to describe the snapshots in his memory only disappoint and depress him: he rejects them as inauthentic, inevitably colored by the concerns of the present. Seeking distraction in society, he is jolted out of his doldrums when, leaping out of the path of a cab on his way into the Guermantes mansion, he stumbles upon two uneven paving stones. At that moment an indistinct vision flutters before him, filling him with happy sensations. Determined to grasp the vision more fully, he repeats the action, stepping again upon the stones. It comes suddenly: a memory of Venice, when, balanced upon two uneven paving stones in the baptistry at Saint Mark's, Marcel had felt this same happiness. For the rest of the evening, his mind seeks triggers that will activate kindred sensations. A stiff napkin, the clanging of a spoon, the sound of running water all serve to bring back past moments imbued with a similar feeling. Later reflections lead him to speculate on the seemingly insignificant sensations that accompany any word or action we have experienced in the past, and which our logical minds filter out, seeing no importance in them. Yet a perception of like character in the present—a physical action, a smell or taste or sound or shape resembling something in the previous moment—can make the earlier experience come flooding to mind with an intensity unlike any we experience when we merely strain to retrieve those "supposed snapshots" we have taken of the past (the photographic analogy is Proust's).

The procedures of memory explored in these two episodes by Schumann and Proust differ as markedly as the circumstances prompting them. In Schumann's song cycle a powerful feeling of loss consumes the moment. The newly widowed protagonist tries intently to transform this absence into a presence, to make the image of her husband reappear before her. Much of the force of the representation comes from making the listener experience a frustration analogous to the protagonist's: a melody fades from our awareness just as her vision evaporates. In contrast, Proust's Marcel, an author by profession, is dejected by the sterility of the distant scenes housed in his imagination. The involuntary memory that emerges when he stumbles upon the paving stones, indistinct as it is, gives him cause to probe the recesses of his mind more deeply. He becomes intent upon retrieving this buried feeling, actively seeking out triggers to dislodge the happy vision so tantalizingly glimpsed. In both instances a creative artist explores his own cognition through a fictional projection of someone near to himself.

In the latter half of the eighteenth century, and well into the nineteenth, the boundary between fictional imagining and empirical science was not as sharply drawn as we are accustomed to imagine it today. As we saw in the previous chapter, Étienne de Condillac tried methodically to explore the nature and limits of human cognition by projecting himself into the place of a lifeless female statue, whom he endowed only gradually with full consciousness. His conclusions were published in the *Traité des Sensations* (1754), a volume that also circulated widely in German translation, especially in the later nineteenth century. One by one Condillac granted his imagined statue the use of her sensory faculties, beginning with smell, then hearing, sight, taste, and finally touch. At each stage he tried to grasp the impact the new sensory input would have on her (that is, his) ability to draw distinctions between self and others, to recall absent things, to form judgments, and the like. The exercise persuaded him that a statue endowed with fewer senses would have enhanced perceptual capacities: with restricted sensory input (blind, deaf, or unable to feel touch), a statue's ability to conjure absent things would be keener, he imagined, as there would be fewer distractions to interfere with her concentration. Indeed, a good portion of his treatise is focused on discovering the precise moment at which the statue would learn to distinguish between present sensation and memory (smell alone is insufficient, he speculated).[1] To be sure, this exercise in empirically derived psychological understanding has its limits, yet it also opened the door to the more precisely controlled experiments of a later age.

---

1. I have relied mainly on Etienne Bonnot de Condillac, *Abhandlung über die Empfindungen*, ed. Lothar Kreimendahl, *Philosophische Bibliothek 25* (Hamburg: Felix Meiner Verlag, 1983).

For William Wordsworth the cultivation of one's ability to make absent things become present was the essence of what it meant to be a poet. In the revised "Preface to the *Lyrical Ballads*" of 1802 he asserted that in addition to such qualities as a lively sensibility and a great knowledge of human nature, the poet

> has added a disposition to be affected more than other men by absent things as if they were present, an ability of conjuring up in himself passions, which are indeed far from being the same as those produced by real events, yet (especially in those parts of the general sympathy which are pleasing and delightful) do more nearly resemble the passions produced by real events, than anything which, from the motions of their own minds merely, other men are accustomed to feel in themselves.[2]

Some pages later, he describes the process of conjuring absent things in the present with greater precision:

> I have said that poetry is the spontaneous overflow of powerful feelings: it takes its origin from emotion recollected in tranquillity: the emotion is contemplated till by a species of reaction the tranquillity gradually disappears, and an emotion, kindred to that which was before the subject of contemplation, is gradually produced, and does itself actually exist in the mind.[3]

The desired result, brought on by contemplation, is here construed as a physical or chemical process—a "species of reaction"—that produces a feeling kindred, but not identical, to the perception previously experienced. Both "actually exist in the mind," and yet there is a qualitative difference between the event lived and relived. We might note that although Proust's quest to recover moments of past happiness dwells on sensory triggers rather than the reflective exploration of feeling that Schumann and Wordsworth rely upon to access memories, each of them is concerned to recover experiences of a strong emotional cast.

The last decades have witnessed a tremendous surge of interest in the mechanisms of memory and consciousness within a community of neuroscientists, psychologists, and philosophers. The recognition of different varieties of remembering (episodic or semantic memory, for example, the rehearsal of so-called autobiographical episodes as distinct from the general knowledge of facts about our surroundings) has led to intensive study of their distinctive modes of encoding and retrieval. Psychologist Daniel

---

2. William Wordsworth, *Revised Preface to the Lyrical Ballads* (1802), reprinted in *Wordsworth and Coleridge: Lyrical Ballads*, ed. W. J. B. Owen (New York: Oxford University Press, 1969), 165.

3. Wordsworth, *Revised Preface*, 173.

Schacter observes that for much of the last century the subjective experience of memory was not thought a proper domain for scientific inquiry, a belief that came under powerful attack in the 1980s—most forcefully by the philosopher John Searle. Resistance was overcome when a series of studies demonstrated that although memories are individual (and highly selective), there is considerable consistency in the way we remember certain classes of events—whether, for instance, we position ourselves as observers, gazing at an image of ourselves in a scene from the past, or whether we reexperience the event from our original perspective. The latter, called a "field" memory, has been shown to be more common when we dwell upon our emotions in a past situation. Memories of early childhood, on the other hand, are frequently reported as observer memories. Further probing of the field-observer distinction by cognitive psychologists has led to the recognition that these perceptions can be manipulated: when asked to focus on their feelings in a given episode, people frequently experienced field memories; asked to focus on objective circumstances surrounding the event, they more frequently reported observer memories. This adaptability of memory to different purposes has been understood to suggest that some memories must not be stored in fixed form but rather are newly assembled from stored elements with each retrieval.[4]

We can easily find the field-observer distinction reflected in literary engagements with memory. There is a remarkable account of a field memory in Adelbert von Chamisso's *Reise um die Welt* (1836), his narration of the three-year journey around the world that he took as a botanist in 1815–18. He recalls an experience in the harbor outside San Francisco. The crew had many regulations imposed on them, including the requirement that lamps had to be extinguished by 10:00 P.M. This led to many hours spent in a kind of half sleep. Waking dreams took over the mind:

> I never dreamt of the present, never of the journey, never of the world that I now belonged to. The cradle of the ship rocked me back to my childhood self, the years were turned back. I was back in my father's house, and my departed ones or those lost to me encircled me again, moving through their everyday tasks as if I had never grown past those years, as if death had not cut them down.
>
> (Ich träumte nie von der Gegenwart, nie von der Reise, nie von der Welt, der ich jetzt angehörte; die Wiege des Schiffes wiegte mich wieder zum Kinde, die Jahre wurden zurückgeschraubt, ich war wieder im Vaterhause, und meine Toten und verschollene Gestalten umringten mich, sich in alltäglicher Gewöhnlichkeit

---

4. Daniel L. Schacter, *Searching for Memory: The Brain, the Mind, and the Past* (New York: HarperCollins, 1996),18–22. The initial resistance within the scientific community is documented at greater length by John M. Gardiner in "On the Objectivity of Subjective Experiences of Autonoetic and Noetic Consciousness," in *Memory, Consciousness, and the Brain: The Tallinn Conference*, ed. Endel Tulving (Philadelphia: Psychology Press, 1999), 159–72.

bewegend, als sei ich nie über die Jahre hinausgewachsen, als habe der Tod sie nicht gemäht.)[5]

And Chamisso's *Frauenliebe und Leben*, published the following year, contains a perfect example of an observer memory. In the penultimate poem (Schumann's final song), the narrating voice shifts briefly into the third-person present—"Es blicket die Verlass'ne vor sich hin"—as the woman sees an image of her own distraught self. Indeed, field and observer memories both are represented in Chamisso's *Frauenliebe und Leben*.[6]

Goethe's poem "Um Mitternacht" (1818) is built around this same perceptual distinction, demonstrating, moreover, a fluid movement from the observation of a body image in the distance to its fusion with a present self. The poet calls up three moments in life, each at midnight. There is a gradual shift from a visually powerful memory of childhood at the beginning of the first stanza ("klein, kleiner Knabe"), which our inner eye surveys from a fixed location, to the more involved reliving of past events (a field memory) in the middle ("mußte, mußte, weil sie zog" "Ich gehend, kommend, Seeligkeiten sog"), to, finally, an intensely illuminated moment of clarity when past, present, and future fuse swiftly into one:

Um Mitternacht ging ich, nicht eben gerne,
Klein kleiner Knabe jenen Kirchhof hin
Zu Vaters Haus, des Pfarrers, Stern an Sterne
Sie leuchteten doch alle gar zu schön,
Um Mitternacht, um Mitternacht.

Wenn ich dann ferner in des Lebens Weite
Zur Liebsten mußte, mußte, weil sie zog
Gestirn und Nordschein über mir im Streite.
Ich gehend, kommend Seeligkeiten sog
Um Mitternacht, um Mitternacht.

Bis dann zuletzt des vollen Mondes Helle
So klar und deutlich mir ins Finstere drang,
Auch der Gedanke willig, sinnig, schnelle
Sich ums Vergangne wie ums Künftige schlang
Um Mitternacht, um Mitternacht.

---

5. Adelbert von Chamisso, *Reise um die Welt* ("Von Unalashka nach Kalifornien. Aufenthalt zu San Francisco"), first published in 1836. In a modern edition: Adelbert von Chamisso, *Sämtliche Werke in zwei Bänden*, vol. 2 (Darmstadt: Wissenschaftliche Buchgesellschaft, 1982), 200. An English translation of the travelogue is available: *A Voyage around the World with the Romanzov Exploring Expedition in the Years 1815–1818 in the Brig Rurik, Captain Otto von Kotzebue* by Adelbert von Chamisso; trans. and ed. Henry Kratz (Honolulu: University of Hawaii Press, 1986).

6. For a more detailed discussion of this, see chapter 3, note 48.

(At midnight I went, not quite gladly,
A small, small boy, to the churchyard,
To father's house, the pastor's; star upon star
O how beautifully they all would shine;
At midnight, at midnight.

When further into life's distance
I went to my beloved, went because she drew me,
Starry heavens and northlights warring above,
I, going, and coming, took in bliss
At midnight, at midnight.

'Til finally the full moon's radiance,
Shone clear into my inner darkness,
And thought itself wound its way willingly,
sentient, swiftly 'round past and future
At midnight, at midnight.)

As modern researchers have probed the mechanisms underlying common subjective experiences of memory, some have turned their attention to the literary and visual arts. Schacter characterizes representations of the rememberer by visual and literary artists as "suggestive" and "provocative" for the direction of scientific research.[7] The careful effort by psychologists to distinguish the many modes of remembering and the new models put forth by neuroscientists may in turn stimulate new awareness of the role of cognitive functioning and its representations in the arts. It is striking that music, the medium perhaps best suited to emulating shifts in consciousness associated with temporal experience, has so far been largely ignored in the cross-disciplinary discussions of the subject that have proliferated in recent years.[8] But musicians have long described certain passages in the repertory—especially from middle-period Beethoven onward—as reminiscences or recollections, as behaving like memories—and not only where there is a poetic

---

7. Schacter, *Searching for Memory*, 18.
8. Two book-length studies must stand for the much wider interest in the humanities. *The Anatomy of Memory: An Anthology* (New York: Oxford University Press, 1996), a stimulating collection edited by James McConkey, brings together writings by such distinguished neuroscientists as Antonio Damasio, Gerald Edelman, and Steven Rose and reflections on memory and related questions of creative process and narrative in writers as disparate as Marcel Proust, Toni Morrison, William Wordsworth, and Henri Poincaré. Perusing these selections, one is easily struck by the frequency with which the poets' introspective accounts resonate with, and often have anticipated, recent neurophysiological models. A volume by Suzanne Nalbantian, *Memory in Literature: From Rousseau to Neuroscience* (New York: Palgrave Macmillan, 2003), more explicitly traces links between shifts in the conceptualization of processes of memory and consciousness over the last two centuries and the representations of literary (and a few visual) artists, suggesting many fascinating avenues of influence and reaction among them. Nalbantian devotes a full chapter to a discussion of Proust's knowledge of the medical and philosophical writings of his time—especially to his adaptations of the work of Henri Bergson.

text to guide our understanding. Moreover, one easily recognizes that these engagements with memory by early nineteenth-century creative minds (whether artists, writers, or musicians) frequently have anticipated the direction of more recent scientific thinking. And they certainly were aware of what they were doing: when the topic of Mozart's instrumental music came up in conversation with Beethoven in 1826, the quartet violinist Karl Holz observed, "One does not find in his works a representation analogous to a state of mind as one does in yours."[9]

Our descriptions of such musical passages until recently have appeared only in isolated brief reflections on the character of especially "poetic" passages, often associated with so-called cyclic returns.[10] Wordsworth's equation of poetic imagination with the art of making absent things present has found a strong echo in music criticism, especially in English-language writing, and cyclic returns have long been characterized as poetic. It will be helpful, therefore, to consider these precedents for Schumann's inspiration as a group. How are such turns to the past marked in Beethoven's music? How are they constructed differently from ordinary formal returns?

All the instances we will be considering here have been characterized by at least one earlier writer (often several) as evoking an act of remembering, and that is much to my point. Yet what strikes me most about them is the extraordinary range of procedures they display (there is no formula), suggesting mechanisms of remembering as varied as any we might discover in Wordsworth or in Proust. The temporal experiences suggested by Beethoven's cyclic returns are equally diverse (sudden flashback, involuntary incursion, meditative rehearsal, quick mental reference to events past), allowing us to discern in each case how a mimesis of mental functioning interacts with commonplace conventions of the local musical discourse.

Let us begin with what is perhaps the most elaborate and the most imaginative of all such descriptive accounts in the critical literature, Donald Francis Tovey's gloss on the famous return in Beethoven's Fifth Symphony of music from the scherzo just before the

---

9. Beethoven, *Konversationshefte*, 8:268. A longer excerpt of the exchange is quoted by Lewis Lockwood in *Beethoven: The Music and the Life* (New York: Norton, 2003), 350.

10. The most systematic discussion of the subject is Elaine Sisman's "Memory and Invention at the Threshold of Beethoven's Late Style," in *Beethoven and His World*, ed. Scott Burnham and Michael P. Steinberg (Princeton, N.J.: Princeton University Press, 2000), 51–87, which places Beethoven's experiments within a wider intellectual history. That same year *Musical Quarterly* published a group of analytic studies reflecting on "Memory and Schubert's Instrumental Music," ed. Walter Frisch, with contributions by Frisch, John Daverio, John M. Gingerich, Charles Fisk, and Scott Burnham (*Musical Quarterly* 84, no. 4 [Winter 2000]). Charles Rosen's *Romantic Generation* (Cambridge, Mass.: Harvard University Press, 1995) is shot through with passing references to memory, and there are others similar in Tovey, Kerman, and elsewhere. Nineteenth-century music encyclopedias are instructive too. For Arrey von Dommer, in the entry "Cyclische Formen" in his *Musikalisches Lexikon* (Heidelberg: Mohr, 1865; an expanded edition of H. Ch. Koch's), cyclic forms referred principally to four-movement sonata cycles whose psychological development spans all four movements. He stressed that to represent subjective impressions coherently a composer must tie expressive departures closely to the structural norms of sonata form. Indeed, as we shall note, many of the passages in question appear at points of retransition.

recapitulation in the finale.[11] Notice that the mode of memory that Tovey locates in this passage has a character again quite distinct from those we have surveyed in Wordsworth, Schumann, or Proust:

> Let us remember that the "scherzo" had a tremendous emotional value, and then consider how it is to be reintroduced into the sustained triumph of the finale. Any one would think that there are only two ways of working the problem: first, to reproduce the mood just as it was. Of course this is impossible. We cannot forget that the terror has passed. Secondly then, could we recover the mood by elaborating the details? This would betray itself as fictitious. If you cannot recover the sensations you felt during an earthquake, it is not much use telling as your own experience things about it that you could not possibly have known at the time. We can easily see, now that Beethoven has shown us, that his is the one true solution which confirms the truth of the former terror and the security of the present triumph; but no lesser an artist could have found it. Beethoven recalls the third movement as a memory which we know for a fact but can no longer understand: there is now a note of self-pity, for which we had no leisure when the terror was upon our souls: the depth and darkness are alike absent, and in the dry light of day we cannot remember our fears of the unknown.

"Beethoven recalls the third movement as a memory which we know for a fact but can no longer understand." Tovey's formulation resonates strikingly with a distinction between *remembering* and *knowing* the past that has come under close scrutiny by neuroscientists and psychologists in recent years. Apparently, reliving a past circumstance and narrating it dispassionately engage very different parts of the brain.[12] Two additional insights are particularly suggestive: the perception that the returning passage is colored by the emotions of the present moment—implied in Tovey's "there is now a note of self-pity"—and his emphasis on the act of relating ("could we recover the mood by elaborating the details?"). The role of emotion in memory storage and retrieval is another topic of intense scientific focus today. Can we match up elements in Beethoven's score with Tovey's account? What exactly is it that comes back before the triumphant C-major recapitulation in the finale?

The thematic material of the passage begins with the second subject of the scherzo, the one whose rhythm also recalls the first-movement subject. Clearly, it is not the first appearance of this material in the third movement that is evoked—where it sounded in a lockstep battalion of strings exhorted on by horns blaring the ♩ ♩ ♩ | ♩

11. Donald Francis Tovey, *Essays in Musical Analysis: Symphonies and Other Orchestral Works* (London, 1935; reprint, London: Oxford University Press, 1981), 59.

12. Schacter, *Searching for Memory*, 23.

figure—rather, it is the mysteriously hushed return of the scherzo emerging from the ruins of the C-major fugal trio that is evoked. Both prior statements stimulate the programmatic imagination (as E. M. Forster's famous account in *Howard's End* confirms), and it is in part the striking contrast between them that, in Tovey's words, lends the return after the trio its "tremendous emotional value." Such illustrative moments are part of an intermittent process in the symphony: certain passages clearly stand out for their capacity to suggest an unfolding dramatic scene. While we can adduce purely structural reasons that the transition from the scherzo into the beginning of the finale should come back before the finale's recapitulation, Tovey's suggestion is that the particular makeup of that return distinguishes it from both previous statements in the third movement as an event recalled, not presently "happening."

How is this effect achieved? Back in the third movement, some twenty bars into the return of the scherzo following the dissolution of the trio, the second theme had reemerged, its eery pizzicato string and bassoon sonority punctuated by isolated clarinet and oboe voices chiming in with the monotone ♩ ♩ ♩ | ♩ figure (m. 255). By contrast, before the recapitulation in the finale (m. 153) the comparable passage is approached from a pounding, full-orchestral force that strains to create a huge dominant upbeat (in analogy with the more modest one that had prepared the return of the exposition) but which ends up spinning in place, weighed down by the bombast of its own—briefly tonicized—mass. At the *Tempo I*, the violins pick up the reverberation of this calamitous psychic noise, making the single note G echo off into the distance. As it fades into nothingness, the pitch mutates into the 3/4 pulsing rhythmic figure with which the second subject of the scherzo had begun. (We might note the gestural similarity here to Beethoven's procedure in the development of the *Eroica*, where after an even greater rhythmic and tonal calamity, a body of strings echoes off into the distance, a blend of shock wave and operatic fade-out, preparing the way for the "new theme" in E minor.) The entire returning passage is completely rescored and much compressed: whereas, in the original statement, the distance between the return of the scherzo (m. 236) and the downbeat of the finale comprised 137 measures, the "recollection" of the event spans only 47 bars. Many of the most characteristic—and, paradoxically, the most memorable—features of the original passage do *not* return: the entire mysterious first theme (the unison cello and bass idea) is absent, as is the distinctive scoring for hushed bassoons in combination with pizzicato strings, punctuated by plaintive, individual wind voices; missing is also the suspenseful *pianississimo* deceptive cadence to a deep A♭ at measure 324 from which the timpani's ominous tapping on the note of resolution, C, emerges; and missing, too, is the basses' agitated pulsing on half steps around the root of the dominant (from m. 340) against which the violins strive to reach into their upper register, repeatedly getting stuck on the sigh figure E♭–D (derived from the first theme of the scherzo). Finally, absent in the later passage is the violins' exhilarating anticipation of the finale's major mode as they break through the stagnant pitch ceiling, rising with ever-increasing momentum into the huge crescendo preparing the hero's welcome of a fanfare at the start of the finale.

All the elements I have just enumerated conspire to create the effects Tovey describes as "depth and darkness" and "terror." They capture the suspense experienced as the event unfolded. If the terror is removed (the emotional envelope filtered out, so to speak), then what is left to return? Before the recapitulation in the finale the scherzo's second subject appears succinctly in a new scoring for pizzicato strings and clarinets (in place of the eerily human voice of that hushed bassoon) in close-position harmony in thirds followed by oboes with the melody. With the tune moved into the wind band, and especially after the dominant pedal is reached (at m. 175), the passage sounds like a hollow distortion of the original moment—an affecting symphonic event transcribed into what in the early nineteenth century was known as *Harmoniemusik*. The divisi violas provide a rhythmic base, reminiscent of the guitar and fiddle in a nineteenth-century *Schrammel* band. Like the wind band that plays numbers from popular operas in the last-act finale to *Don Giovanni*, this is music imported from another setting, a transcription, whose very sonority points to a reenactment or replaying. The use of clarinets in an accompanimental role points especially to a change of scene or time. (In imitation of a popular entertainment style, Mozart gave both melody and accompaniment to two clarinets in the trio of the E♭ Symphony K. 543—yet Schubert notably left away the clarinets when he tried to write a symphony of more typical Mozartian proportion and scoring, the B♭, D 485 from 1816.)[13]

This is not to suggest that all music for wind band is about memory of course: the device depends on the listener having a more fully scored setting in ear. We might draw an analogy with an artifice that has recently shown up in everything from Hollywood films, to television commercials and sitcoms: the filtering out of color to suggest a movement into the past. To work upon us this device depends on our experience with the world of black-and-white film, just as *Harmoniemusik* could draw on the wider experience of hearing easily transportable wind instruments play popular arrangements of opera or concert music in a variety of settings. The wind band scoring is heard as the "later" statement just as the black-and-white scene is understood to have taken place "earlier." The new scoring in a symphonic setting, like the filtering out of color, could function either in the service of realism (if the passage invoked was already scored for winds) or as a purely conventional sign—in much the same way that the device of black and white can create an aura of historical realism in one instance, depicting events from the era of black-and-white film, and merely signal a shift to the very recent past in another, sometimes no more than fifteen minutes ago, which really

---

13. Mozart's K. 543 is a special case. There is implicit social commentary in its lavishly scored 3/4 march masquerading as a minuet (trumpets, drums, even clarinets; with a chorus of doubled voices sounding the cadence like some revolutionary hymn). The minuet crashes back in after the trio, silencing the amiable *Ländler*, in which clarinet yodels (wordless signals) are echoed by a flute, and the horns urge us to listen up.

is quite absurd when you come to think of it. But we accept it and instantly get what it means.[14]

While essential thematic material is brought back before the recapitulation in the finale, the distinctive harmonic diversions and crucial orchestrational and registral effects of the earlier passage are not. In this synoptic view of previous events, the consequent phrase of the melody moves directly to prepare a dominant pedal, the augmented sixth at measure 174 a mere trace of the former mysterious turn to the flatted submediant. Instead of the ominously pulsing timpani C's and rumbling double basses that gradually built up tension before, horns, clarinets, and also violas vamp percussively on the ♩ ♩ ♩ | ♩ figure in tightly voiced chords, as the oboes, later joined by flutes and bassoons in plangent octaves, arpeggiate the diminished triad at the top of a dominant seventh. This wallowing in diminished harmony without any of the former suspense is, I presume, what Tovey hears as "a note of self-pity." The whole thing sounds hollow and static. The wide registral span of the original passage is compressed into a narrow middle range, its programmatically evocative instrumentation replaced with a wind band sonority that rings false. Only in the final bars do the timpani come in with a roll on C, blurring the texture, as the orchestral forces make an upbeat into the triumphant recapitulation. With the strings and timpani joining in for the final bars of crescendo, a compressed version of the earlier buildup into the beginning of the finale is produced.

In this account of the later passage, I have emphasized all that is missing from the original event. But that is precisely what makes this intrusion work in its new context: if Beethoven's return were any more exact, if indeed it brought back the pacing and the unique effects that we might understand as simulating the emotions and consciousness during an event whose outcome is yet uncertain, it would not sound like an act of conjuring, like a retracing of past experience. The placement of this passage at the point of retransition in a sonata movement allowed Beethoven to exploit the feeling of inevitability and compression characteristic at this point in the form; nothing in the conventional form, however, dictated his choice of thematic substance or his decisions about instrumentation and register, or even the particulars of pacing. These elements are introduced in the service of some descriptive idea.

Tovey's choice of subjective descriptive words like "self-pity," "fear of the unknown," and "terror" should not distract us from his principal insight: Beethoven's return

---

14. In time such a device can become tradition. Was Brahms playing with this idea in the nostalgic opening of the slow movement of the violin concerto, where the theme is presented *first* in a wind band with solo oboe and only then elaborated by the soloist? Michael Steinberg hears in this music a residue of the ensemble from the end of *Fidelio*, "O Gott, O welch' ein Augenblick," also in F major, also with solo oboe and prominent winds. Brahms's opening has a familiar aura long before we begin to place the affective worlds it echoes: it sounds like a reminiscence of things past that we may or may not ever have heard. Michael Steinberg, *The Concerto: A Listener's Guide* (New York: Oxford University Press, 1998), 127.

emulates a familiar perceptual process, the intrusion of an unforgettably suspenseful past event into the experience of a more secure, predictable present. The later passage is a reflection on the first, rehearsed from a distance, until by some "species of reaction" an emotion kindred—but not identical—to that of the original is gradually produced "and does itself actually exist in the mind." The final measures of Beethoven's highly pressurized buildup into the recapitulation are indeed a close, and only slightly abbreviated, facsimile of the earlier event, as if, in drawing closer again to the present triumph, the recollection had finally gained access to some of the original emotion.

Convention and invention work perfectly in tandem here, as is the case with so many of the most characteristic moments in nineteenth-century music. To look briefly at a later instance, consider the dual facets of Schumann's artistic personality as he portrayed them in *Carnaval*, op. 9: Eusebius is a romance—a song form whose refrain is enhanced by sympathetic voices—and Florestan is a stormy waltz (with a maelstrom in place of a trio) that spirals out of control at the end like a furious whirlwind, refusing to cadence. These most intensely personal characterizations are based on conventional forms. But the composer's own striking observation about memory has shaped his portrayal of Florestan too. In a vivid 1836 review of Schubert dances, Schumann depicts a convivial *Hauskonzert* attended by fictional and living characters intermixed. Florestan offers a running verbal commentary on the dances as they are performed. The narrator reports that Florestan suddenly broke off in the middle of the waltz, observing: "Florestan, you know, has a habit of breaking off just when his enjoyment is at its height, perhaps to impress it in all its freshness and fullness on the memory."[15]

For representations of a very different type of recall again conceived within the symphonic genre, we may turn to the evocations of each of the earlier movements in the finale of Beethoven's Ninth Symphony. The reviewer of the first performance for the London *Harmonicon* perceptively singled them out. "But it is in the finale," he wrote, "that the genius of this great master shines forth most conspicuously. We are here in an ingenious manner presented with a return of all the subjects in short and brilliant passages, and which, as in a mirror, reflect the features of the whole."[16] Unlike the Fifth Symphony, where those fading violin G's suggest that something in the preceding calamity has sparked the recollection (a flashback?), here there is no change of scene, nothing that negotiates a movement into the past. Introduced by instrumental bass recitative, the recollections seem to illustrate an ongoing discursive argument, like

---

15. The full review appears in Ruth A. Solie, *The Nineteenth Century*, vol. 6 of *Source Readings in Music History*, ed. Oliver W. Strunk; rev. ed., gen. ed. Leo Treitler(New York: Norton, 1998), 112–15 or, in the single-volume edition, Oliver W. Strunk, ed., *Source Readings in Music History*, rev. ed., gen. ed. Leo Treitler (New York: Norton, 1998), 1154–57.
16. *The Harmonicon*, vol. 2 (London: W. Pinnock, 1824), 178–81.

sonic equivalents of visual images projected onto a screen. Unlike a still photograph, however, the musical images projected in time do not faithfully capture a slice of some earlier experience. (To be sure, art historians will be quick to tell us that a still photograph does not either.) Rather, each recollection is a construction, putting together distinctive features of the original events in a new configuration. When we review quickly a musical work in our minds, a few distinctive elements must stand for the whole: Beethoven's vignettes of the earlier movements are crystalline images, more sharply focused than any single moment in the original, yet calculated to make us instantly recognize their source. The evocation of the *Adagio molto e cantabile*, drawn from that movement's opening phrase, is merely two bars long. The slow movement begins with a lush combination of woodwinds slowly unfolding a murky dominant harmony, heavy with appoggiaturas. Two measures later, the strings give out a beautiful *mezza voce* melody, and we are drawn into an expansive lyrical space. The winds play an increasingly prominent role as the double variations unfold; at one point they even do take over the string melody—though in a different key and with different counterpoint from the opening. When Beethoven calls up the adagio in the finale, he fuses the two features we would certainly retain from a distance into a single phrase, borrowing from the strings the beautiful melody, but scoring it for a complement of woodwinds. In this marked use of the wind band, realism and recollection merge, for the slow movement's winds leave a lasting impression. Decontextualized in this way, without the rhythmic impetus of a clear dominant upbeat resolving into the melody, the phrase stands out of time. It does not so much evoke a single memorable phrase as stand for the totality of the movement.

The eight measures of first-movement material are even more static, and while they elaborate elements drawn from three distinct places in the first movement—the opening bars, the beginning of the development, and the recapitulation—the fragment sounds like none of these exactly. The passage is marked *pianissimo* throughout, and the fifth on A–E is held by instruments in every register for the full duration. There is no gradual buildup in register and sonority, no increase in rhythmic articulation, all of which were essential features at the opening of the symphony. The third in the bass, of course, was not present in the opening bars, but it was hinted at in the development, and it played a critical role at the recapitulation, both times, however, in connection with the triad on D, not A. Tiny rhythmic punctuations in the timpani and trumpets at the start of the development gave the first signals that the events of the exposition were not going to be retraced before continuing on. They register here too, small signs of activity within a static halo of winds, disposed, like so many oracular pronouncements in accompanied recitative, as a first-inversion triad. A performance splicing together the finale's recitative with the actual beginning of the first movement will demonstrate more efficiently than any prose how completely ineffective a more literal return would be at this point: a literal return would not behave like an act of conjuring the past but would take us back through the event in all its slowly unfolding process.[17] One thing this stasis achieves is to make *us* concentrate and focus our attention inward. (In a review of Michael Tye's book *Consciousness Revisited*, Jerry Fodor reminds us, "*The mind is active in perception*; but it is *passive in experience*; which is to say that *perception is inferential but experience isn't*."[18] And memory is a mode of perception, or at least active recollection is.)

Finally, the little wisp of a phrase calling up the scherzo also will not be found anywhere exactly in the earlier movement. Its pitches come closest to the passage approaching the scherzo's most memorable surprise—the sudden intrusion of the timpani with the shift from four- to three-bar phrase groupings not far into the development (the spot that reportedly elicited spontaneous applause at the first performance). While this tiny snippet of scherzo material cannot reproduce the metric thrill of the earlier moment, we may nonetheless perceive a dull echo of the timpani's sharp octave F's in the descending fourth, F–C, with which the bass recitative resumes its argument. The difference in timbral resonance between the explosive timpani and the more muffled basses is no less a factor than the motivic relation in making this feel like something recalled.

These fleet phrases in the finale of the Ninth Symphony are a special case, designed to call up the earlier movements in a flash. They are decidedly not set up as musical ruminations on some past event (even if considerable effort went into their crafting). Heard in real time, in performance time, these passages mimic the mental experience of pausing to bring familiar pieces to mind, of internal hearing.[19] More frequently Beethoven's intrusions of thematic material from earlier movements are staged in a way that distances them from the surrounding discourse, as with the Fifth Symphony.

---

17. Richard Kramer understands the phrase as "a commentary, a gloss" and asks of it: "How, precisely, does this phrase enter into the text of the symphony, standing, as it does, outside both the first movement and the finale proper? We cannot invoke the phrase when we read the text of the first movement, it cannot alter how the first movement actually goes. The phrase means in a way that no other phrase—and certainly not the three phrases on which it comments—can be said to mean. It is here that a new strategy of interpretation—this hermeneutical dialogue—is called into play." Richard Kramer, "Between Cavatina and Ouverture: Opus 130 and the Voices of Narrative," in *Beethoven Forum* I (Lincoln: University of Nebraska Press 1992), 170–71. I am reminded here of Wagner's observations on analytical programs and the act of listening to music in performance. The two are incommensurable modes of mental engagement, he reflects —but when we merely rehearse a work in memory, it is easier to bear such analogies in mind. This was prompted by his own analytical program for the C♯ minor quartet in the 1870 Beethoven essay. *Gesammelte Schriften und Dichtungen* (Leipzig: C. F. W. Siegel's Musikalienhandlung, 1904), 96.

18. Jerry Fodor, "The Truth Is Not Out There," *Times Literary Supplement*, October 2009.

19. Sketches rarely record the kind of labor we might expect such inspired passages to have cost, but a telling little snippet of surviving sketch material for the finale's recollection of the first movement—showing a return built on the fifth above E, not A—documents the considerable distance Beethoven had traveled from his first instincts. Gustav Nottebohm, *Zweite Beethoveniana: nachgelassene Aufsätze* (Leipzig, 1887; reprint: New York: Johnson Reprint Corporation, 1970), 190.

Another manner of achieving this has been described by Joseph Kerman. Characterizing the cyclic returns in Beethoven's *An die ferne Geliebte*, the C-major cello sonata, op. 102, no. 1, and the A-major piano sonata, op. 101, as "momentary nostalgic recollections" and "distant half-visions, unexpected, muted, nostalgic in effect," Kerman points out that the sonata returns both come within a cadenza-like passage hovering on dominant harmony (this is akin to the transition into the finale in the "Emperor" concerto, as Kerman notes, although in that work the thematic material looks forward, not past), and in both the song cycle and the piano sonata the recollection is introduced by arpeggiation.[20] All three works were composed very near each other in 1815–16 after an extended compositional lull, and in all three works the thematic return "wells up" at the peak of an arpeggio or similar gesture rising from the registral depths. Elaine Sisman understands such passages as invoking the rhetoric of *Phantasia*, an improvisatory genre conceptually allied with eighteenth-century discourses on memory and imagination.[21] It is noteworthy that the language of *Phantasia* (characterized by arpeggiations and other stock figurations, instrumental recitative, stark harmonic juxtapositions linked by the barest of acoustic threads, and so on) is most prevalent in those works that feign extemporization at various points—not only at the point of a cyclic return. The recapitulation in the first movement of the "Emperor" concerto, too, is worth considering in this connection, since the entire movement puts the topic of improvisation on display. While a recapitulation is of course an expected formal return, this one is constructed with remarkable attention to a listener's recollection of the unusual earlier event. The concerto opens with a simulated extemporization by the pianist, embellishing each step in the simple cadential progression stated in the orchestra. This is masterfully reworked into a new "improvisation" at the recapitulation. But the progression from chord to chord the second time through is much more urgently directed, the changes of harmony come more swiftly and predictably until the action stalls again with the arrival of the dominant. The listener's past experience is thus a calculation in the new proportions and timing: from the arrival of the first chord in the recapitulation (after a suspenseful retransition), we know how the progression will go, and our expectation is quickly confirmed. (What oddly proportioned performances we might hear were these embellishments left entirely to the performer!) In the "Emperor's" first movment Beethoven has not so much written a return that behaves like a memory as constructed one whose impact *relies* upon what every listener will recall of the unexpected "improvisation" at the concerto's opening. To put it another way, the impact of the recapitulation depends on our memory of the earlier moment, but the passage itself does not represent one.

---

20. Joseph Kerman, "An die ferne Geliebte," in *Beethoven Studies*, ed. Alan Tyson (New York: Norton, 1973), 138.
21. In "Memory and Invention at the Threshold of Beethoven's Late Style" (note 10), Sisman gives an excellent account of late eighteenth-century ideas on memory, fantasy, and invention, pursuing parallels with the rhetorical language of *Phantasia*.

The most pronounced alignment with the rhetoric of *Phantasia* among the works from 1815–16 comes in the A-major piano sonata's surprising return to material from the opening of the first movement between the pensive slow movement, "Langsam und sehnsuchts-voll," and the finale. The mimetic component in the passage setting up the return may again be illuminated by a comparison with modern-day cinematographic convention—the blurring of focus just prior to a flashback, a stylized device that, unlike the filtering out of color, clearly has its origins in physical perception. We in fact lose visual focus when we turn our attention inward.[22] In like manner, a wash of heavily pedaled, arpeggiated sonority perched on dominant harmony dissolves the previous thematic substance as it releases a blur of overtones, setting up the expectation of a new arrival. The cyclic return is not the only point in the sonata where the pianist is invited to strike an extemporary pose, creating the illusion that some moments are unrehearsed inspirations. Spontaneity erupts in those bare octaves that collapse the finale's wide initial gesture ("with conviction" at first appearance) into a major third to launch the development's eccentric fugue and, likewise, in the off-the-cuff, impatient cadence that so abruptly ends the sonata (after weight gradually has shifted to the last movement with incrementally bigger cadential arrivals along the way). All this shines a spotlight on the moment of performance, the here and now. It should come as no surprise to us, then, that the return in the piano sonata is the most *literal* of any of Beethoven's cyclic returns. That is because what is inscribed into this moment is a performer's memory, as if the pianist's hands had landed unwittingly back on the opening phrase of the first movement (marked "Zeitmaß des ersten Stückes," to be played softly, and with maximal resonance). The only recomposition involves the pauses between phrases, a kind of stage direction suggesting a performer straining to recall what comes next, a feigned memory lapse, a pose struck in the real time of performance. The beginning of the sonata is shown in example 4.1a, the later return in example 4.1b. By definition, the musician playing a piece by heart must cultivate an uncommonly literal mode of memory.

Charles Rosen has also described this passage in terms of a process of memory:

> A fermata *subito piano* on the dominant introduces a cadenza that starts slowly, quickens slightly and arpeggiates into the opening theme of the first movement. Marked *dolce* at first, this theme returns in fragments, like a memory difficult to

---

22. Perhaps the most remarkable engagement with this phenomenon is Schubert's song "Ihr Bild," and Heinrich Schenker's beautiful account of it. As the persona in Heine's poem gazes at a portrait of his beloved, the picture gradually comes alive to him. Schenker takes the hollow B♭ octaves, sounded twice at the song's opening, and separated by a pause, as representing the very act of staring. At the point of return (and retransition) in the ABA form when the warm G♭ major melts away, the poet no longer gazes at the portrait but instead "stares into memory." Schubert has extended the B♭ octave frame into a muddier register an octave below, and creates a blurry wave of movement by an inner-voice augmented sixth (G♭–E) expanding to octave F's. Overpowered by the acoustic pressure of those B♭'s sounded in three octaves at the bottom of the range, this creates a warped sonority. Schenker's essay was printed in *Der Tonwille* (1921), 46–49.

EXAMPLE 4.1a Ludwig van Beethoven, piano sonata in A major, op. 101/1, mm. 1–16.

recall with confidence. The technique was first worked out by Beethoven in the finale of the Sonata in G major op. 31 no. 1, where the main theme returns at the end, punctuated by pauses, and with some of the phrases at a very slow tempo. The technique reconstructs the effort of recalling something from the past.[23]

23. Charles Rosen, *Beethoven's Piano Sonatas: A Short Companion* (New Haven, Conn.: Yale University Press, 2002), 216.

EXAMPLE 4.1b Ludwig van Beethoven, piano sonata in A major op. 101/3 transition into movement 4.

The *effort* of recalling something from the past: this looks ahead to Schumann's post-lude in *Frauenliebe und Leben*. But did Schubert likewise associate these two sonatas of Beethoven? The close structural parallels between the rondo finale of Schubert's A-major sonata, D 959 and the finale of op. 31, no. 1 in G major are widely appreciated today. Following Beethoven's procedure, Schubert also brings back his rondo theme in fragments in the coda, adding contrasts in tonality as well as tempo, and follows this with a raucous

EXAMPLE 4.2a Ludwig van Beethoven, piano sonata in A major, op. 101/1, recapitulation.

presto. But there are elements that resemble Beethoven's procedure in op. 101 as well. A part of what makes the cyclic return in Beethoven's A-major sonata so satisfying is that the tessitura of the opening phrase was withheld at the recapitulation in the first movement (as is shown in ex. 4.2a). Coming to a pause with a fermata on V/iii at the end of the development, the harmony is gently nudged toward the dominant, and the opening theme reenters over it in the tonic minor an octave above its initial statement before slipping into the tonic major, still in the upper octave, at measure 58. Two bars into the

A-major return the register is abruptly brought down, continuing with a "cut" directly to the equivalent location of bar 8. (This little glitch in continuity sets the stage for the hesitation between phrases at the transition to the finale.) The register spikes up several times more before the end of the movement, to be only gradually brought back down.

Schubert's recapitulation in the finale of D 959 is similarly placed in the higher octave and makes an even more intense tonal contrast. (There is no equivalent in op. 31, no. 1 for this special moment.) Schubert's retransition has set up a "false reprise" into F♯ major. A small tonal adjustment in place of a cadence in the consequent phrase (requiring an expansion of the phrase from four to five bars) returns the harmony to A major, where the theme begins anew at the *a tempo* (ex. 4.2c), still an octave above its original placement at the beginning of the rondo (shown in ex. 4.2b). Later, like the cyclic return in Beethoven's op. 101, the first phrase of Schubert's coda has an especially satisfying feel because it restores the tuneful theme into its original register, following a complete break in continuity with a bar-long rest and fermata in measure 329 (this is shown in ex. 4.2d). Almost immediately, after another full-measure pause, its second phrase enters with a change of mode to A minor at the *a tempo*, and back up the octave. Another pause (this one replacing an absent bar), and the theme continues back in the proper register but on F, the flatted submediant. Then, another leap up the octave, where we are left perched on an augmented sixth. Schubert's fractured return in the coda gives the impression of a pianist searching for the right placement of the hands on the keyboard: the fragments sound like familiar pieces of a puzzle (each of the tonal areas touched upon has played a role earlier in the sonata), but they are too brief, too isolated, to coalesce. Memories are merely stirred to build up suspense before the closing *presto*.[24] It is interesting to consider the very different roles register plays at these points in the two A-major sonatas. Several times in Beethoven's lyrical first movement delicate melodic lines straddle multiple ranges, teasing open the registral space, which billows out, then collapses again. The recapitulation arrives as the melody is pushed into the higher octave before the development has fully wound to a close. Schubert, working with a theme of very different character in the rondo, takes over nothing of this distinctive textural development. The stark registral contrasts in his coda coincide with shifts in tonal orientation: each phrase is a transposition, resituated as a block in tonal-registral space, making us intensely aware of location.

---

24. Schubert's propensity to return to the tonal site of earlier striking events (both across movements and within) is explored in some detail by Charles Fisk in *Returning Cycles: Contexts for the Interpretation of Schubert's Impromptus and Last Sonatas*, California Studies in 19th-Century Music, ed. Joseph Kerman (Berkeley: University of California Press, 2001).

EXAMPLE 4.2b Franz Schubert, piano sonata in A major, D 959/4, theme, mm. 1–8.

EXAMPLE 4.2c Schubert, piano sonata in A major, D 959/4, recapitulation, mm. 213–230.

EXAMPLE 4.2d Schubert, piano sonata in A major, D 959/4, coda, 325–353.

In *An die ferne Geliebte* Beethoven's ingenious construction of two melodies resembling one another to the point of confusion takes the mimesis of cognitive functioning in still another direction. The nostalgic effect of the return of the melody of the opening song with the final strophe of the last song depends not only on the cadenza-like arpeggio on the dominant preceding it that Kerman points to, but on the half-concealed statement

of "Nimm sie hin denn" (the tempo I melody) *in the piano alone* as the singer's declama-
tory repetition of the words "nur der Sehnsucht sich bewusst" comes to an expectant
pause at the top of the vocal register, on scale degree 2.[25] The two melodies are thus
brought right up against each other in the piano, which, like some figurative inner voice,
arrives at the opening notes of "Dann vor diesen Liedern weichet . . ." a split second before
the singer brings back the melody of song one (ex. 4.3). Like a thought that is "on the tip
of the tongue" or a scent that carries strong associations of time and place, this exposed
premonition of the returning melody in the piano prompts the listener to sense the
impending return a moment before it issues from the singer's mouth. We learn from Kerman's study of the sketches that the inspiration for the poetic foreshadowing in the piano
came late in the compositional process. Likewise, the wonderfully nostalgic opening
melody of the last song also was not a starting point in Beethoven's conception; the
original plan was to bring back the tune of song one for all four stanzas.[26] It seems right
that these poetic moments should have come about only in the act of composing, symptoms of the composer's own intense attention to memory: yet there is no reason to think
that Beethoven began with the ambition of representing a process of memory.

   Beethoven's staging of the far more inexact return in the C-major cello sonata is
equally impressive, creating the effect of an improvisation passed between two musicians. The thematic links between all four movements and the return of first movement
material between the slow movement and the finale have been widely explored, most
exhaustively by Lewis Lockwood.[27] I shall rehearse only the minimum detail necessary
for intelligibility here. Of special interest for an understanding of the passage as an act
of recollection is once again the preparation for the return, something that past discussions, focusing mainly on the motivic continuities within the return itself, have tended
not to linger over. Beethoven adapts a familiar technique of his sonata retransitions[28]—
the introduction of thematic premonitions over a dominant pedal—in the cello sonata, where the music that intrudes from an earlier movement is sparked by a chain of
associations that coalesce, as if inadvertently, into the unexpected thematic return. To
appreciate this preparation, we must first think back to the opening page of the sonata,
to see how the events that will be brought back have been set up. The entire opening
movement is shown in example 4.4.

---

25. Was it this phrase that coursed through Robert Schumann's mind in his evocation of *An die ferne Geliebte* in
    the C-major Fantasy? Schumann's much-discussed reminiscence is molded into a statement with both an
    antecedent and a consequent phrase. The latter's opening incipit builds to an expressively drawn-out rolled
    chord on the dominant, similar to Beethoven's arpeggio, whose crowning pitch is similarly scale degree 2.
26. Kerman, "An die ferne Geliebte," 136–38.
27. The most detailed account of shared motivic elements across these movements is in Lewis Lockwood,
    "Beethoven's Emergence from Crisis: The Cello Sonatas of Op. 102 (1815)," *Journal of Musicology* 16 (1998):
    301–22. See also Sisman, "Memory and Invention at the Threshold of Beethoven's Late Style," 58–66.
28. The distinctive rhetoric of sonata retransitions deserves closer attention. For a stimulating discussion of
    Mozart's handling of these crucial formal moments, see Roman Ivanovitch, "Mozart's Art of Retransition,"
    Music Analysis 29 (forthcoming).

EXAMPLE 4.3 Ludwig van Beethoven, "Nimm sie hin denn diese Lieder," Op. 98/6, transition into the return of the melody from song one.

EXAMPLE 4.4 Ludwig van Beethoven, cello sonata in C major, op. 102, no. 1, opening movement.

EXAMPLE 4.4 (*continued*).

A tune built of the simplest of tonal materials is introduced in the cello alone at the beginning of the sonata. It is answered by the piano, in a variant exchanging the order of the two structural fourths with which the melody opens and closes. Separated by rising sixteenth-note figuration with striking repeated tones at the top of the phrase, the cello's scalar descent of a fourth, C–B–A–G, and its cadential fourth, G–F–D, are reversed in the piano's answer in bars 3 and 4. The lyrical *Andante* that unfolds from these elements is generated by a process of variation involving three loose countermelodies—two voices that shadow the contours of the cello's opening theme at the fourth and sixth below (numbered 2 and 3 on example 4.4, reserving 1 for the opening melody) and a related syncopated line descending from scale degree 5 (number 4). The counterpoint is invertible: the four variation-like elaborations are generated by shifting the position of the melodic strands in the texture. The middle elaborations, beginning at bars 6 and 11, start off with two bars of "inner voice" writing (strands 2, 3, and 4) before piano and cello vie for greater melodic definition as the phrases press toward a cadence. Closure in the tonic is evaded as each phrase culminates in a prolongation of dominant harmony preparing the next strain, each dominant made more intense than the previous one (by added chromaticism, greater length, a trill, etc.). While the harmony never departs from the tonic key, the shape of the original cello melody is absent in the two middle strains. This memorable opening theme sits squarely within the key, outlining its most basic melodic functions. The sharpness of melodic contour and its isolation at the beginning of the movement etch it into memory much like a fugue subject, and there is a great sense of arrival when it returns at measure 17 as part of the densest texture yet, the tune shadowed by contrapuntal lines that create a long chain of parallel six-three harmonies elaborating V of IV en route to the final cadence.[29] A new element, a sustained trill on G, further enriches the thick sonority, driving this expanded statement to a sweeping, heavily pedaled arpeggio on a dominant seventh before a fade-out on tonic harmony closes the introductory movement.

It is the quality of this culminating arrival at bar 17 that will be conjured in the final two bars of the *Tempo d' Andante*, which links the rhapsodic, improvisatory slow movement to the finale (as is shown in ex. 4.5). Despite the partial presence of the principal melody in the piano the *Tempo d'Andante*, marked *dolce*, begins midparagraph, like another of the inner elaborations beginning from bars 6 and 11. The crucial cadential fourth, G–F–D, is replaced with a distended dominant, delaying the even more powerful return that restores the entire theme into the original lyrical tenor register in the cello. The sustained trill on G and rich accompanimental figuration in the piano clearly recall the effect of the return at bar 17 of the first movement. This memory comes in waves.

Once again, notably, it is the staging of the return as much as the return itself that invites us to hear the passage as a memory. The intrusion of thematic material from the *Andante* is preceded by three bars of wonderfully nostalgic music, marked *teneramente*, like the music at the beginning of the sonata. From the ponderous tones at the end of the slow movement, as a deep augmented sixth gives way to a dominant, the cello suddenly leaps up into its upper singing register, with the piano entering imitatively in the following bar, approximating the interaction between the two instruments in the opening measures of the sonata. Just a bar into this *teneramente* passage the piano's chordal backdrop slips into the distinctive sound of six-three position harmonies,

---

29. A rigorous exploration of this technique for multiple instruments may be found in both outer movements of J.S. Bach's second Brandenburg Concerto, where sharply profiled ("outer voice") themes rotate through the texture combined with subsidiary countersubjects that trace the contour of the principal subject in blunter intervals, as is typical of "inner voices."

EXAMPLE 4.5 Ludwig van Beethoven, cello sonata in C major, op. 102, no. 1, transition from the slow movement into the finale.

bringing back a characteristic sonority, if not yet fully the characteristic texture of the opening movement.

The nostalgic new phrase in the cello ends with a transposition of the familiar cadential fourth, D–C–A, which then comes at pitch at the end of the piano's answering phrase. Soon this closing gesture begins to permeate the texture in all registers—it sounds first in the cello, preceding the trill in the second measure of the passage, then in the piano right hand at the end of the measure, in the left hand on the following downbeat, then twice more as the cello dips into its deepest register and brings up the repeated-note figure that had prepared each new melodic strain in the *Andante*.

The falling cadential fourth of the *teneramente* passage was in fact also present in the opening bars of the slow movement, marking the close of the piano's sixty-fourth-note flourish, but it is not distinctive enough to qualify as motivic or structural in any ordinary sense of these terms. Its presence in more than a single movement has nothing to do with a typical Beethovenian process of motivic development—nothing, in fact, is developed. The very ordinariness and triviality of the cadential gesture are what is exploited to simulate a process of memory in the transition. The recollection seems to be sparked by the reappearance of the two soloists in a spatial configuration resembling their interaction at the opening of the sonata. The cadential fourth, arrived at by seeming happenstance at the end of the new lyrical *teneramente* phrase (like the cadence of a familiar voice), coalesces into a dominant pedal in which a concentrated focus on this motivic contour, together with the distinctive six-three-position harmonies in the piano, the trills, and finally the cello's repeated sixteenth-note G's gradually predict the reappearance of the first-movement melody. Beethoven's return simulates the effect of an involuntary memory, one that we can feel gradually coming on, and one triggered by an association that on the face of it is completely insignificant.

Such attention to the spatial configuration of an event, a feeling for its location even before the content becomes clear, has been described by Toni Morrison in an essay entitled "Memory, Creation, and Writing." Morrison elaborates the concept of a "galaxy of feeling," the specific environment that accompanies any scene, emphasizing that memories need not be primarily visual, but that they are always based on a feeling of our own location in relation to the remembered image, a feeling for the light, or the sounds, or the smells that were a part of our perception of the moment. Morrison writes, "Memory (the deliberate act of remembering) is a form of willed creation. It is not an effort to find out the way it really was—that is research. The point is to dwell on the way it appeared and why it appeared in that particular way."[30]

The registral distribution of thematic materials at the *Tempo d' Andante* may also contribute to our sense that this material intrudes like a memory. Sounding in the treble with added octave doubling and with pitches carried over from the *teneramente* phrase (marked

---

30. Toni Morrison, "Memory, Creation, and Writing," in *The Anatomy of Memory*, ed. James McConkey (New York: Oxford University Press, 1996), 213.

on example 4.5), the return of the opening melody has a particularly nostalgic aura. It is the first time the cello's principal theme has sounded in the piano. In Schubert's songs, the return of a vocal melody in the piano an octave, sometimes two, above its original register becomes a stock device for creating an effect of distance, an analogue for the elevated emotional pitch accompanying a vivid internal image. Men's voices especially are higher in childhood: this plays into it too, perhaps. "Frühlingstraum" from *Winterreise* is a good example of this use of the treble, or the final version of "Greisengesang" on a poem explicitly about memory in which an aging poet takes comfort in his ability to call up the past at will. Even in the *Moment Musical* in A♭, op. 94, no. 6, the right-hand octave doubling in the trio gains its expressive power from this timbral cue: essentially a song without words, the entire piece observes the characteristic melodic limits of a Schubertian vocal tenor. Beethoven's return shows a similar sensitivity to the emotional impact of registral placement, and to the primacy of the cello as the bearer of melody. Both in the cello sonata and in *An die ferne Geliebte*, Beethoven precedes the thematic return with a new melody sharing certain of its features, just enough to create a feeling of familiarity. When the returning material breaks in, its character is substantially altered, colored by strong present emotions.

As we can see from these few instances, the postures of memory to be discovered in Beethoven's oeuvre are richly varied and involve every aspect of the music, not just thematic shape and pitch: texture, register, instrumentation, the use of doublings, pacing, all play a role. The cyclic returns are only the most obvious cases perhaps, but these also are the immediate models for Schumann's postlude. That such intense engagement with the mechanisms by which we remember past events and especially past music should have come from a composer whose ability to hear fresh music was fast eroding is poignant and probably not entirely coincidental. And although the overt staging of returns to resemble familiar forms of mental experience fell away in later years, Beethoven's fascination with resemblance and familiarity continued with the late works (think, for example, of the string quartet op. 131, where the brief G♯-minor *Adagio* preparing the last movement inevitably puts us in mind of the opening fugue). With this, Beethoven cleared a path for the intense nostalgic effects in Schumann, Mendelssohn, and Brahms. They all learned from him the power of inexact, fragmentary recall, often mingling memories from the music-historical past with the immediate musical past of earlier movements or songs. It remained for Schumann, however, to discover in the postlude to *Frauenliebe und Leben* how to draw the listener actively into the experience by supplying only the stimulus for a memory, making the feeling of absence into a central part of his representation.

5

A Curious Measure of Changing Beethoven Reception

This brief meditation on the surprising language of an episode in the Goethe-Zelter correspondence, and on its garbled transmission by Adolph Bernhard Marx, traces a story of changing Beethoven reception, from Zelter's reluctant fascination with him to Marx's blinding championship. Occasionally it is useful to remind ourselves how deeply the resistance to Beethoven ran, that there was a time, still in the middle of his career, when admiration for his music was a minority taste. The unexpected way in which Goethe's *Elective Affinities* is brought into this exchange of letters will shed light once more on Schubert's treatment of the "matrimonial anomaly" in the Graf von Gleichen legend, and Zelter's casual linking of Beethoven's music with psychological and sexual abnormality reminds us how much was at stake in Schubert's oblique depictions of same-sex passion, explored in chapter 6. Goethe himself came under moral attack for his portrayal of unorthodox social structures in novels and in plays, and he could not stand the prevalent strain of thinking in his time that equated nature with the social norm (the merely customary). As a matter of intellectual principle, he celebrated the variety in nature and the freedom of creative minds to explore whatever intrigues them. On those grounds alone, hearing Beethoven's music decried as unnatural can only have provoked his sympathy for the man.

I

At the close of a well-known letter dated 2 September 1812 from Carlsbad, Goethe shared with Carl Friedrich Zelter his impressions of a momentous encounter:

> I got to know Beethoven in Töplitz. His talent leaves me in a state of amazement; he is, however, a completely intractable personality, who may not be wrong in

finding the world detestable, but who surely does not thereby make it more pleasant, either for himself or for others. On the other hand, he may be forgiven this, and is to be pitied, for his hearing deserts him—a factor which perhaps afflicts the musical part of his being less than the social. He, who is already of laconic nature, now becomes doubly so through this loss.[1]

If Goethe was put off by Beethoven's social manner, he was quick to pardon it and astute in his estimation that Beethoven's loss of hearing likely interfered more with his social dealings than with his musical being. This is a far cry from the assessments that only a decade later routinely ascribed the difficulties of Beethoven's late style to a damaged faculty of hearing, or from the even more fanciful later ones, collected by Adorno, that sought to understand his deafness as a consequence of his ceaseless concentration and stress on the ear, a deafness half willed for the sake of a hermetic art. The latter thesis, fostered by Romain Rolland, echoes Walter Benjamin's provocative analysis of Proust's asthmatic condition as a creative necessity, partly nurtured by the artist, partly physiological. Indeed, that may be what attracted Adorno's attention. Which analysis came first is difficult to establish with any certainty, since Rolland's discussion of Beethoven's deafness appeared at almost exactly the same time as Benjamin's essay "The Image of Proust" (1929).[2] More significant than the question of priority, however, is how strained an explanation of deafness it is.[3] No such mythologizing had set in by 1812. In Goethe's sympathetic no-nonsense view, the hearing loss is simply an unfortunate blow that will only magnify the composer's already lamentable lack of social grace. Musical functioning remains largely unaffected.

What a surprise it is, then, to find Zelter's animated reply asserting a direct link between this intractable personality and Beethoven's music, which fills him with marvel but also with terror. The question of hearing is sidestepped, in tacit agreement, perhaps, with Goethe's diagnosis that this would only amplify an existent failing; deafness

---

1. "Beethoven habe ich in Töplitz kennen gelernt. Sein Talent hat mich in erstaunen gesetzt; allein er ist leider eine ganz ungebändigte Persönlichkeit, die zwar gar nicht Unrecht hat, wenn sie die Welt detestabel findet, aber sie freilich dadurch weder für sich noch für andere genußreicher macht. Sehr zu entschuldigen ist er hingegen und sehr zu bedauern, da ihn sein Gehör verläßt, das vielleicht dem musikalischen Teil seines Wesens weniger als dem geselligen schadet. Er, der ohnehin lakonischer Natur ist, wird es nun doppelt durch diesen Mangel." Johann Wolfgang von Goethe, *Briefwechsel zwischen Goethe und Zelter in den Jahren 1799 bis 1832*, ed. Edith Zehm et al., *Sämtliche Werke nach Epochen seines Schaffens: Münchner Ausgabe* (Munich: Carl Hanser Verlag, 1991), 20.1:281–83.

2. Walter Benjamin, "The Image of Proust," in *Illuminations*, ed. and with an introduction by Hannah Arendt, trans. Harry Zohn (New York: Schocken Books, 1969), 201–16.

3. See Theodor W. Adorno, *Beethoven: Philosophie der Musik: Fragmente und Texte*, ed. Rolf Tiedemann (Frankfurt am Main: Suhrkamp, 1993), fragment 76, 58, quoted from Romain Rolland's *Beethovens Meister-jahre* (Leipzig: Im Insel Verlag, 1930 [French edition, 1928]). The Adorno volume has been issued in English: Theodore W. Adorno, *Beethoven: The Philosophy of Music*, ed. Rolf Tiedemann, trans. Edmund Jephcott (Stanford, Calif.: Stanford University Press, 1998).

is not at the psychological core of Beethoven's problem. But for Zelter the personality and the music are clearly inseparable, and there already is too much of Beethoven in Beethoven's music:

> What you say about Beethoven is certainly true. I, too, admire him with terror. His own works seem to cause him secret horror—a perception that is dismissed all too lightly in our contemporary culture. His works seem to me like children whose father is a woman or whose mother is a man. The most recent work of his I have come to know (Christ on the Mount of Olives) seems to me like an impurity whose very foundation and goal are eternal death. Music critics, who seem better able to grasp and agree upon almost anything but singularity and the natural, have gushed over this composer in the most curious manner, in both praise and reproach. I know musical persons who used to find themselves alarmed, even indignant, upon hearing his works, but who are now gripped with an enthusiasm for them like the partisans of Greek love. The attraction of this is not difficult to understand, and yet what can come of it you have demonstrated clearly enough in your *Elective Affinities*.[4]

The progression of ideas in Zelter's letter is arresting: (1) Beethoven's works, the offspring of twisted parentage, must make even him secretly shudder; (2) musical critics who once responded with indignation and alarm to Beethoven's music have since been seized with a passion for it akin to the devotees of Greek love; (3) the appeal of this is easy enough to understand, but what comes of it has been amply demonstrated by Goethe's own *Elective Affinities*.[5]

---

4. "Was Sie von Bethofen sagen ist ganz natürlich. Auch ich bewundere ihn mit Schrecken. Seine eigenen Werke scheinen ihm heimliches Grauen zu verursachen. Eine Empfindung die in der neuen Kultur viel zu leichtsinnig beseitigt wird. Mir scheinen seine Werke wie Kinder deren Vater ein Weib oder deren Mutter ein Mann wäre. Das letzte mir bekannt gewordene Werk (Christus am Ölberge) kommt mir vor wie eine Unkeuschheit, deren Grund und Ziel ein ewiger Tod ist. Die musikal. Kritiker, welche sich auf alles besser zu verstehen scheinen als auf Naturell und Eigentümlichkeit, haben sich auf die seltsamste Weise in Lob und Tadel über diesen Komponisten ergossen. Ich kenne musikal. Personen, die sich sonst bei Anhörung seiner Werke alarmiert ja indigniert fanden und nun von einer Leidenschaft dafür ergriffen sind, wie die Anhänger der griechischen Liebe. Wie wohl man sich dabei befinden kann, lässt sich begreifen, und was daraus entstehen kann, haben Sie in den *Wahlverwandtschaften* deutlich genug gezeigt." Goethe, *Briefwechsel zwischen Goethe und Zelter*, 20.1:285–86.

5. And shudder he did before publishing *Christ on the Mount of Olives* in 1811, but not for Zelter's grounds. Lewis Lockwood tells it well: "revising it for publication at long last eight years later, he described it defensively and apologetically to Breitkopf & Härtel as 'my first work of that kind [a sacred oratorio] and, moreover, an early work . . . written in a fortnight during all kinds of disturbances and other unpleasant and distressing events in my life (my brother happened to be suffering from a mortal disease).' Significantly, Beethoven adds that 'what is quite certain is that now I should compose an absolutely different oratorio from what I composed then.'" Lewis Lockwood, *Beethoven. The Music and the Life* (New York: Norton, 2003), 269–70. The strongest contemporary criticisms of the work charged Beethoven with a miscalculation of genre, a missing grasp of proper religious demeanor, and an excessively dramatic style that made Christ's

Zelter's startling opening image is already a veiled reference to a central moment in Goethe's *Elective Affinities* (*Die Wahlverwandtschaften* [1809]), a novel that portrays the collapse of a marriage after the content but restless spouses invite two others to stay with them, the wife's niece, Ottilie, and an old friend of her husband's, the Captain. At the outset of the novel the well-kept gardens and lovingly maintained landscaping of their estate are described in meticulous detail, a perfect picture of psychological and social harmony. As new attractions begin to form among the four elements of the household (a "Wahlverwandtschaft" describes a chemical attraction), the narrating voice, ever the keenest of observers, dwells on the first signs of developing trouble—the increasingly neglected grounds. The once neatly cultivated borders of the garden path have become overgrown, and Eduard for the first time finds fault with Charlotte's vision for the garden. Nature does not know to keep up appearances, indiscriminately making every inner impulse legible. Late one night, Eduard and Charlotte, husband and wife, each yearning for the company of the ones they secretly love, fall into each other's arms. The features of the child born of this displaced passion betray the adulterous fantasies on the minds of his parents: the baby boy resembles the two absent lovers more than his parents. Eduard cannot bear to be present at the birth of his only son, and neither one of the parents is able to bond with the child, who later drowns in an accident caused by Ottilie, the object of Eduard's erotic fascination.

Zelter hence judges Beethoven's musical creations to be products of a similarly alarming psychic displacement, children whose father is a woman or whose mother is a man, and he imagines that like Eduard, Beethoven must recoil at his offspring. The implication—not far from the surface—that Beethoven's music is against nature (or, truer to Goethe's portrayal in *Elective Affinities*, that nature is permitted to run wild in it) is reinforced with a psychological truism: like the partisans of Greek love, Beethoven's advocates too have found their initial indignation transformed into passionate enthusiasm. The purple thread running through this whole network of associations is the theme of same-sex eros, but precisely because this is not explicitly Zelter's subject (merely a deliberately jarring analogy), the underlying cultural beliefs are left nakedly exposed: the affiliation of same-sex relationships with notions of displacement or surrogacy; the supposed path from distaste to enthusiasm; such emotional triggers as

---

suffering too human (the latter in 1828 from an advocate of Protestantism writing for the *Berliner Allgemeine musikalische Zeitung* who understood this to reflect Catholic taste). In 1812, a critic for the *Allgemeine musikalische Zeitung* wrote "Ein Oratorium? Nun. Das eben nicht! Weder in der Anlage, noch im Styl des Ganzen ist auch nur die leiseste Tendenz bemerkbar, welche auf religiöse Gefühle im Innern des Zuhörers wirken möchte. Ueberall ein heftiges Drängen, ein feuriges, leidenschaftvolles Wogen, eine kunstvolle Rhapsodie, das ganze ein dramatischer Torso. . . . berechnet für den Concertsaal, nicht für die Kirche oder das Bethaus." And further: "Das Gemüth unsers Tonsetzers scheint ein treues Abbild unsers Zeitgeistes zu seyn, der nach dem Ungeheuern trachtet, das Sinnbetäubende ergreifet; aber das rein Geistige unberührt lässt." For the full text of these reviews, see Stefan Kunze, ed., *Ludwig van Beethoven: Die Werke im Spiegel seiner Zeit: Gesammelte Konzertberichte und Rezensionen bis 1830* (Laaber: Laaber-Verlag, 1987), 232–48.

"impurity" and "eternal death."[6] If it was the similarly shocked reaction of readers to *Elective Affinities* that motivated Zelter's comparison in the first place, he masked this with the shrewd suggestion that Goethe's treatment of his disturbing subject ultimately reaffirms social order—unlike Beethoven's unbridled music. Goethe himself maintained that the novel's tragic close upheld the orders of society, an assertion that left Walter Benjamin skeptical as I have noted earlier in connection with the *Graf von Gleichen* story (chapter 2).

We have no immediate reply from Goethe to Zelter's provocation of 14 September. When the correspondence picked up two months later, a personal tragedy had altered its tone: Goethe responded to the distressing news that Zelter's eldest son had committed suicide by changing his mode of address from "Sie" to "Du," a moving offer of friendship to fill the painful gap. Nevertheless, in the coming years, both the novel and Beethoven were recurring topics of conversation between them. Recalling an 1827 letter of Goethe to Zelter, Walter Benjamin once remarked that Goethe sensed the discomfort of his audience even through the respectful posturing with which his works were customarily met: readers had reacted to *Elective Affinities*, Goethe then reminded Zelter, and perhaps gently admonished him, "as if to the Robe of Nessus."[7] (As the myth has it, when Nessus tried to ravish Herakles's bride Deianeira, Herakles shot the centaur with a poisonous arrow. As he lay dying, Nessus told Deianeira that mixing his seed with his blood would make a powerful love potion. But when Deianeira sought to ensure her husband's eternal fidelity by dousing his robe with the potion, it became burning hot, searing him to death.) This drastic image emerges out of nowhere, two decades after the novel's publication, in a diatribe about the unwillingness of literary consumers to accept clothes that are not an easy fit.[8] The public's taste could be as great a barrier to authorial ambition as the threat of official censorship—to which taste accommodated itself all too readily—and reaction to this creation, over which Goethe claimed to have labored like no other, had left him stung.

Goethe protests the reception of the novel as a garment too hot to touch: Would he have pushed the analogy so far as to avow the folds of his robe held a genuine prescription for marital fidelity? It is worth recalling that *Elective Affinities* was not a work of Goethe's rebellious youth like *The Sorrows of Young Werther* or *Stella* but one produced by the most celebrated of German poets approaching his sixtieth year, and a work he counted among his greatest achievements. Benjamin notes "the speechless irony" of a

---

6. This resonates, of course, with recent work in disability studies. Joseph Strauss explores the role of "disability" in shaping critical narratives in "Normalizing the Abnormal: Disability in Music and Music Theory," *Journal of the American Musicological Society* 5 (2006): 113–84.

7. Walter Benjamin, "Goethe's Wahlverwandtschaften," in *Illuminationen: Ausgewählte Schriften*, ed. Siegfried Unseld, 2nd ed. (Frankfurt: Suhrkamp Verlag, 1980), 78.

8. Goethe, *Briefwechsel zwischen Goethe und Zelter* (21 November, 1827), 20.1:1083.

scene reported by Heinrich Laube: "A lady addressed Goethe on the subject of *Elective Affinities*: 'I do not approve of this book at all, Herr von Goethe; it is truly immoral and I do not recommend it to any woman.'—Thereupon Goethe kept a serious silence for awhile, and finally, with great civility, replied: 'I am sorry, for it is my best book.'"[9] Zelter can only have ignited Goethe's curiosity about Beethoven's music with the analogy to *Elective Affinities*. And Goethe may well have had the 1812 letter fresh in mind when he reflected on the novel's reception in 1827, since the two friends had recently begun to exchange old packets of letters in preparation for the eventual publication of their correspondence.

It is noteworthy that the tone of Zelter's remarks about Beethoven's music began to shift soon after this 1812 conversation, in which Goethe had expressed both amazement and a good measure of sympathy for Beethoven (and Zelter outdid himself to find adequate words in reply).[10] In the coming years Zelter would write admiring accounts to Goethe of Beethoven's works, including *Egmont* (27 February 1813) and the popular but contested *Wellington's Victory*. "Beethoven has written a Victory Symphony that'll make his audience just as deaf as he is," stated a caustic first report on 8 May 1816. The next day, after the concert—he had sat in the rear to protect his ears—he sheepishly took it back, giving a detailed account of the entertaining piece ("denn Gestern hat es mir ungemeinen Spaß gemacht"). The high quality of its craftsmanship had surprised and impressed him. The final verdict: "Vivat genius and to hell with all the critics!"[11] The turnaround seems calculated to win Goethe's approval, a posture that surfaces time and again in this correspondence. Not that Goethe's estimation of Beethoven's accomplishment was particularly astute, but he certainly recognized Beethoven's growing stature as well as his talent. More important, the comparison to Goethe himself was becoming inevitable, and Goethe bristled whenever any product of the creative imagination was maligned as "unnatural": in 1831 this same raw nerve touched off Goethe's impassioned defense of the minor third, which he mistakenly believed music theorists had declared the product of human invention, not a given in nature. As man belongs to nature, he explained to Zelter,

9. Walter Benjamin, *Selected Writings*, vol. 2, *1927–1934*, ed. Howard Eiland, Gary Smith, and Michael W. Jennings (Cambridge, Mass.: Belknap Press of Harvard University Press, 1999), 328.

10. The earliest discussion of Beethoven in the correspondence was also prompted by Goethe. On 12 November 1808 Zelter complained that the most significant musical talents of the age, chief among them Cherubini and Beethoven, employed Hercules's club to swat flies (like the one wielded by Liberty?). If music as an art is to survive, he predicted, such music will have to be forgotten. This came in reply to a letter of Goethe bemoaning the self-indulgent humor and lack of technical command in younger poetic talents, particularly Jean Paul and Görres. Goethe had specifically asked Zelter for similar examples from the field of music. In the same letter he expressed his concern for the proper education of the young composer Carl Eberwein. Goethe, *Briefwechsel zwischen Goethe und Zelter* (30 October 1808), 20.1:197–205.

11. Goethe, *Briefwechsel zwischen Goethe und Zelter*, 20.1:424–25. For a wider study of the reception of this piece, see Nicholas Cook, "The Other Beethoven: Heroism, the Canon and the Works of 1813–14," *19th Century Music* 27 (2003): 3–24.

we are wrong to dismiss as arbitrary artifice the inventions of a creative mind.[12] The subject matter here may seem remote from Zelter's 1812 letter, but the terms on which Goethe mounted his defense of the minor mode—so well suited, he found, to rendering "das unnennbare Sehnsüchtige" (indefinable yearning)—brings to mind charges leveled against his own creations. Man belongs to nature, thus the inventions of a creative mind are not unnatural: an 1828 discussion by the conservative critic Wolfgang Menzel held that although the personal relationships—the breaches of marital contract?—that Goethe explored in *Elective Affinities* and *Stella* do in fact arise in nature, they are obscene and repellent aberrations of nature from which young persons must be shielded. Continuing his attack with a preemptive appeal to Plato's authority, Menzel sought to isolate Goethe as a degenerate modern. (Even Plato, he argued, reproached Homer and Hesiod for revealing so many things about the gods that are obscene and against nature.)[13] Was culture an expression of nature, or did it stand as its opposite? Menzel happily conflated the two so long as nature accorded with social proprieties. Of course the inflexible term in his scheme was cultivated life, not nature: all that stood outside the behavioral norm he simply declared unnatural.

There are other indications that Zelter's changing view of Beethoven arose in dialogue with the figure of Goethe—the figure of the poet as much as the man, since their friendship flourished mainly by correspondence (and Goethe's letters so often are circumspect even as they are warm). Writing to Goethe on 13 May 1820, Zelter returned to the subject of musical "painting" in such works as Beethoven's "Victory" symphony and Haydn's "Chaos" and "Seasons." He maintained that in the hand of an imitator such literal painting is a disaster, yet in works of genius it is enthralling and spellbinding—so long as we are able to relinquish our former expectations. (Goethe once demonstrated the same

---

12. Goethe, *Briefwechsel zwischen Goethe und Zelter* (March, 1831) 20.2:31, 1460–61. Goethe's role as defense attorney for the minor third is discussed by Dieter Borchmeyer, "Anwalt der kleinen Terz: Goethe und die Musik," in *Beethoven, Goethe und Europa: Almanach zum Internationalen Beethovenfest Bonn 1999*, ed. Thomas Daniel Schlee (Laaber: Laaber-Verlag, 1999), 41–61.

13. "Schon Platon tadelt mit strengem Ernst die Entweihung der Dichtkunst durch die Enthüllung unnatürlicher Gelüste. Er wirft es dem Hesiod und Homer vor, daß sie so viele obszöne und naturwidrige Dinge von den Göttern erzählen. Er sagt mit vollem Recht: 'wenn sich dergleichen auch in der Natur vorfände, so muß man sie doch unmündigen und jungen Leuten nicht vorerzählen, sondern mehr als irgendetwas verschweigen. Sollte jedoch irgendeine Notwendigkeit eintreten, davon zu reden, so müßten diese Dinge nichts anders, denn als Mysterien gehört werden, von so wenigen als möglich. . . .' Es ist wahr, daß sich jene geheimnisvolle Wahlverwandschaft, das Prinzip des Ehebruchs, es ist wahr, daß sich Gelüste, dergleichen in der *Stella* geschildert sind, wirklich in der Natur vorfinden, aber als Auswüchse, und wir sollen uns über die Natur, oder vielmehr über die Unnatur dieser Dinge nicht durch eine einnehmende poetische Beschönigung, durch eine Verwechslung derselben mit den heiligsten Gefühlen reiner Liebe täuschen lassen. . . ." Reprinted in full in Karl Robert Mandelkow, ed., *Goethe im Urteil seiner Kritiker: Dokumente zur Wirkungsgeschichte Goethes in Deutschland*, Teil 1, 1773–1832 (Munich: C. H. Beck, 1975), 396–97. For more, in English, on Menzel's view of Goethe as a pernicious influence, see *German Literature*, translated from the German of Wolfgang Menzel by C. C. Felton, 3 vols. (Boston: Hillard, Gray and Company, 1840), vol. 3.

thing to him in connection with Molière, he recalls.)[14] A stirring personal encounter between Zelter and Beethoven near Mödling in September 1819 had called forth a wave of sympathetic feeling. Zelter was on his way to see the celebrated composer when their carriages crossed paths. Beethoven got out and they hugged before continuing in opposite directions: "I could barely hold back my tears, for the unfortunate man was as good as deaf."[15]

Zelter's appreciation for Beethoven only continued to grow as the years went by. In 1825 he picked up the thread again, observing that although one could detect in Beethoven's music some of the excess that is a pervasive sign of the times (no longer, we note, is that excess seen as a mark of perversity), he had far outstripped his contemporaries—"one might compare him to Michelangelo."[16] This came at a time when both Zelter and Goethe were captivated by the young Felix Mendelssohn's music, so openly indebted to the latest works of Beethoven: the impact and importance of Beethoven's music had become plain even to those who resisted its manner.

Just how thoroughly Zelter's attitude to Beethoven had shifted later in life is captured in a letter of 19 April 1831 when, at the age of seventy-two, he penned a gushingly enthusiastic account of *Christus am Ölberge*, the very work that once had seemed such a monstrosity to him! There is a fascinating discussion of Christ's opening lament. After high praise for the robust orchestral writing in the introduction ("like an overflowing heart, a pulse of superhuman power, I was seized"), Zelter gives the following marked-up text and commentary:

Jehova, du mein Vater! O sende
Trost und Kraft und Stärke mir!
Sie nahet nun, die Stunde meiner Leiden,
Von mir erkoren schon, noch eh die Welt
Auf dein Geheiß, dem Chaos sich entwand. U. s. w.

With marvelous artistry, the underlined words stand in the most felicitous of relations to one another, like so many painterly motives. It is like an exercise in drawing: to carve from five or more randomly given points a beautiful form or group portrait, all with the hand of a master. The nonsense contained in the words disappears; the most familiar tones appear as if heard for the first time; one is swept away.[17]

---

14. Goethe, *Briefwechsel zwischen Goethe und Zelter*, 20.1:603–5.

15. Goethe, *Briefwechsel zwischen Goethe und Zelter*, 20.1:584–85.

16. Goethe, *Briefwechsel zwischen Goethe und Zelter* (4 June 1825), 20.1:849.

17. "Die unterstrichnen Worte stehn mit bewunderns[würdi]ger Kunst als lauter malerische Motive im glücklichsten Zusammenhange, wie eine bildliche Aufgabe: zwischen 5 oder mehr gegebenen Punkten, eine schöne Gestalt oder Gruppe von Meisterhand einzuzeichnen. Der in den Worten enthaltene Unsinn verschwindet; wohlbekannte Töne erscheinen als nie gehört, man wird hingerissen." 19 April 1831, Goethe, *Briefwechsel zwischen Goethe und Zelter* (19 April 1831), 20.2:1465–67.

Already a few days earlier, following a performance of *Fidelio*, Zelter had simultaneously recalled and softened his own resistance to Beethoven: "Above all else, Genius has this advantage: it offends and reconciles, wounds then heals; one has little choice but to follow, no amount of barricading or tarrying can hold it at bay."[18]

II

These vignettes from the Goethe-Zelter correspondence offer a remarkably up-close view of the mechanisms of changing taste, the gradual melting of resistance to a challenging new style felt by many to be brash and uncompromising. But the story of Zelter's picturesque 1812 letter does not end there, for it gained a certain notoriety after the publication in 1833 of the Goethe-Zelter correspondence. We find a surprising invocation of it in A. B. Marx's study of the *Eroica*, in the 1859 volume on the life and works of Beethoven, where Zelter's response is mistakenly attributed to Goethe—its central image spectacularly misinterpreted to say that Beethoven had transformed music's feminine nature into one of mind and spirit (*Geist*). Marx evidently only knew the letter by word of mouth, and—like a party game of "telephone"—any relation to the original sense of the passage is obliterated in the transmission. His topic is music's capacity to impart ideas, when suddenly he is reminded of Goethe's famous lines on the eternal Feminine from the conclusion to *Faust*:

> Alles vergängliche/ Ist nur ein Gleichniß:/ Das Unzulängliche,/ Hier wird's Ereigniß,/ Das Unbeschreibliche,/ Hier wirds gethan,/ Das ewig Weibliche/ Zieht uns hinan!

Inspired, Marx now stands Zelter's genealogical postulate (he thinks it is Goethe's) on its head:

> The eternal Feminine—that is what music is, mysteriously harboring life and spirit in her womb. If it is true that Goethe said of Beethoven that "while listening to Beethoven's works it appeared to him as if this man's father had been a woman, his mother a man," then the clear-eyed poet has once again gazed penetratingly and deeply. The father, the spirit, directed him to music and in him music [*die Musik*] became Man, became Spirit.[19]

---

18. "Das ist der Vorteil den man beim Genie voraus und davon hat: es beleidigt und versöhnt, es verwundet und heilt; man muß mit, da hilft kein Sperren und Weilen." Goethe, *Briefwechsel* zwischen Goethe und Zelter (6 April 1831), 20.2:1461–62.

19. "Das ewig Weibliche, das ist die Musik, die das Leben, den Geist, geheimnißvoll in ihrem Mutterschooße birgt. Wenn es wahr ist, daß Goethe von Beethoven gesagt: es komme ihm beim Anhören Beethovenscher

The subject of discussion has shifted from Beethoven's work to Beethoven's own lineage, a symbolic patrimony that Marx wished to believe molded Beethoven's creations. Engendered by the father's Spirit, Beethoven's musical offspring are emphatically masculine. Marx's gloss so thoroughly transforms the sense of the original image by tapping into a biographical trope that mushroomed in midcentury accounts of composer's lives: like the kiss with which Beethoven himself was purported to have anointed an eleven-year-old Franz Liszt, here the most esteemed of all German poets has recognized the wellspring of Beethoven's genius, certifying his patrimony within a genealogy of spirit.[20] Perhaps even the misattribution of the letter to Goethe was unconsciously conditioned by this model: it would not really have done much for Marx's conviction had Beethoven's genius been grasped by a second-rate talent like Carl Friedrich Zelter! Comically, a footnote actually acknowledges that the insight arose in an exchange of letters with Zelter, who is dismissed indignantly, however, as an impudent Berliner and philistine known to

---

Musik vor, als ob dieses Menschen Vater ein Weib, seine Mutter ein Mann gewesen sein müsse: so hat der sonnaugige Dichter wieder einmal klar und tief geblickt. Der Vater, der Geist, hat ihn in die Musik gewiesen, sie ist in ihm Mann—Geist—geworden." Adolf Bernhard Marx, *Ludwig van Beethoven: Leben und Schaffen*, 2 vols. (Berlin: Otto Janke, 1859; reprint in facsimile, 2 vols. in 1, Hildesheim: Georg Olms Verlag, 1979), 1:280. Marx's German allows for a fuzziness of meaning, which the characteristic greater precision and directness of English will not support. Much of it here comes from the friction between culturally reinforced gender associations ("geheimnißvoll . . . Mutterschooße," on the one hand, and "sonnaugige . . . klar und tief," on the other) and the arbitrary grammatical feminine gender of "die Musik."

20. Allan Keiler has made a strong case for the presence of the trope whereby a renowned figure attests to the great promise of an aspiring artist in the transmission of the so-called *Weihekuss* myth, based at least as much in wishful thinking as in fact. See his "Liszt and Beethoven: The Creation of a Personal Myth," *19th Century Music* 12 (1988): 116–31, and "Liszt Research and Walker's *Liszt*," *Musical Quarterly* 70 (1984): 374–403. He returns to the issue with rich insight in his recent translation and commentary to "Ludwig Rellstab's Biographical Sketch of Liszt," in *Franz Liszt and His World*, ed. Christopher H. Gibbs and Dana Gooley (Princeton, N.J.: Princeton University Press, 2006), 335–60. Several contradictory variants of the story emerged at midcentury, and Liszt did nothing to discourage (or correct) them. Indeed, it may be no coincidence that the *Weihekuss* story parallels so closely the account of Beethoven's supposed 1787 meeting with Mozart, related by Jahn in the biography of 1856–59. (Impressed by Beethoven's skill in improvisation, he reportedly predicted, "Keep your eyes on him; some day he will give the world something to talk about.") Thayer quotes Jahn's narrative in full, presenting it as a sober account stripped of the fanciful embellishments earlier supplied by Seyfried (Alexander Wheeloch Thayer, *Thayer's Life of Beethoven*, revised and edited by Elliott Forbes [Princeton, N.J.: Princeton University Press, 1967], 87). Maynard Solomon is skeptical in this instance, too, speaking of a possible rejection by Mozart, who faced significant personal and professional challenges during the two weeks of Beethoven's stay in Vienna (Maynard Solomon, *Mozart: A Life* [New York: HarperCollins, 1995], 395). In any event, there is a notable difference between Marx's distortion, several times removed, and the Liszt story in that we cannot ascribe *Marx's* misreading to what Kris and Kurz called "enacted biography"—a psychological mechanism by which artists (consciously or unconsciously) have molded occasions in their lives to fit stereotypes of their profession (Ernst Kris and Otto Kurz, *Legend, Myth, and Magic in the Image of the Artist: A Historical Experiment* [New Haven, Conn.: Yale University Press, 1979], 132). In line with this mechanism is an alternative scenario that might account for the story: the child Liszt did receive Beethoven's kiss on that occasion only it was not Ludwig's but his brother Johann's. (We know Johann was present at the performance and conversation book entries suggest he gave Ludwig a report).

speak disrespectfully of Beethoven.[21] One cannot help but suspect that if Marx knew about Zelter's 1812 letter, he may also have known that Zelter regularly denounced the editor and chief music critic of the *Berliner Allgemeine musikalische Zeitung* in his reports to Goethe on the musical life of the city. Marx, of course, had also attacked Zelter's *Singakademie* in the pages of his journal.[22] But thinking the letter to be Goethe's, it does not occur to Marx to imagine that the enigmatic characterization might have been a reproach, leaving him free to discover in it confirmation of an already established judgment: Beethoven has elevated the art of music to a serious masculine endeavor, rescuing it from the taint of the feminine. Among other things, this weirdly skewed transmission of Zelter's letter illustrates well how some of the most conspicuous assertions of an era's dominant social ideology come about incidentally, when an excited author reaches for ready, nominally acceptable cultural images (things so pervasive that even those who find them disagreeable routinely let them pass unchallenged) to make an emphatic point about another matter entirely.

Within a few decades after Beethoven's death and to so strong an advocate of his music as A. B. Marx, it had become unthinkable that anyone, least of all the great Goethe, should have spoken about Beethoven with anything but reverence. Ironically, both the passions of Zelter and of Marx were kindled by an anxiety over Goethe's estimation of Beethoven: in 1812 Zelter seized upon Goethe's slightest adverse reaction to Beethoven to steer his opinion deeper into the negative with psycho-sexual innuendo that he must have believed would be favorably received, and Marx, still irked by Goethe's acceptance of Zelter and anxious for some sign of the great poet's recognition of Beethoven's superiority, makes of the same terms a panegyric to a mystical form of masculine procreation. Would Beethoven have recognized anything of himself in these fanciful critical extremes?

---

21. Marx's language is too lively to pass up: "Gewährsmann und Anreger ist Zelter, der mit der ganzen plumpen Frechheit eines berliner Philisters (denen er 'unser Zelter' hieß) von Beethoven gesagt: er gebe ihm den Namen eines Thiers, das man lieber gebraten, als lebendig im Zimmer suche." The stimulus for Goethe's insight, he says, came from "Zelter who, with all the pompous insolence of a Berlin philistine (among whom he was called 'our Zelter') said of Beethoven: he'd give him the name of an animal that one would prefer to see roasted than running loose in our living quarters." A turkey? A goose? A rooster? Marx, *Ludwig van Beethovens Leben und Schaffen*, 1:280.

22. One tirade in particular is revealing for what it tells of the changing cultural climate: Marx's call in the *Kunst des Gesanges* for the renewal of German music in an era dominated by Italian style infuriated Zelter, who argued that there is no such thing as German music, or Italian. Dürer, Hackert, Goethe, and Handel, Graun, Hasse, Mozart all had traveled to Italy to strengthen their art and to share their own talent. If only the gentlemen occupying honorary chairs would allow music to be music! Thus in one swipe, he dismisses the emerging nationalist agenda as a problem invented in the academy. Goethe, *Briefwechsel zwischen Goethe und Zelter* (26 September–5 October 1830), 20.2:1376–77.

6

Schubert, Platen, and the Myth of Narcissus

In the years since this essay first appeared, our understanding of the literary and social circles around Schubert has been enriched above all by the work of Ilija Dürhammer, whose systematic sifting through poetic texts, letters, and other documents has turned up, among other things, much additional evidence of Schubert's engagement with the topic of same-sex love and friendship. Many biographical puzzles still remain, especially concerning the activities of the various organized social groups with which Schubert was affiliated. But if the precise nature of Schubert's intimate life remains elusive, his temperament and intellectual leanings have come into sharper focus for us.[1]

So many of Schubert's songs on poems addressing male lovers have a special intensity—perhaps the greatest of them all is "Suleika" ("was bedeutet die Bewegung," D 720), dedicated to Franz von Schober. After an ecstatic climax at the words "dort find' ich bald den Vielgeliebten" (there, soon I shall find my Beloved), energy tapers, the tempo pulls back, and a throbbing F♯ accompanies the following lines repeated over and over again:

Ach die wahre Herzenskunde, Liebeshauch erfrischtes Leben, wird mir nur aus seinem Munde, kann mir nur sein Athem geben . . . sein Athem geben.

---

1. Ilija Dürhammer, *Schuberts literarische Heimat: Dichtung und Literatur-Rezeption der Schubert-Freunde* (Vienna: Böhlau Verlag, 1999), and *Geheime Botschaften: Homoerotische Subkulturen im Schubert-Kreis, bei Hugo von Hofmannsthal und Thomas Bernhard* (Vienna: Böhlau Verlag, 2006). One of these societies came into the spotlight with the publication of Rita Steblin, with Erich Benedikt, Walther Brauneis, Ilija Dürhammer, Herwig Knaus, Michael Lorenz, and Gerhard Stradner, *Die Unsinnsgesellschaft: Franz Schubert, Leopold Kupelwieser und Ihr Freundeskreis* (Vienna: Böhlau Verlag, 1998). Might there be a connection between the 1817–1818 "Unsinnsgesellschaft" and eighteenth-century English satirical literary clubs like the Nonsense Club? See Lance Bertelsen, *The Nonsense Club: Literature and Popular Culture, 1749–1764* (Oxford: Clarendon Press, 1986).

Ah, the heart's true message, life renewed in love's exhale, comes to me only from his mouth, is given to me by his breath alone . . . by his breath alone.

Next to the breathtaking intimacy of Schubert's thirty-five-bar coda, Marianne von Willemer's poem (which appeared under Goethe's name) pales, even if its expression of passion directed toward a male lover would have stood out to contemporary readers. Schubert seized the opportunity, finding a model for his own ambition in the embrace of plural perspectives in the *West-östlicher Divan*, and in Goethe's understanding that contemporary culture was an amalgam of distinct traditions: the secular world, the Christian sacred, the ancient Greek, the Roman, the more remote Persian heritage. Each tradition carries with it its own history and pictorial imagery. Separating them out or allowing them to intermingle could bring out distinct strains of experience for readers and listeners attentive to those traditions. Reading circles cultivated such sensitivities (so basic to the prized ambiguity of German Romantic poetry), and Schubert's exceptional skill in drawing out specific associations through word repetition, or various means of emphasis (register, dynamics, duration, tonality, rhetorical gesture) is unmatched. The study that follows explores some implications of one stunning example in a song based on a poem by August von Platen.

I

When Schubert's first setting of a text by the poet August von Platen was published as one of four songs in op. 23, an anonymous critic for the *Allgemeine musikalische Zeitung* (*AmZ*) of Leipzig singled it out for attack. Of the entire opus the reviewer wrote:

> Herr Schubert does not write *Lieder*, properly speaking, and has no wish to do so . . . but rather free vocal pieces, some so free that they might better be called caprices or fantasies. In view of this intent, the poems, mostly new but of greatly varying quality, have been favorably chosen and their translation into music is generally praiseworthy, for the composer invariably succeeds in mapping out the whole and each detail in accordance with the poetic idea; but in the execution he is frequently less successful, seeking to make up for the want of inner unity, order and regularity by eccentric, and even wild actions which are hardly or not at all justified. Naturally, the former characteristics alone do not suffice to elevate an ordinary work to a work of fine art, but without them, only bizarre, grotesque works can arise.[2]

---

2. "Hr. Fr. S. schreibt keine eigentlichen Lieder und will keine schreiben . . . sondern freie Gesänge, manche so frei, daß man sie allenfalls Kapricen oder Phantasien nennen kann. Dieser Ansicht gemäß sind die meist neuen Gedichte, deren Wert jedoch verschieden ist, günstig gewählt und die Übertragung derselben in Töne im allgemeinen zu loben, da dem Verfasser durchaus die Anlage im ganzen und einzelnen, der Idee nach, aber bei weitem nicht so glücklich die Ausführung gelingt, die durch wenig oder gar nicht motiviertes exzentrisches, oft recht wildes Wesen und Treiben den mangel innerer Einheit, Ordnung, und Regelmäßigkeit zu ersetzen versucht; durch welche letzten Eigenschaften allein freilich kein Werk der Kunst zum schönen

Fixing his attention on one of the most confounding measures in the entire collection, the critic continued: "This reviewer does not trust himself to decide whether the tone-configuration three bars from the end of Op. 23, no. 1 should be considered as truly new and original, if quite dreadful, or as a printer's error, though he has considerable reason for believing the former."[3] The song in question is the deceptively simple "Die Liebe hat gelogen," based on a poem later published in Platen's *Vermischte Schriften* of 1822:

Die Liebe hat gelogen,	Love has Lied
Die Sorge lastet schwer,	Anxiety weighs heavily,
Betrogen, ach, betrogen,	Betrayed, alas betrayed
Hat alles mich umher!	By everything around me!
Es rinnen heiße Tropfen	Hot tears stream
Die Wange stets herab,	Steadily down my cheek,
Laß ab, laß ab zu klopfen,	Let up, let up from pounding
Laß ab, mein Herz, laß ab.	Let up, my heart, let up.

Schubert's source was not the *Vermischte Schriften* but evidently a prepublication manuscript prepared for him by the poet.[4] Beyond bringing the opening stanza back at the end, his setting departs from the published poem only in minor textual detail.[5] The tone configuration that so disturbed the reviewer for the *AmZ* is the surprisingly unprepared, then frustrated harmonic motion on the word "betrogen" in the final measures, shown in example 6.1.

The song is in the key of C minor. At the final outcry, "betrogen, ach, betrogen," a dominant seventh chord built on F explodes unexpectedly from the tonicization of F minor at the end of the preceding phrase. The sudden harshness of the major third and the extremity of the added seventh have barely registered before their effect is magnified. Behaving as an augmented sixth, the seventh chord is wrenched outward to the half-note octave E♮'s that frame an unstable A-minor six-four chord. The conventionally powerful tendencies of this progression are in turn evaded, the quadrupled E♮'s in the six-four chord treated as a paradoxical preparation for the final cadential progression to C major,

---

Kunstwerk wird, ohne welche Eigenschaften aber auch bestimmt nur bizarre, groteske Produkte entstehen" Otto Erich Deutsch, *Schubert: Die Dokumente Seines Lebens*, Neue Ausgabe sämtlicher Werke, ser. 8, suppl. 5 (Kassel: Bärenreiter Verlag, 1964), 243–45. Opus 23 appeared in 1824, three years after all four songs were composed. Deutsch raises the possibility that the anonymous critic was G. W. Fink.

3. Deutsch, *Dokumente*, 244.

4. The evidence for this is reviewed in Walther Dürr's commentary to the New Schubert Edition: *Franz Schubert: Neue Ausgabe sämtlicher Werke*, ser. 4, vol. 2a (Kassel: Bärenreiter Verlag, 1975), xvii.

5. The final lines in the second stanza of Schubert's text read: "Laß ab, mein Herz, zu klopfen, Du armes Herz, laß ab."

EXAMPLE 6.1 Franz Schubert, "Die Liebe hat gelogen," D 751, mm. 14–18.

where the song ends. "Love has Lied . . . [I have been] betrayed by everything around me," Schubert's singer lashes out.

The only other surviving song of Schubert to a text by Platen, "Du liebst mich nicht," was again isolated in the pages of the *AmZ* for the extravagance of its harmonic language.[6] The reviewer commented on the first two songs in op. 59, no. 6, "Du liebst mich nicht" and the Rückert song "Dass sie hier gewesen," as follows:

> Herr Schubert rather excessively probes and constructs artifice—not in melody, but in harmony. In particular he modulates in such alien ways and so unexpectedly to the most remote regions in a manner unlike any other composer on the face of the earth, at least of Lieder and other small vocal pieces. (As here, for example, in the first song, the very short and simple melody is torn practically through all keys of the entire scale, often with as little as two chord changes between one virtual

6. Opus 59 contains "Du liebst mich nicht" together with the three Rückert songs "Dass sie hier gewesen," "Du bist die Ruh," and "Lachen und Weinen." The three Rückert poems, each contemplating different facets of love, were first published in *Östliche Rosen: Drei Lesen* (Leipzig: F. A. Brockhaus, 1822). There are minor divergences between Schubert's texts and the published poems, which suggest that Schubert may have worked from a different *Textvorlage*. Rückert and Platen were in close contact in the months before the publication of *Östliche Rosen*.

extreme and another.) But equally true is the fact that (even in this case) he does not probe in vain; that he really does succeed in drawing out Something, which if performed with complete assurance and ease, truly speaks, and says something substantial, to the imagination and the sensibility. May one thus both try them and try oneself on them.[7]

There is a certain grudging appreciation in this latter assessment. Yet what strikes me foremost about the response of the contemporary press to these songs is the stark contrast of its criticism to the abundant and no less emphatic testimony on the subject of Schubert's text setting from among his circle of friends, who almost routinely celebrated the remarkable fit of his translations of poetry into music. One of the most famous and characteristically effusive passages comes from the singer Johann Michael Vogl, whose enthusiasm is notably expressed against a backdrop of widespread public misapprehension of Schubert's songs:

Nothing has made the lack of an adequate school for singing so sorely apparent as have Schubert's songs. For otherwise, what a universal and extraordinary effect these truly divine inspirations, these displays of a musical clairvoyance, would of necessity have had on the entire German-speaking realm. How many would perhaps have come to understand for the first time what is meant by: language, poetry in music, words in harmonies, thoughts clothed in music. They would have learned how the loveliest verbal poem by our greatest poets, when translated into such a music-language, might be heightened—yes, even surpassed.[8]

The only surviving response specifically to one of the Platen songs from a member of Schubert's circle is in a letter to Platen from Franz von Bruchmann, a philosophy and law student who frequently headed the reading group Schubert and his friends had formed

---

7. "Hr. Schubert sucht und künstelt—nicht in der Melodie, aber in der Harmonie, gar sehr, und besonders modulirt er so befremdlich und oft so urplötzlich nach dem Entlegensten hin, wie, wenigstens in Liedern und anderen kleinen Gesängen, kein Componist auf dem ganzen Erdboden: (so wird z. B. hier, im ersten Liede, die ganz kurze und sehr einfache Melodie ziemlich durch alle Tonarten der gesamten Leiter und mehrmals nur durch zwey Griffe beynahe von einem Aeussersten zum anderen gerissen); aber eben so wahr ist, dass er (wie hier auch) nicht vergebens sucht; dass er wirklich etwas herauskünstelt, das, wird es dann mit vollkommener Sicherheit und Zwangslosigkeit vorgetragen, der Phantasie und der Empfindung wirklich Etwas sagt, und etwas Bedeutendes. Möge man darum sich an ihnen, und sie an sich versuchen" (25 April 1827; reprinted in Till Gerrit Waidelich, ed., with preliminary work by Renate Hilmar-Voit and Andreas Mayer, *Franz Schubert, Dokumente 1817–1830*, vol. 1, *Texte. Programme, Rezensionen, Anzeigen, Nekrologe, Musikbeilagen und andere gedruckte Quellen*. Veröffentlichungen des Internationalen Franz Schubert Instituts, ed. Ernst Hilmar,vol. 10.1, [Tutzing: Hans Schneider, 1993], 332–33).

8. The full text of this diary passage is given in Andreas Liess, *Johann Michael Vogl: Hofoperist und Schubert-Sänger* (Graz: Hermann Böhlaus Nachf., 1954), 153.

and who knew both Platen and his poetry very well. In keeping with Vogl's enthusiastic tone, Bruchmann characterized the effect of Schubert's "Du liebst mich nicht" on him quite simply as "entrancing,"[9] with no mention of the radical nature of its harmonic language. Indeed, the choice of a word like "entrancing" presupposed that he found the setting persuasive, and that its tonal language, however novel, posed no barrier to his appreciation. Perhaps Schubert's friends were simply less troubled by his departures from principles of unity and order, less concerned with academic definitions of the Lied, than was a distant music critic writing for the *Allgemeine musikalische Zeitung*. Not all of them had extensive musical training, after all, though Vogl surely did. Perhaps, too, his friends had access to performances of greater sophistication and nuance than did the anonymous critic(s), allowing congruences between poem and music to speak to them more readily. Indeed, Vogl decries the inadequate school of singing that has blocked the path to universal appreciation of Schubert's songs. Yet explanations that appeal to disparities in the level of technical expertise or the quality of performance serve largely to skirt a more provocative issue unleashed by these conflicting testimonies: the claim that there was a genuine difference in perception among listeners. In order to privilege another kind of question, I would like to set aside the obvious differences in polemical intent and partisanship underlying these diverging assessments, drawing into focus only the fundamental disagreement in perception they seem to describe. Then it becomes possible to ask: Could it have been precisely their personal proximity to Schubert that gave his friends a special insight, that allowed them to appreciate aspects of his work the critic(s) did not, and perhaps could not, fully comprehend? For while the *AmZ* critic—at least the author of the first review—appears to share with Vogl the conception of songwriting as an act of translation (he writes of the *Übertragung* of the poems into music), he finds Schubert's eccentricities to be only barely motivated, if at all. His complaint is only partially that Schubert's bold departures from regularity and unity are insufficiently prepared: the underlying charge is that they are not justified by the poetic text. If Schubert's musical response to the poem appears to him exaggerated, inappropriate, unmotivated, could this be at least in part because the anonymous critic does not share Schubert's understanding of the text?

---

9. "Aus diesen ersten Gh[aselen] wird Schubert einige setzen, worauf ich mich sehr freue, wie hat Ihnen seine Composition Ihres Liedes gefallen? . . . Schelling seine Schrift über Mythologie [!] kommt nicht! Schreiben Sie mir doch etwas über Goluchowsky, ich habe ein Buch von ihm, worüber sich vieles sagen läßt.—Soeben höre ich von Schubert Ihre Ghasele: *Zerrissen, du liebst mich nicht*, die mich ganz bezaubert; wenn noch eine sich anreiht, u. Sie mir bis dahin etwas über ihn schreiben, erhalten Sie beyde" (Schubert plans to set several from the first [book of] *ghazals*, which I look forward to. How did you like his setting of your Lied? . . . Schelling's work on mythology [!] hasn't appeared! Do write me something about Goluchowsky; I have a book of his about which there is much to be said.—Just now I am hearing your *ghazal* "Zerrissen, du liebst mich nicht" by Schubert, which completely entrances me. If another should follow, and if by then you have written me about him, you shall receive both). August Graf von Platen, *Der Briefwechsel*, 4 vols., ed. Paul Bornstein (Munich, 1914; reprint, Hildesheim: Georg Olms Verlag, 1973), 2:320 [end of July/early August 1822].

The later reception history of the Platen songs reveals that the concerns raised by Schubert's contemporaries have only been magnified, not resolved. A century after the publication of "Du liebst mich nicht," the impression of the song's novelty had not faded, but the power of the work to express vivid psychological states was addressed less guardedly. In a 1928 centennial volume on Schubert's songs Carl Lafite wrote that

> "Du liebst mich nicht" leaves a remarkably modern impression with its listless and impassioned modulatory turns that conjure the image of one wandering aimlessly. An unaccustomed nervous streak governs the beautiful, grand, and pathetically conceived work. Something of this unstable surge of feeling has also penetrated the central section of "Die Liebe hat gelogen," whose beginning and end replaces this flare-up of unrest with a still, but perhaps even more painful, resignation.[10]

By 1953, something in the psychology of the Platen songs had evidently touched a raw nerve. In *Der Klassiker Schubert*, Walther Vetter felt obliged to launch an emphatic defense of Schubert's moral reputation, in a scarely veiled effort to fend off any hint of suspicion over the composer's sexual orientation. (The section bears the telltale heading "Der gesunde Grundzug.") Troubled by the fact that the vast majority of Schubert songs are conceived to be performed by a male interpreter, Vetter concluded:

> Although on purely artistic grounds it is necessary to warn against an overvaluation of the masculine component in Schubert's complete song output, we may nonetheless emphasize that the indisputably strong masculine tone of Schubert's lyricism, which is foe to anything soft or weak, conveys a healthy character through and through and sustains a high moral level.

The discussion begins with the observation that in "Du liebst mich nicht" Platen strictly avoided revealing the sex of the object of the poet's passion. Vetter remarks that "the innocent reader [der harmlose Leser] must take these verses as a normal love song, and nothing speaks for the composer's awareness of the poet's true feelings. Lafite calls the song 'Du liebst mich nicht' strangely modern and uncharacteristically nervous, and in the central section of 'Die Liebe hat gelogen' he discerns an unstable surge of feeling." Be that as it may, Vetter continues, Schubert never set any additional texts by Platen after these

---

10. "'Du liebst mich nicht' macht einen merkwürdig modernen Eindruck mit der unruhigen, leidenschaftlichen Führung seiner Modulationen, die an einen ziellos Umherirrenden erinnern. Ein ungewohnt nervöser Zug beherrscht das schöne, groß und pathetisch aufzufassende Stück. Und etwas von diesem unsteten Gefühlsdrang ist auch in den Mittelsatz des anderen Platenliedes, 'Die Liebe hat gelogen,' eingedrungen, während anfangs und am Ende an die Stelle jener flackernden Unruhe hier eine stillere, aber vielleicht noch schmerzlichere Resignation tritt" Carl Johann Sigismund Lafite, *Das Schubertlied und seine Sänger* (Vienna: Strache, 1928), 62–63.

two.[11] (There is, however, evidence that he at least considered setting several others.)[12] For Vetter, writing in an era that equated homosexuality with infirmity—it was generally considered a from of nervous disorder—Lafite's choice of the descriptive terms "nervös," "pathetisch," and "unsteter Gefühlsdrang" must have set off alarms.

Well into our own time, the extravagant harmonic language of "Du liebst mich nicht" has continued to preoccupy critics, who have repeatedly described it as forward-looking, more characteristic of the music that would be written decades later than of the 1820s.[13] Recent assessments of the song's "abnormal" harmonic language have generally concluded that it is in the end an experimental, not entirely persuasive work. In an essay on "Du liebst mich nicht" and "Dass sie hier gewesen," Kofi Agawu admonished those who would turn only to the poems for explanations of remarkable harmonic events:[14]

> It is tempting to evade the difficult questions by ascribing to text-music relations those bold harmonic strokes that we find in songs like "Die Stadt, "Am Meer," and "Der Doppelgänger," and therefore to refuse to deal with their harmonic logic. But even if we grant Schubert his fair share of textual inspiration, we cannot escape the fact that what that motivation produces are musical objects clothed in specific, pitch-based identities. It is hard to imagine that Schubert with all his facility could somehow suppress (or miraculously "lose") his competence as a harmonist when setting a text.[15]

---

11. "Obwohl also vor einer Überschätzung des Anteils der Männlichkeit am Gesammtbestande des Schubertliedes aus rein künstlerischen Gründen gewarnt werden muß, darf doch betont werden, daß die unleugbar vorhandene starke männliche Note der schubertschen Lyrik, die allem Weichlichen [a word choice only one phoneme removed from 'Weiblichen'] feind ist, einen durch und durch gesunden Grundzug verleiht und einen hohen sittlichen rang gewährleistet." "Der harmlose Leser muß die Verse als normales Liebeslied hinnehmen, und nichts spricht dafür, daß sich der Komponist über des Dichters wahre Gefühle im klaren gewesen wäre. Nichts freilich auch dagegen. Lafite nennt das Lied 'Du liebst mich nicht' merkwürdig modern und ungewohnt nervös, und im Mittelsatze des Liedes 'Die Liebe hat gelogen' verspürt er einen unsteten Gefühlsdrang." Walther Vetter, *Der Klassiker Schubert*, 2 vols. (Leipzig: Peters, 1953), 1:334–35).

12. Letter from Bruchmann to Platen, 8 November 1821: "Schubert setzt nicht nur das kleine Gedicht, das Sie mir sendeten, sondern noch mehrere aus den *Lyrischen Blättern*, unter andern d. 2 Winterlieder" (Platen, *Briefwechsel*, 2:275–76). See also the letter from late July/early August, quoted in note 9.

13. See especially V. Kofi Agawu, "Schubert's Harmony Revisited: The Songs 'Du liebst mich nicht' and 'Dass Sie hier gewesen,'" *Journal of Musicological Research* 9 (1989): 23–42; and Susan Youens, "Schubert and the Poetry of Graf August von Platen-Hallermünde," *Music Review* 46 (1985): 19–34.

14. Agawu hedges, but leans toward a negative evaluation: "But precisely because the overall effect of the song transcends what we would expect from a normative tonal-functionality, the song may be seen to aspire toward (but perhaps miss?) a higher status, the status of a masterpiece" ("Schubert's Harmony," 32).

15. Agawu, "Schubert's Harmony," 24. Surely this need not be the implication. A compelling musical portrayal of a poetic image of incoherence, for example, demands a calculated manipulation of patterns of harmonic expectation and denial, which—if it is not to sound merely muddled—requires a composer's utmost competence as a harmonist. Nonetheless, the musical surface in such a representation must appear at least partly unintelligible without reference to the text.

Agawu was of course right to remind us that if no underlying musical logic governed those ear-catching moments of syntactic disruption associated with poignant lines of text, the song would be unintelligible to us. But there is another equally important, if less rule-governed, component to the intelligibility and persuasiveness of Romantic song, which has to do with the comprehensiveness and consistency of the poetic vision governing the musical response to the poem. I do not mean to invoke the tangle of aesthetic questions that ask whether the composer's setting is true to the poet's intent—that is largely irrelevant here—but only whether the setting presents a coherent response, a *plausible* reading of the poem. More specifically, if a composer's music addresses aspects of poetic meaning not universally available, meanings lying "below the surface" of the text, so to speak, must this not have consequences for the comprehensibility of the music's surface? No demonstration of harmonic integrity will satisfy us if we are unpersuaded by the poetic or interpretive impulse that motivated the emphatic musical effects in the first place. The explication of "Du liebst mich nicht" I offer in the following pages will align the extravagance of Schubert's setting with the representation of a culturally specific, extreme affective state that is enciphered in a network of oblique images in Platen's poem.

Mein Herz ist zerrissen, du liebst mich nicht!
Du ließest mich's wissen, du liebst mich nicht!
Wiewohl ich dir flehend und werbend erschien,
Und liebebeflissen, du liebst mich nicht!
Du hast es gesprochen, mit Worten gesagt,
Mit allzugewissen, du liebst mich nicht!
So soll ich die Sterne, so soll ich den Mond,
Die Sonne vermissen? du liebst mich nicht!
Was blüht mir die Rose, was blüht der Jasmin?
Was blühn die Narzissen? du liebst mich nicht![16]

(My heart is torn apart, you love me not!
You have let me know it, you love me not!
Though I have pleaded with you, wooed you,
Appeared in ardent pursuit, you love me not!
You have spoken it, cast it in words,
In all too certain ones, you love me not!
So shall I the stars, so shall I the moon,
The sun relinquish? you love me not!
What to me are blossoming rose, jasmine,
The narcissi in bloom? you love me not!)

---

16. First published in Graf August von Platen, *Ghaselen* (Erlangen: Carl Heyder, 1821).

Platen's poem is a Persian-style *ghazal* of five couplets reflecting on the obsessive agony of unrequited passion. The emphatic declamation of its insistent refrain abruptly bumps up against the suppliant dactylic meter of the surrounding lines each time it recurs, inevitable and unyielding in its conclusion. The disjunction in meter arises from the fact that the word "liebst" has only one stressed syllable instead of the strong-weak accent the underlying meter demands. This can be simply illustrated by declaiming the second couplet with an additional syllable added to the refrain, substituting "liebest" for the word "liebst":

⏑ /‒ ⏑ ⏑/‒ ⏑ ⏑ /‒ ⏑ ⏑/‒
Wiewohl ich dir flehend und werbend erschien,

⏑/‒⏑⏑/‒ ⏑ ⏑/‒ ⏑ ⏑ / ‒
Und liebebeflissen, du lieb(est) mich nicht.

While smoothing out the metric irregularity, this alteration of course destroys the meaning of the refrain, for the softly insistent dactyls cannot support the harsh words of the conclusion, and, indeed, the clash in metric gears is integral to the effect of the poem. Each upcoming refrain replicates the poet's anxiety in the reader, for it is extremely difficult to tell precisely when to change metric gears and where to lay the strong stresses—on "du," on "liebst," or only on "mich." Each occurrence of the refrain is preceded by a harsh, almost hissing, interior rhyme that captures the tone of bitter reproach with which the poet assaults his unbending lover—*zerrissen, wissen, liebebeflissen, allzugewissen, vermissen,* and *Narzissen.* The emotional pitch rises with each formulaic iteration as the poet's self-indulgent ruminations turn from anguished, bitter reproach to suicidal despair.

At the opening of the song, the shifting rhythmic accents, closely spaced chords, and resonant middle register prepare the way for a series of cadential motions away from the tonic (ex. 6.2). Published in A minor (although originally composed in the remote key of G♯ minor), the first half of the song progresses with surprising rapidity to cadences on a series of chromatically descending key centers, all but one coinciding with a statement of the insistent refrain. The piano introduction anticipates these unsettling ventures to remote keys, ending its first phrase with a cadential movement to the submediant, F. The singer's first two cadences are firmly rooted in A minor, the tonic pitch squarely centered in the middle of the vocal range with the fifth scale degree forming the upper and lower melodic boundary. After the second A-minor cadence in measure 12, the music creates an impression of agitated, nervous movement, for the formulaic cadential articulations between measures 12 and 28 each come about through concise close-positioned voice leading only at the last possible moment, generally with the piano doubling the singer's melodic cadential formula in an inner voice. A movement toward G minor is abruptly cut off with the swerve to A♭ on the refrain at measure 20. Mostly upward-pushing semitone inflections and enharmonic reinterpretations of pitch lead to a somewhat weaker pause on G in measure 24

EXAMPLE 6.2. Franz Schubert, "Du liebst mich nicht," D 756.

and, at the next refrain, to a cadence on G♭ at measure 28. The music after measure 29, the exact midpoint of the song, is given to couplets 4 and 5, sung twice. From here on, the setting becomes more expansive as the regular four-bar phrase rhythm, which lent a certain predictability to the otherwise surprising cadential motions in the first 28 measures, breaks down. Between measures 29 and 40 and again in measures 41 to 52,

EXAMPLE 6.2. (*continued*)

couplet four is set as a five-bar phrase, and couplet five as a five-bar phrase, intensified by a two-bar extension.[17]

Significantly, these lines mark a decisive psychological shift in the poem. Torn by the hopelessness of his passion, the poet works himself into a state of frenzied despair, envisioning himself driven to take leave of the stars, the moon, the sun, of roses and jasmine—and of narcissus, a flower whose name resonates with a symbolism of mythic proportion. As the vocal line in the second half of the song gradually begins to creep upward, the singer's growing passion is reinforced by the register of the right hand, which doubles the singer as an outer voice for the first time at the refrain in measure 32. A return to the

---

17. Thus the two halves of the song take up exactly the same number of measures: The four-bar introduction is balanced by a four-bar postlude; the first three couplets each span 8 measures (4 + 4), totaling 24; couplets 4 and 5, sung twice, are asymmetrically divided 5 + 5 (+ 2), again totaling 24. Interestingly, in the early G♯-minor version, the piano postlude was five measures long, not four.

EXAMPLE 6.2. (*continued*)

tonic, but major, is brought about by a violent paroxysm that partially duplicates the shocking tone configuration in "Die Liebe hat gelogen": beginning in measure 35, a strong tendency to the neapolitan minor, B♭ minor, emerges together with the impassioned question "was blühn die Narzissen?" At the refrain in the following bars the expected resolution is emphatically denied: a dominant seventh on F is wrenched outward by half step to octave E♮'s framing an implied A-minor six-four, which resolves first to A minor and, at the convulsive repetition of the phrase, an octave below in the piano, to A major, in measure 40.[18] This major structural arrival coincides with the end of the poem. But Schubert repeats the poet's final couplets in the thus hard-won A major, which is twice threatened by a perilous phrase that sends out a shock wave of reverberations—harmonic, rhythmic, and registral—threatening to destroy the stability of the latter half of the song. The extraordinary rhyming phrases are boxed off on the score in example 6.2.

Schubert uses a turn to the parallel major within a predominantly minor context in a great number of his songs—especially in the song cycles—to represent a sudden immersion in memories, projections, or other forms of vivid imagination. Psychologically, the gesture seems right on the mark here, for with the repetition of the final couplets we imagine the poet transported ever more deeply into his terrible fantasy. The underlying horror of what he contemplates reverberates in the rhyming phrases that threaten to wrest the music to C♯ minor at "die Sonne vermissen" in measures 42 and 43 and again at "was blühn die Narzissen?" five bars later. The sudden harmonic instability is underscored by an explosion in register, with the singer hitting the melodic high point as the left hand extends the bass into the piano's deepest octave. Even the appearance of the notes on the page—the jagged cluster of sharps amassed above a G♯ root to form the distended dominant sevenths emphatically marked *fortissimo*—mirrors the intensity of the psychic disturbance. (These passages underwent striking revision between composition and eventual publication. For a discussion of the sources and plates of Schubert's autographs see appendix 6.2.)[19]

---

18. Nearly the same gesture—harmonic and registral—involving the same pitches as the G♯-minor version of "Du liebst mich nicht" occurs at the cadence before the trio in the *Moment musical*, op. 94, no. 6 in A♭ (from m. 66). *Les Plaintes d'un troubadour* was the suggestive title given to it in the first edition, published by Sauer und Leidesdorf in December 1824, as Edward T. Cone notes in "Schubert's Promissory Note: An Exercise in Musical Hermeneutics," in *Schubert: Critical and Analytic Studies*, ed. Walter Frisch (Lincoln: University of Nebraska Press, 1986), 30. An earlier version of Cone's essay appeared under the same title in *19th Century Music* 5 (1982): 233–41. Cone links the extreme language of this piece to Schubert's syphilis, so it is worth noting that Schubert's Platen settings predate that illness: the musical devices themselves do not have fixed meanings attached.

19. In the original version of the song in G♯ minor (both versions are printed in the old Breitkopf/Dover edition), this effect was somewhat weaker, for these measures were notated as a swerve to C minor. The extant autographs for the song are shown in plates 6.1 and 6.2 in appendix 6.2. Because the song veers to so many distant key centers, the transposition from G♯ minor to A minor affects the relationship between background home key and the places to which the song modulates. One might liken the relationship between the two conceptions to the relationship between a photographic negative and its print: in the G♯-minor version the key of the background is the most remote, and the modulations tend in the direction of the more familiar. In the A-minor version that relationship is reversed: the modulations move in the direction of greater tonal extremity from a more normative background. It is tempting to speculate that the original extreme choice of key, G♯ minor, may have held some symbolic significance for Schubert. If so, a residue of this significance is transferred in the A-minor version from the level of background key to the catastrophic measures on "vermissen" and "Narzissen" that swerve to C♯ minor. Charles Fisk is especially sensitive to Schubert's treatment of C♯ minor as a distant space in such pieces as the C-major "Wanderer" Fantasy, D 760, or the C♯-minor slow movement in the late B♭ sonata, D 960. Fisk, *Returning Cycles: Contexts for the Interpretation of Schubert's Impromptus and Last Sonatas*, California Studies in 19th Century Music, ed. Joseph Kerman (Berkeley: University of California Press, 2001). See also Vivian Ramalingam's further reflections on Schubert's transposition in a colloquy in *Journal of the American Musicological Society* 50 (1997): 530–36.

The tonal stability and, indeed, the very coherence of the song are placed in jeopardy with these two rhyming phrases, not because the harmony itself is so radical (unlike the abrupt modulations in the first half of the song, the harmonic tracks for a swerve toward C♯ minor have been carefully laid in the preceding measures) but because of the magnitude of the gesture, which on the face of it seems disproportionate to the underlying text. The stress on "vermissen" is intelligible enough, for it is this word that signals the suicidal intent in the poem. But why is the poet's invocation of the flower narcissus made to echo the psychological peril of the earlier phrase? There is no underlying musical necessity for a repetition of the phrase—of the sort dictated by a strophic setting, for example—and indeed, on the first pass through these lines in measures 29 through 40, Schubert does not treat the two passages as rhyming phrases. An inflection of this magnitude in Schubert's music cannot be without significance.

Why the two catastrophic phrases at "vermissen" and "Narzissen"? I shall propose a way of approaching this question, but first I would like to consider briefly two earlier critics' observations on the same passages. My point is to illustrate how profoundly our reading of the poem in fact affects the way we account for the musical events. In Agawu's analysis, full of astute insight into many aspects of the song, the two rhyming phrases peaking at measures 43 and 48 pass by surprisingly almost without comment. Although a graph representing the rising emotional temperature in the setting (as measured by the rising vocal line) explicitly identifies measure 43 as the high point of that process,[20] the rhyming phrase at measure 48 falls away in this representation, and neither the first high point nor its echo receives more than a fleeting mention in the text of the article. This is all the more striking as Agawu has earlier set aside his reluctance to address text-music relations to comment on the effect of Schubert's obsessive repetition of the refrain, which occurs only six times in Platen's poem but nine times in Schubert's song. "Because repetition generally implies emphasis," he writes, "it is reasonable to assume that Schubert's decision to give prominence to this phrase is motivated in part by a desire to dramatize the poem's tragic sentiment."[21] This would seem to be all the more true for the repetitious treatment of the two final couplets, which places the two climactic disturbances only three measures apart. But Agawu offers no poetic motivation for these inflections, and the analytic tools he draws on to account for the song's tonal construction and voice leading largely overlook nonteleological expressive effects, such as those depending on agogic accent or repetition. Voice-leading reductions, because they are primarily concerned with pitch trajectories, invariably give priority to the *first* instance a melodic high point is attained, even though the rhetorical effect of a later peak may be much more powerful.

A second critic addresses the events in bars 42 and 43 and 47 and 48 in even more telling fashion. In a 1985 article on the Platen settings, Susan Youens duly notes "both

---

20. Agawu, "Schubert's Harmony," 26.
21. Agawu, "Schubert's Harmony," 25.

fortissimo full cadences to C♯ minor," but she promptly deflects attention away from them with a parenthetical remark: "however emphatic, [they are] short-lived and immediately melt away."[22] In a song of fifty-six measures, a disturbance of this power cannot be short-lived: the disruption at "die Sonne vermissen" does not subside into a stabilizing cadence until the downbeat of measure 45, and the second rupture, beginning halfway through measure 47, sustains tension at the top of the singer's range—the high F♯ is repeatedly attacked—until the final vocal close in measure 52, just before the piano postlude sinks back into the minor mode. Youens not only fails to scrutinize the verbal impetus behind these emphatic inflections but also deliberately minimizes their effect. This is all the more surprising as she painstakingly accounts for virtually every other verbal inflection in the song.[23] Does this impulse of both critics to gloss over the events beginning in measures 42 and 47 result from a sense that the music in these bars is somewhat "out of sync" with the expressive import of the words it accompanies? This conjecture is lent some support at least in Youens's case by her revealing discussion of the language of Platen's poem at an earlier point in the essay. She does not conceal her distaste for Platen's poetry and, like Vetter, is concerned to account for why Schubert evidently never set any additional texts of Platen:

> The grief the poet so often expresses is stylized in the extreme, at times disconcertingly impersonal in tone, a curious amalgam of chiseled word-sculpture and a

---

22. Youens, "Schubert and the Poetry," 32. While I believe that Youens's observation in this case stems from a deeper wisdom, her account of the harmony in these songs is unreliable. For example, in "Die Liebe hat gelogen," she identifies the crucial chord on the downbeat of measure 16 merely as "the parallel major triad" (30), suppressing the seventh that allows it to behave as an augmented sixth (see ex. 6.1). The A-minor six-four chord this moves to in the middle of the measure and the similarly functioning incomplete chord in measures 37 and 39 of "Du liebst mich nicht" are repeatedly identified as first-inversion C-major triads (32). With characteristic generosity, David Gramit has replied to my comments in the previous sentence, granting the validity of either explanation of the voice leading in "Du liebst mich nicht," the one Youens put forth back in 1985 or mine. I happily accept his refinement that the arrival of the actual 6–4 against the bass E♮ is delayed by the contrapuntal descent 8–6, 7–5, then 6–4, 7–5–3, before resolving to A minor, but his defense of the 8–6 chord (with quadrupled E♮ and approached by a dominant-defining augmented sixth, F–E♭ [D♯]) as a possible dominant to F (the outnumbered C construed as root) simply does not reflect harmonic practice. When Schubert sends genuinely mixed harmonic signals to represent a distraught state of mind (as he does at the climactic *Geschrei* in "Der Doppelgänger," for instance), he becomes more, not less, attuned to the implications of voice leading. There often are problems when we attempt to reduce Schubert's harmony to four-part writing because he was enormously sensitive to the acoustics of doubling and to the pressure this exerted on the surrounding tones. See David Gramit, "Orientalism and the Lied: Schubert's 'Du liebst mich nicht,'" *19th Century Music* 27 (2003): 104.

23. So, for example: "Five times—on one occasion, twice in succession—we hear, not Platen's repeated phrase 'Du liebst mich nicht,' but a variant: 'du liebst, du liebst mich nicht' (the daisy-petal invocation, 'He loves me, he loves me not," comes irresistibly to mind). Schubert, whether consciously or unconsciously, understood the poet's self-torturing use of the phrase, the masochistic insistence on the simple and devastating words, and carries the repetition a step farther. The initial words 'Du liebst . . .' imply the reciprocal, returned love the poet so desperately wanted, followed by the truth, its polar opposite, 'Du liebst *mich nicht*'" (Youens, "Schubert and Poetry," 32).

certain obsessive quality, at times very unpleasant and grating, not because of any roughness of expression or want of craft and refinement but because everything but a single-minded insistence on grief is obliterated. The resulting poems appear as if within a vacuum, the result being a distinctive but often claustrophobic atmosphere. There *are* flowers—lilies, narcissuses, and roses—in "Mein Herz ist zerrissen, du liebst mich nicht!" but the nature imagery in which Schubert took such delight is not central to the poem—indeed, the poet asks bitterly why they should even bloom any longer.[24]

If indeed the flowers invoked in Platen's poem are to be understood as mere decorous nature imagery "not central to the poem," then Schubert's emphatic spotlighting of "Narzissen" makes absolutely no sense, for it would be simply a mindless echo of the earlier phrase. Why, then, the cataclysmic stresses on both "vermissen" and "Narzissen"? The internal rhyme that courses through Platen's *ghazal* is an invariant feature of that form. The poet must invent both a refrain that can be sustained and a resonant image from which to generate the subsequent rhymes. Which, then, is the central image here: "zerrissen," "vermissen," or "Narzissen"? A special emphasis is conferred on the culminating instance of the rhyme by another convention of *ghazal* writing, for in the Persian models Platen studied, the poet almost invariably identifies himself in the final couplet, sometimes only by oblique allusion. For Platen, the figure of Narcissus was a recurring object of reflection, an idée fixe, to which he returned again and again in his poetic oeuvre as well as in his diaries. The significance of the image for him is unequivocally associated both with his own powerful attractions to young men and with the social conditions that defined this "homosexual" experience above all as painful and frustrating for him. The *ghazal* "Mein Herz ist zerrissen, du liebst mich nicht" is an expression of autobiographical experience elevated to the universal through the evocation of myth.

II

It will be recalled that in Greek myth Narcissus is a young boy of astonishing beauty whose cold rejection of his admirer's advances drives one after another to despair, even suicide. Ovid opens the story of Narcissus in Book 3 of the *Metamorphoses* with a prophecy by the blind poet Tiresias, the only mortal to have experienced the world both as a woman and as a man. Asked how long a life the infant boy will lead, Tiresias replies with a cryptic reversal of the famous Delphic injunction to know thyself: Narcissus will grow old only if he does not know himself.

One of those most cruelly spurned by Narcissus was Echo, a nymph whom Juno (Hera) had robbed of her capacity to initiate speech, in retaliation for the verbal distractions she devised to protect Jove (Zeus) when he abandoned himself with the other nymphs.

---

24. Youens, "Schubert and the Poetry," 27–28.

Henceforth, Echo was capable only of repeating that which she had just heard. The first encounter between Echo and Narcissus is a disaster in communication. Unable to initiate dialogue, Echo must rely on her ability to inflect Narcissus's words to convey her own meaning. "Is anyone here?" Narcissus calls out. "Here!" Echo replies. "Come to me!" Narcissus shouts and Echo returns his words. Yet when Echo rushes forward to meet her beloved, Narcissus cries out, "Hands off! Embrace me not! May I die before I give you power over me!" "I give you power over me," Echo responds. Narcissus, not recognizing the aural reflection, only grows increasingly angry—and Echo increasingly distressed. The force of his rejection proves too great to bear. Poor Echo literally wastes away, all save her voice, which remains behind in the valleys and the hills as a plaintive reminder.

Narcissus does not learn from this lesson, continuing to disdain those drawn to him. Finally, when a young man Narcissus has held in contempt prays that he may love himself in vain as others have loved him, nature is transformed into a place of retribution. Narcissus, tired from hunting, comes upon a pool. Quenching his thirst, he becomes transfixed by the image he sees reflected in the water. When we fall in love, the ancients held, we are really falling in love with an image of ourselves in the eyes of the beloved. Narcissus carries this idea to its impossible extreme. Reaching out to embrace the vision over and over again, he becomes distraught with frustration: his beloved mimics his every move, yet a thin barrier of water prevents their union. Even the words Narcissus calls out to his beloved are mouthed on the lips of the statuesque figure in the pool, yet they produce no sound. In the end, the lack of an echo forces Narcissus to recognize himself, to acknowledge the impossibility of this union. As he dissolves into a flood of tears, which in turn causes the reflected image in the pool to dissolve, his passion is so overwhelming that it eventually consumes him. A flower, the narcissus, springs up in his place.[25]

Platen wrote the *ghazal* "Mein Herz ist zerrissen, du liebst mich nicht!" in the wake of the most emotionally turbulent affair of his life. As a student in Würzburg, in the early summer of 1818, he had been passionately drawn to a young man named Edouard Schmidtlein. Fearful of making contact with the object of his obsession, Platen charted the day-by-day course of his passion in his diary for nearly a full year before he finally learned Schmidtlein's name and paid him a visit. (The following discussion is based on the selection of entries from Platen's diaries given in appendix 6.1.) The diary entry of 14 June 1818 marks the beginning of the extended affair: "My age, my entire being calls out for love. As I am unable and uninterested in finding it in reality, I seek it in the ideal. I doubt that this youth, whom I shall call Adrast, though I do not know his name, could become something to me. I even avoid making his acquaintance so as not to rob myself of the beautiful deception."[26]

---

25. My retelling of the myth has benefited from Kenneth J. Knoespel's superb book *Narcissus and the Invention of Personal History*, Garland Publications in Comparative Literature (New York: Garland, 1985).

26. August von Platen, *Die Tagebücher des Grafen August von Platen*, ed. Georg von Laubmann and Ludwig von Scheffler, 2 vols. (Stuttgart: Cotta'sche Buchhandlung Nachfolger, 1896–1900; reprint, Hildesheim: Georg Olms Verlag, 1969), 2:66–67.

By the next day Platen noted with surprise his indifference to Adrast, an indifference at least partially spawned by the sobering recognition that "a relationship punishable by law can exist between men."[27] Precisely what significance the name Adrast—the young king who led the seven against Thebes to victory—may have held for Platen is not clear, but on other occasions in his life Platen also assigned mythological aliases to the objects of his passion. (Incidentally, there exists an early opera fragment by Schubert entitled *Adrast*, based on a libretto by Johann Mayrhofer, the troubled and ultimately suicidal poet with whom Schubert lived for several years as a young man. That libretto unfortunately has not survived in its entirety, but the opera is based on the story of Atys and Adrast as told by Herodotus. See also the remarks on *Adrast* in chapter 1, note 27.)

Over the following months, Platen's emotional pendulum continued to swing back and forth with increasing frequency. If on one day he would brood that no true friendship could ever be sustained between them, for Adrast showed no signs of interest in foreign languages or history, he would console himself soon after with a vision of teaching his young friend the southern languages. "Your beautiful soul would grasp them easily," he writes in his diary on 10 December 1818; "then we would read Calderón and Ariosto together. Your resonant voice would rise gently with the undulations of Spanish verse." Within hours, as the fantasy is once again shattered, Platen cries out in despair, "Wohl sah ich, daß du liebst, aber du liebst nicht mich."[28] The language comes uncannily close to the stresses Schubert has given the climactic final statements of the refrain in the Platen song—"Du liebst, du liebst mich nicht!"—and I am reminded of the singer Vogl's famous characterization of Schubert's poetic insight as clairvoyant, for Schubert could not have known the diary entry.

In the summer of 1819, Platen finally learned the young man's name and made direct contact with him. From this point on, for the next seven months, the language of the diaries shifts to French, which Platen had formerly reserved for correspondence with his parents. The most candid confessions and intimate reflections on the nature of his own sexuality are cast in a language both foreign and deeply personal. Within a matter of weeks the fear Platen had harbored the preceding winter—"you love, but it is not me you love"[29]—has been transformed in a letter to Schmidtlein, inscribed in the diary on 13 July 1819, into the bitter accusation "You love me . . . [but refuse to admit it!]"[30] Climactic revelations about his own sexuality, and Schmidtlein's, are recorded in the late summer of 1819, only months before Platen was to leave Würzburg to continue his

27. Platen, *Die Tagebücher*, 2:67.
28. Platen, *Die Tagebücher*, 2:155–57.
29. Platen, *Die Tagebücher*, 2:156.
30. Platen, *Die Tagebücher*, 2:298.

studies in Erlangen. On 26 July 1819 he writes: "Oh why, why has providence made me in this way? Why is it impossible for me to love women, why must I nourish such doomed inclinations, which never will be permitted, which never will be mutual?"[31] On 23 August Platen records:

> I met with Edouard at seven in the morning.. . .I told him that I know his secret and that there is no longer need for him to conceal it. I did not name it, and he continued to try to deceive me for a long time. But finally he could no longer deny that which I had clearly understood, just as he understands me. His secret is none other than the inability to love women and an overwhelming inclination toward his own sex. Those words were not spoken, but there no longer is any doubt.[32]

The poem "Mein Herz ist zerrissen, du liebst mich nicht" could almost be carved out of the diary entries, so closely do their words correspond. Note the excerpts of 25 March and 10 April 1819 (appendix 6.1), in which the image of the torn heart is explicitly linked to the prospect of suicide.[33] The emotional force of the repeated refrains echo language like that in the letter to Schmidtlein of 13 July 1819: "You love me or you would possess an ability to deceive surpassing the darkest of demons."[34] Interspersed with his reflections on this affair, Platen remarks in the diary on the literature he has been reading: he admires, among other things, the myth of Narcissus in Ovid's *Metamorphoses* and Calderón's play on the same subject.[35] In a private poem in the diary addressed to Adrast (21 November 1818), Platen explicitly associates him with Narcissus: "Have you, like Narcissus, perhaps seen your image in the pool, to disdain all that is foreign, whose likeness does not match yours?" And in a series of private poems composed on subsequent days, Adrast is compared to two other beautiful youths in Greek myth, Hyacinth and Ganymede.[36] Hyacinth, the beloved of the sun god, Apollo, was tragically killed when he resisted the advances of Zephyr, the West Wind; and—like Narcissus—his remains gave rise to a flower, the hyacinth. Ganymede, the favorite of Zeus, was chosen to serve as cupbearer to the heavenly father, much to Hera's dismay.

The three beautiful youths have frequently been brought into close association with one another in both literary and visual representations from vastly remote historical periods. Often made to look almost interchangeable—boyish figures with curly locks— each one nonetheless conjures up distinctly different emotional resonances. In his book *Ganymede in the Renaissance*, James Saslow showed that over a three-year span

---

31. Platen, *Die Tagebücher*, 2:302.
32. Platen, *Die Tagebücher*, 2:310–11.
33. Platen, *Die Tagebücher*, 2:231–34, 245–47.
34. Platen, *Die Tagebücher*, 2:295–97.
35. Platen, *Die Tagebücher*, 2:309, 312–13.
36. Platen, *Die Tagebücher*, 2:134–39.

Benvenuto Celllini produced statues on the subjects of Narcissus, Apollo and Hyacinth, and Ganymede and the Eagle. Even the block of marble used to carve Narcissus was taken over from the Ganymede project.[37] In Thomas Mann's homage to Platen, *Death in Venice*, the figure of Tadzio is explicitly likened to all three beautiful youths in the same chapter of the novella.[38] Some years later, in an essay on Platen, Mann speculated that Platen's choice of poetic forms and indeed his preoccupation with formal beauty were a direct consequence of his eros:

> His only masquerade lay in the selection of traditional lyric forms in which
> he poured himself out and which also extended a sense of tradition to his

37. James M. Saslow, *Ganymede in the Renaissance: Homosexuality in Art and Society* (New Haven, Conn.: Yale University Press, 1986), 142–74. Readers familiar with Maynard Solomon's work on Schubert's sexuality will recognize the connection to Eduard von Bauernfeld's [August 1826] diary entry associating Schubert's ailment with the "young peacocks" of Benvenuto Cellini. Solomon, "Franz Schubert and the Peacocks of Benvenuto Cellini," *19th Century Music* 12 (1989): 193–206. I place the date in square brackets because Bauernfeld's original diaries do not survive, only the copy does of selected entries that he produced many years after the fact. Thanks to our colleagues nearer Vienna, we now know that the parenthetical remark about the young peacocks actually appears in the margin with a caret showing its point of insertion into Bauernfeld's text. A facsimile of this page of the copied diary is shown in Dürhammer, *Schuberts literarische Heimat*, 269, and in the exhibition catalog by Till Gerrit Waidelich and Ilija Dürhammer, *Schubert 200 Jahre* (Heidelberg: Braus, 1997), 34. Interest in the passage was sparked by Solomon's 1989 proposal. In a subsequent special issue of *19th Century Music* devoted to Solomon's proposal (he too has another contribution), I noted some of the textual problems surrounding Bauernfeld's diaries, but this was before I had seen the manuscript myself and knew only Glossy's introduction to the published excerpts (*Aus Bauernfelds Tagebüchern*, ed. Carl Glossy [Vienna: Carl Konegen, 1895]). Kristina Muxfeldt, "Political Crimes and Liberty, or Why Would Schubert Eat a Peacock?" *19th Century Music* 17 (1993): 47–64. That an editor would have silently added those quotation marks seemed to me sufficiently improbable to allow an exploration of what "young peacocks" meant, but I noted that I was relying on the transcriptions in Deutsch and the Bauernfeld literature; I was glad to learn that the manuscript bears me out. Even less certain now is whether Bauernfeld's parenthetical solution to his circumspect riddle "Schubert half-ill (he requires 'young peacocks' like Benv. Cellini!)" genuinely dates from 1826 or whether it was added a half century later with a view to publication. The entries omitted from the early twentieth-century publications, incidentally, are all clearly indicated in Bauernfeld's manuscript, which is housed in the Handschriftensammlung of the Wienbibliothek im Rathaus, and which I have since examined long enough to know that an unexpurgated modern edition would be welcome. (I am not the scholar to do this, I realized, after spending the better part of a day hunting down a reference to a person from someplace that sounded like a town, but which turned out to be the name of a local wine that my hosts knew instantly.)

38. Thomas Mann, *Death in Venice*, trans. and ed. Clayton Koelb, Norton Critical Edition (New York: Norton, 1994), 39–43 (chap. 4). In a letter to Carl Maria von Weber of 4 July 1920, Mann reveals that the story he initially intended to tell "was not homoerotic at all," but was to concern the aged Goethe and a young girl in Marienbad. This idea was abandoned after a "personal, lyric travel experience . . . made me determined to carry things to the pinnacle by introducing the motif of 'forbidden' love." Earlier in the letter he recalls, "I strove for the balance of sensuality and morality that I found ideally perfected in *Elective Affinities*, which I read five times during my work on Death in Venice, if I remember correctly" (quoted in the Norton Critical Edition, 96–97). The considerable influence of Platen on Mann's work generally, and on *Death in Venice* specifically, is discussed in the epilogue to August von Platen, *Lyrik: Werke*, vol. 1, ed. Kurt Wölfel and Jürgen Link (Munich: Winkler Verlag, 1982), 963–82.

mode of feeling: the persian *ghazal*, the Renaissance sonnet, the pindaric ode all knew the cult of youths and lent it literary legitimacy. Because he took them over from the past—and with what unheard of artistic brilliance he recast them!—their emotional content could also appear borrowed, as an archaicizing convenience, impersonal and therefore possible in this world. I am thus convinced that his choice of [the] poetic genres he so excelled in stemmed from the source of all his enthusiasm and his suffering—not solely as an accommodation, out of fear, as Heine believed, but rather especially because the markedly formal and form-oriented character of these genres shared an artistic-psychological affinity with his own eros. "The degree and character of a person's sexuality," says Nietzsche, "extends into the highest reaches of his spiritual constitution."[39]

Mann's analysis builds upon an ancient trope, for the association of male same-sex desire with a love of formal beauty goes back at least as far as Diotima's address to Socrates in Plato's *Symposium* on the nature and proper constitution of erotic bonds between men.

But what could Schubert possibly have known about any of this? He certainly did not have access to Platen's diaries, and there is no reason to believe the two ever met personally. They did share a mutual friend. Franz von Bruchmann, one of the most intellectually ambitious members of the circle around Schubert, spent a semester in the spring of 1821 at the University of Erlangen, where both he and Platen attended Schelling's lectures on, among other things, mythology.[40] The two quickly became fast friends. Bruchmann took a lively interest in Platen's poetry, even delaying his trip back to Vienna in the summer to

---

39. "Seine einzige Maskerade lag in der Wahl der überlieferten lyrischen Formen, in denen er sich ausströmte und die auch seiner Gefühlsart eine Überlieferung boten: Das persische Ghasel, das Renaissancesonett, die Pindarsche Ode kannten den Knabenkult und verliehen ihm literarische Legitimität; indem er sie übernahm—und mit wie unerhörtem Kunstglanz neu bildete!—, konnte auch der Gefühlsinhalt als übernommen, als archaisierende Konvenienz und als unpersönlich wirken und damit Weltmöglich werden. So bin ich überzeugt, daß die Wahl der poetischen Gattungen in denen er glänzte, vom Quellpunkte all seiner Begeisterung und seiner Leiden her bestimmt war; doch nicht allein aus Rücksicht, aus Furchtsamkeit, wie Heine meinte, sondern vor allem, weil der stark formale und formenplastische Charakter dieser Gattungen eine Kunstpsychologische Affinität zu seinem Eros besaß. 'Grad und Art der Geschlechtlichkeit eines Menschen,' sagt Nietzsche, 'reichen bis in die höchsten Gipfel seiner Geistigkeit.'" Thomas Mann, "Platen-Tristan-Don Quichotte" [1930], in *Thomas Mann Essays*, ed. Hermann Kurzke and Stephan Stachorski, vol. 3 (Frankfurt am Main: S. Fischer, 1994), 252. For another appreciation of the role of Platen's sexuality in his oeuvre, see Hubert Fichte, "I Can't Get No Satisfaction: Zur Geschichte der Empfindungen des Grafen August von Platen-Hallermünde," in *Homosexualität und Literatur 2: Die Geschichte der Empfindlichkeit, Paralipomena 1*, ed. Hubert Fichte (Frankfurt am Main: S. Fischer, 1988), 183–234.

40. Bruchmann returned to Erlangen for a formal series of lectures on mythology in the late summer of 1823. Platen, *Tagebücher*, 2:588–90 [24 August–6 September 1823]. See also the letter to Platen from the end of July/early August 1822, partially quoted in note 9.

await the publication of the *Ghaselen*. He brought multiple copies back home with him, delivering them to the important community of Persian scholars in Vienna, to Friedrich Schlegel, and to various other acquaintances, and he frequently headed the reading circle Schubert and his friends had formed.[41]

Bruchmann and Platen continued to correspond over the next years, even forging plans—which never materialized—for an ambitious poetic-philosophical journal. Schubert's name regularly courses through their correspondence. Bruchmann even promised to send Platen several of Schubert's Goethe settings, and he sent the setting of "Die Liebe hat gelogen" through the mail. Around the same time, Platen began to take piano lessons.[42] Bruchmann announced the composition of "Du liebst mich nicht" in the letter of late summer 1822, alluded to earlier, in which he described the song as "entrancing."[43] We can presume, I think, that Platen received a copy of "Du liebst mich nicht" as well, though there is no record of this in either his diary or his correspondence. Bruchmann and Platen met in the city of Linz only weeks after the song was composed, however. That meeting was laden with resonant implications, for Bruchmann's stop in Linz was part of a larger walking tour through Linz, Salzburg, and ultimately Innsbruck, where Bruchmann was headed to convey greetings and support from his Viennese friends to Johann Chrisostomus Senn, the gifted young poet whose lodgings in Vienna the police had raided (after his diary had fallen into the hands of an informant) during a celebration for a fellow student.[44]

As frequently as the story of Senn has been repeated in the Schubert literature, it has remained the most mystifying event in the lives of this circle of friends. Schubert and

---

41. Platen's correspondence from that autumn is filled with references to people who received copies. See especially Bruchmann's letter from 11 September 1821 (Platen, *Briefwechsel*, 2:260–62). Deutsch notes that in 1822 Bruchmann subscribed to fifty copies of Platen's second volume of *ghazals* (*Lyrische Blätter*) and purchased an additional forty copies for his Viennese friends (Deutsch, *Dokumente*, 158 [1 July 1822]). The extent to which this poetry was circulating among Schubert's friends is further suggested by the fact that Matthäus von Collin (encountered also in chapter 1), a cousin of Joseph von Spaun as well as a friend of Bruchmann's, wrote an extensive review of Hammer-Purgstall's translations of Persian poetry together with the Persian collections of Goethe, Platen, and Rückert for the Vienna *Jahrbücher der Literatur* in 1822 (vol. 19, 142–68). Schubert's settings of Collin date from this period as well, and in 1822 and 1823, toward the end of his life, Collin hosted several Schubertiads.

42. Platen, *Tagebücher*, vol. 2: 1 April 1821 (Platen anticipates publication of the *Ghaselen* the following week. Bruchmann will delay his departure until then, he notes; he has also shown Bruchmann two earlier volumes of his poetry); 7 April 1821 (Schelling and Bruchmann receive the first two copies, each with dedicatory sonnets; in the following days, Platen sends copies to members of his family, to Rückert, to other friends, and to Goethe); Platen, *Briefwechsel*, vol 2: 2 August 1821 (Bruchmann offers to send Platen Goethe settings by Schubert); 5 (11) September 1821 (Bruchmann announces that he is sending Platen several Goethe settings by Schubert, and "Ihres erhielt Schubert noch nicht, weil er nicht hier ist"); 8 November 1821 ("Schubert setzt nicht nur das kleine Gedicht, das Sie mir sendeten, sondern noch mehrere aus den *Lyrischen Blättern*, unter andern d. 2 Winterlieder"); 17 April 1822 ("Beyliegend finden Sie Ihr Gedicht in Musik nach Wunsch"—presumably, "Die Liebe hat gelogen"). See also Deutsch, *Dokumente*, 134 [2 August 1821].

43. Platen, *Briefwechsel*, 2:320, end of July 1822 (see n. 9 above). The earliest autograph of "Du liebst mich nicht" bears the date July 1822.

44. Platen, *Tagebücher*, 2:554–57 [22 September–3 October 1822]; Deutsch, *Dokumente*, 162 [8 September 1822].

Franz von Bruchmann had escaped that incident in January 1820 with only police reprimands (Schubert also with a black eye), but Senn was incarcerated for fourteen months before being exiled from Vienna for life. In the two months before this drastic sentence was handed down, Bruchmann left the country to study in Erlangen, where he soon met Platen, Schubert moved out of the room he had shared for several years with the poet Johann Mayrhofer, and the first of the Schubertiads was held (further ramifications are considered in chapter 1).[45] In this context I should like to recall the internal police memorandum on the incident, a document whose official bureaucratic prose is at once reticent and full of innuendo. The purpose of the investigation, the memo stated, was to determine the nature of Senn's *"vita ante acta*, his private and personal affairs, his *Gemüthsbeschaffenheit*, and finally, his moral and political beliefs and actions."[46] Last on this list are Senn's political actions, and even after months of investigation the charges against him were never clarified. It is perhaps no coincidence that August von Platen would use very similar language to allude to his own homosexuality: he begged forgiveness from the future readers of his diaries for his "unfeste und unglückliche *Gemüthsart*."[47]

This brings me back to the emotional extremity conveyed by those wrenching harmonies on the phrase "betrogen, ach betrogen, hat alles mich umher" in the first of the Platen songs. Walther Dürr, editor of the song volumes of the New Schubert Edition, has speculated that op. 23, containing "Die Liebe hat gelogen" as well as two songs on poems by Johann Senn, "Selige Welt" and "Schwanengesang," and one by Franz Schober, "Schatzgräbers Begehr," is to be understood as Schubert's show of solidarity with Senn.[48] The hypothesis is buttressed by a passage from Senn's memoirs,

---

45. Deutsch, *Dokumente*, 115 [30 January 1821]; 116 [Schubert's letter to his brother Ferdinand, from early 1821]; and 134 [2 August 1821].

46. "In Erwartung des umständlichen Berichts über die Constituirung des ganz mit recht in das Polizeyhaus verschafften Privatstudierenden Joh. Senn und der näheren Aufklärung über seine vita ante acta, seine Privat und persönlichen Verhältnisse, Gemüthsbeschaffenheit, dann moralische und politische Denkungs und Handlungsweise, wird der Pol.Ob.Dir., der anher vorgelegte Rapport des Pol.Ob.Coars [Polizeioberkommissärs] Ferstl über das unanständige Benehmen dieses Verhafteten bey der angeordneten Visitation und Beschlagnahme seiner Schriften sowie über die gegen die Regg [Regierung] von ihm ausgestossenen Beleidigungen im Anschlusse mit dem Bedeuten zurückgestellt, daß es dem Zwecke der wider ihn anhängigen Untersuchung angemessen zu seyn scheine, die Studenten Bruchmann und St[r]einsberg über ihre Bekanntschaft mit Senn, und über die Natur, Zwecke, dann Entstehungsweise, so wie über ihre etwaige Theilnahme am Commersiren, endlich über ihr bei Senns Verhaftung beobachtetes Benehmen streng zu constituiren und nach Befund gegen selbe die Amtshandlung einzuleiten, deren Erfolg die Pol.Ob.Dir. sofort hieher anzuzeigen haben wird." This is the second of two police memos reproduced by Moriz Enzinger; the first memo also names Schubert as a participant (Enzinger "Franz v. Bruchmann, der Freund J. Chr. Senns und des Grafen Aug. v. Platen: Eine Selbstbiographie aus dem Wiener Schubertkreise nebst Briefen," *Veröffentlichungen des Museum Ferdinandeum in Innsbruck* 10 [1930]: 285–87). See also Deutsch, *Dokumente*, 87–89 [March 1820].

47. Platen, *Tagebücher*, 2:iii.

48. Walther Dürr, "Lieder für den verbannten Freund: Franz Schubert und sein Freundeskreis in Opposition zum Metternich-Regime," in *Zeichen Setzung: Aufsätze zur musikalischen Poetik* (Kassel: Bärenreiter Verlag, 1992), 135–40.

written in 1849, in which the poet alludes to the veiled political meanings in the two poems he contributed:

> The German struggles for liberation, from 1813 to 1815, had left in their wake a significant spiritual upheaval in Austria as well. Among other things, there gathered in Vienna at the time, quite by instinct rather than by design, a tremendous, companionable circle of young writers, poets, artists and intellectuals, which, after its dissolution, sowed seeds of the future in every direction. . . . It was in this environment that Franz Schubert composed his songs. . . . My poems, too, some of which Schubert set to music, originated in this circle in part, or were connected with it or are to be regarded as echoes of it, even though the inconstant present also maintains its claims. As unworthy as these works are to be placed alongside the works of the others alluded to above, they do not conceal their origins, in both narrow and broader senses of the term, which, indeed, they often acknowledge by the language in which they are clothed.[49]

All four songs were composed fairly close to the time of Bruchmann's visit to Senn, and while no autograph corresponding to the selection of songs in the publication has survived, it is hard to imagine that Schubert would not have had a hand in this decision. The opus contained songs based on the poetry of a man banished from the city, and its publication hinged on the approval of the censorship bureau, headed by chief of police Joseph Sedlintzky, the same man who directed the investigation of the Senn affair (and whose office held up the publication of the opus containing "Ganymed"—op. 19—for nearly three years).[50] Heard against the backdrop of these incidents, the terrible harmony on "betrogen"

---

49. "Die deutschen Befreiungskämpfe 1813 bis 1815 hatten auch in Österreich eine bedeutende geistige Erhebung zurückgelassen. Unter anderem hatte sich in Wien damals gleichsam instinktmäßig, ohne alle Verabredung, ein großartiger geselliger Kreis von jungen Literaten, Dichtern, Künstlern und Gebildeten zusammengefunden, der nach seiner Auflösung nach allen Richtungen Samen der Zukunft streute. . . . In diesem Kreise dichtete Franz Schubert seine Gesänge. . . . Auch meine Gedichte, von denen Schubert einige in Noten setzte, entstanden in diesem Kreise zum Teil oder stehen in Beziehung zu demselben oder sind als Nachklänge zu betrachten, wenn auch die wechselvolle Gegenwart ihr Recht behält. So wenig würdig dieselben sind, den oben angedeuteten anderen Erzeugnissen anderer an die Seite gesetzt zu werden, so verleugnen sie meist nicht ihren Ursprung im engeren und weiteren Sinne des Wortes, die sie häufig auch durch ihre Einkleidung bekennen." Cited in Harry Goldschmidt, *Franz Schubert: Ein Lebensbild* (Leipzig: VEB Deutscher Verlag für Musik, 1976), 142–43. Also quoted in Dürr, "Lieder für den verbannten Freund," 135. For a discussion of the close associations between political and sexual freedom in early nineteenth-century Vienna, see my "Political Crimes and Liberty," 47–64.

50. In any case, Senn's name was suppressed in the first edition of op. 23. Deutsch doubted the validity of the official explanation for the delay in publishing op. 19 that it was necessary to obtain permission from Goethe for the dedication (*Dokumente*, 288 [6 June 1825]). Ernst Hilmar has discussed the suppression of Senn's name in op. 23. He notes, too, that the documents concerning the Senn affair that one would expect to find in the police archives are all either missing or being withheld (Hilmar, *Franz Schubert in seiner Zeit* [Vienna: Hermann Böhlaus Nachfolger, 1985], 21).

seems hardly extravagant. Whatever specific events Senn's poems may have recalled to Schubert's friends, Platen's poem makes explicit that the world's betrayal is a betrayal of eros.

Just how much Schubert might have known through Bruchmann or others about Platen's private life is not entirely clear (though certainly the European intellectual community was small, and news traveled quickly). But his setting of this passage and, even more conclusively, his treatment of the two rhyming phrases in "Du liebst mich nicht" suggest he had a fairly good idea. The perilous phrase on the word "vermissen" and its echo a few bars later on "Narzissen" identify the two terms in the poem needed to call up the myth of Narcissus—with all its attendant resonances. Schubert's music conveys an indirect meaning by the same strategy Echo used to communicate with Narcissus: he inflects the meaning of a deceptively bland text—"Was blühn die Narzissen?"—by means of a well-placed echo, thereby jeopardizing the surface coherence of the song. Indeed, the part of the myth that deals with Echo's mode of communication may be understood as a lesson in the creation of hidden meaning.[51]

If this seems an unduly subtle interpretation, one need only look at the poems surrounding "Mein Herz ist zerrissen, du liebst mich nicht!" in the edition of the *ghazals* that Schubert worked from to see how he might have arrived at the same poetic insight with little if any additional outside stimulus. Before turning to several of these poems, however, I must interject that the homoerotic aspect of Platen's poetry was an almost immediate factor in its reception, as evidenced by Heinrich Heine's famous attack on Platen in *Die Bäder von Lucca*, contained in part 3 of the *Reisebilder* (published in 1828). Nor was Heine alone in his judgment. Adalbert von Chamisso reproached not only Platen but also Goethe, the latter for the poetic precedent he set in "coquetting" with the foreign practice of "Knabenliebe" in the *West-östlicher Divan*.[52] Ludwig Robert, the brother of Rahel Varnhagen and a friend of Heine's, wrote a review of Platen's poetry in 1829, in which the poems addressed to Franz von Bruchmann and Carl Theodor German are explicitly held up as evidence that what might have been considered merely a poetical conceit in the orientalizing *Ghaselen* reflects a fundamental trait in the poet's nature:

> Up to this point—as is proper for an honest criticism—this critique has quietly kept pace with the hand of the poet, strictly perhaps, but yielding to his thoughts

---

51. The communicative power of carefully placed verbal stress is humorously illustrated in a 1988 cartoon by Kate Charlesworth entitled "Benjamin Britten met Peter Pears..." (reproduced in Philip Brett, "Musicality, Essentialism, and the Closet," in *Queering the Pitch: The New Gay and Lesbian Musicology*, ed. Philip Brett, Elizabeth Wood, and Gary C. Thomas [New York: Routledge, 1994], 20). Unusual inflections, syntactic breaks, extravagant punctuation, or ruptures in the normal rhythm of a discourse are common methods of signaling veiled meanings. Eduard von Bauernfeld's reference to Schubert's need for "young peacocks" (in which the quotation marks signal a metaphorical usage) is one example. For references to literature on this diary passage, see this chapter, note 37.

52. See Paul Derks, *Die Schande der heiligen Päderastie: Homosexualität und Öffentlichkeit in der deutschen Literatur 1750–1850*, Homosexualität und Literatur 3 (Berlin: Rosa Winkel, 1990), esp. 271, 617.

and feelings with as much benevolence and as impersonally as possible. So that, for example, it took the *ghazals*, which sing the praises of the beautiful cup-bearer, as mere fictions, as imitations of oriental life. But now, with the friend-ship-poems directed to F. v. B and C. T. G. it is violently torn from this attitude. In shock it now lets drop the hand of the young poet and addresses him earnestly and with indignation, stepping into the office of judge accorded it, which must censure even the appearance of publicly offended custom. Surely these friend-ships, since they show themselves to the world so openly, so uninhibitedly, surely, they are sacred and pure. But the feverish manner in which these feelings of friendship are expressed does not elevate the heart, but rather enrages it. The sight of the most grotesque misbirth could not be more repugnant than the glowing physical praise of youths in these beautiful poems, this weak hankering, these petty jealousies, this sniveling over rejection, this unfeminine femininity in the feeling of friendship!⁵³

This much said, table 6.1 gives three *ghazals* found on the pages adjacent to "Mein Herz ist zerrissen, du liebst mich nicht!" in the edition of 1821. Most immediately illumi-nating is "Komm und brich des jungen Jahres Hyazinthen," a delicately erotic poem that uses the hyacinth as its refrain. In its second couplet—the only couplet where the word order forces us to strain to make sense of the refrain—the hyacinth is defined as having a secret meaning. A proper word order would put the flowers at the beginning of the sentence—"hyacinths point to a sweet secret, a still one, known only to the two of us"—whereas the imperative of the poetic form conveniently shifts them to this remote

---

53. "Bis hierher—wie es einer redlichen Kritik geziemt—schritt sie ruhig an der Hand des Dichters fort: streng zwar, doch seinen Gedanken und Gefühlen so wohlwollend und so unpersönlich als möglich sich hinge-bend. So z.B. nahm sie die Gaselen, welche den schönen Schenken besingen, als blosse Fictionen, als Nach-bildungen des Orientalischen Lebens. Nun aber, bei den Freundschaftsgedichten an *F. v. B.* und *C. T. G.* wird sie gewaltsam aus dieser Hingebung herausgerissen. Erschreckt lässt sie die Hand des jungen Dichters fahren, und redet ihn Ernst an und entrüstet, das ihr auferlegte Amt einer Richterin verwaltend, die auch selbst den Anschein nur der öffentlich verletzten Sitte zu rügen hat. Sicherlich sind diese Freundschaften, da sie sich der Welt so offenkundig, so ungefangen zeigen, sicherlich sind sie heilig und rein; aber die fie-berische Art, mit welcher sich dieses Freundschaftsgefühl ausdrückt, erhebt das Herz nicht, empört es. Der Anblick der eckelhaftesten Missgeburt kann nicht widerlicher seyn, als, in diesen schönen Versen, das glüh-ende Körperlob der Jünglinge, dieses für sie kraftlose Schmachten, diese Eifersüchtelei, dieses jammervolle Verschmähtseyn, diese unweibliche Weibheit im Gefühle der Freundschaft!" (quoted in Derks, *Die Schande der heiligen Päderastie*, 505). Robert's calculated expression of his moral outrage through the feminine voice of "Die Kritik" resists translation into English. The only poem of Platen explicitly addressed to Franz von Bruchmann is the dedicatory sonnet the poet inscribed in Bruchmann's copy of the *Ghaselen*, made public in 1828 (see Platen, *Lyrik*, 371). It is not one of Platen's more effusive expressions of friendship, which may lead one to wonder if Robert was basing his judgment on other information. The "schöne Schencke" is a

TABLE 6.1

Three poems from August von Platen's *Ghaselen* (Erlangen: Carl Heyder, 1821)

Es tagt, es wirft aufs Meer den Streif der Sonne;	It dawns, casting upon the sea a trail of sun;
Aufflatternd sucht der junge Greif* die Sonne;	Fluttering up the young condor seeks the sun;
Auch du blick auf und singe Morgenhymnen,	You too: gaze up and sing morning hymns,
Als aller Wesen bild begreif die Sonne;	As an image of every creature grasp the sun;
Die Sonne sei dir jede volle Rose,	Let every vibrant rose be to you the sun;
Und jeder Pfirsich, rund und reif, die Sonne;	And every peach, round and ripe, the sun;
Du siehst den Pfau, der durch den Garten schreitet,	You see the peacock, strutting through the garden,
Und dir enthüllt sein schöner Schweif die Sonne;	And his beautiful fan unveils to you the sun;
Und schmückt den Schah die Krone mit Demanten,	And the shah, adorned with a diadem of diamonds,
Bedeutet ihm der goldne Reif die Sonne.	To him its golden rays stand for the sun.
Komm und brich des jungen Jahres Hyazinthen;	Come and pluck the young year's hyacinths;
Laß mich locken deines Haares Hyazinthen;	Let me curl [entice] your locks' hyacinths;
Auf ein süß Geheimniß deuten, auf ein stilles,	Pointing to a sweet secret, a still one,
Und allein uns Beiden klares, Hyazinthen;	Known only to the two of us, hyacinths;
Nicht allein im Morgenlande, allenthalben	Not solely in the orient, in all places
Blühn des frohen Liebespaares Hyazinthen;	Blossom joyful lovers' hyacinths;
Brach doch auch der Muselmann im Abendlande	For even the Moslem in the West did pluck,
Am Xenil und Manzanares Hyazinthen.	On the Genil and Manzanares, hyacinths.
Nach lieblicherm Geschicke sehn ich mich,	For a lovelier destiny I yearn,
Wie nach dem Stab die Wicke, sehn ich mich;	Like the sweet pea for the pole I yearn,
Nach deines Mundes Duft, nach deines Haars	For your mouth's scent, for your locks'
Geringel am Genicke sehn ich mich;	Ringlets at the nape I yearn;
Ich sehne mich, daß poche mir dein Herz,	I yearn that your heart should beat for me,
Daß mich dein Arm umstricke, sehn ich mich;	That your arms should encircle me, I yearn;
Du gehst, o Schönheit, mich so stolz vorbei,	O Beauty, you pass by me so proudly,
Nach einem zweiten Blicke sehn ich mich!	For a second glance I yearn!

*An image of Ganymede?

---

recurring theme in these Persian imitations. On the double meaning of the word "Schenke" ("cupbearer" and "inn") in Goethe's "Schenkenbuch," the part of the *West-östlicher Divan* most explicitly concerned with homoerotic motifs, see Robert D. Tobin, "In and against Nature: Goethe on Homosexuality and Hetero-textuality," in *Outing Goethe and His Age*, ed. Alice A. Kuzniar (Stanford, Calif.: Stanford University Press, 1996), 99.

position, half concealing, half insisting on their hidden meaning. And if the simile of the curled locks as hyacinths plays upon a subtly gendered trope, the joyful lovers' blossoming hyacinths in the third couplet leaves little to the imagination.[54]

Similarly gendered images pervade the other two *ghazals*, despite their careful avoidance of revealing pronouns. In "Es tagt, es wirft aufs Meer den Streif der Sonne," the celebration of the masculine sun—Apollo, Helios—is intermixed with the exotic imagery of the southern fruit, the peacock, the bejeweled shah, and the rose, all staple images in the vocabulary of Platen's model, the *ghazals* of the fourteenth-century Persian poet Hafis, much of whose poetry is explicitly homoerotic.[55] "Nach lieblicherm Geschicke sehn ich mich" may similarly be understood to conjure up a masculine beloved: "for your mouth's scent, for your lock's ringlets at the nape I yearn." The dictates of nineteenth-century fashion would only allow the locks of one sex to converge at the nape, and as for "mouth's scent," "sweet lips" would perhaps have been a more likely feminine image. But the most highly gendered term in this network of associations is the one that defies the gender of the article with which it is implicitly paired: *Schönheit*, Beauty personified, is always obliquely defined as masculine in Platen's poetry. Thomas Mann would later explore this usage in his essay on Platen:

For what is "the Beautiful"? For what to us in the present is this concept made of alabaster, this at once sweet and schoolmasterly concept of proportion, regularity and golden mean, and what was it already at that time, a time of rising realism and the dawn of a social modernity? The Beautiful—is it the knee of the youth, upon

---

54. In his critical notes to the *West-östlicher Divan* (1819), Goethe discussed two ways in which hidden meanings are constructed in oriental poetry. The first involves the language of flowers. It is not that specific flowers have fixed meanings and are used as a coded language, he argues, but that devising and solving puzzles is part of the "oriental national character." The recipient of a love poem cast in flower language must try out various rhymes until he or she is able to divine the intended message. A second way of enciphering meaning in oriental poetry is based on the fact that in the East everyone learns the Koran by heart, so that just the hint of an allusion will speak to a reader practiced in this art. A similar effect can be achieved in the West through the use of biblical or classical allusion: "Gleicherweise bedient man sich klassischer Worte, wodurch wir Gefühl und Ereignis als ewig wiederkehrend bezeichnen und aussprechen" ("in the same way one may draw upon classical expressions, whereby feelings and events are characterized and expressed as eternally recurring). Johann Wolfgang Goethe, *West-östlicher Divan* (Stuttgart: Cottaische Buchhandlung, 1819; reprint, Frankfurt: Insel Verlag, 1981), 193–98.

55. This was directly acknowledged by the most important Viennese orientalist, Josef von Hammer, with whom Franz von Bruchmann was in close contact upon his return to Vienna from Erlangen (Platen, *Lyrik*, 794). It should go without saying that Hammer's attention to the matter has no necessary bearing on his own erotic propensities, only on his worldly and generally open-minded spirit. In recollections of his youth Hammer good-naturedly recounts how, in fending off the unwelcome advances of his close colleague, the historian Johannes von Müller, he informed the latter of his own "ganz antigriechischen Geschmackes." It seems the verbal protest did not suffice, and a permanent understanding between the two was reached only after Hammer struck his colleague's wandering hand with a metal ruler (Derks, *Die Schande der heiligen Päderastie*, 106). Hammer's attitude stands in sharp contrast to that of Schelling, who, though admittedly moved by Platen's diaries, shamefully opposed their publication out of concern for his own reputation. The Schelling story is recounted in Laubmann and Scheffler's preface to Platen, *Tagebücher*, 1:viii.

which Pindar rested as he rose in sleep to the gods in the theater? Yes, this is how Platen meant it, how it lay in his mind, how it intoxicated him: his idea of Beauty was of classically sculpted, erotically platonic origin, the product of an absolute aesthetic, to whose priesthood he felt himself ordained by fate, a naked idol of perfection of Greek-oriental slant of eye, before which he knelt broken-heartedly with the pain of infinite yearning.[56]

Platen's idea of the beautiful is tied to a long tradition of aesthetics, renewed in German culture above all through the writings of Johann Joachim Winckelmann. Among Schubert scholars the best-known, if not always recognized, instance of this homocentric tradition of usage probably is Goethe's "Ganymed."[57] Because it is also one of the most subtly crafted, it deserves our closer examination. No doubt the linguistic challenge posed by this kind of indirect expression was a part of its attraction for Goethe. For ease of reference, I give the entire poem:

---

56. "Denn was ist 'das Schöne'? Was ist uns Heutigen dieser Begriff aus alabaster, dieser zugleich süße und schul-meisterliche Begriff von Ebenmäßigkeit, Regelrechtigkeit und Goldenem Schnitt, und was war er schon jener Zeit, einer Zeit des heraufkommenden Realismus und des Frührots einer sozialen Modernität? Das Schöne—ist es das Jünglingsknie, auf dem Pindar im Theater zu den Göttern entschlief? Ja, so meinte es Platen, so lag es ihm im Sinn, und so berauschte es ihn: Seine Schönheitsidee war klassizistisch-plastischer erotisch-platonischer Herkunft, das Produkt einer absoluten Ästhetik, zu deren Priester er sich schick-salsmäßig geweiht fühlte, ein nacktes Idol der Vollkommenheit von griechisch-orientalischem Augenschnitt, vor dem er in Zerknirschung und unendlichem Sehnsuchtsschmerz kniete" (Mann, "Platen," 249–50).

57. In her introduction to Tobin, *Outing Goethe and His Age*, Alice Kuzniar discusses the influential concept of beauty elaborated in the works of Winckelmann and later Hölderlin (especially in his poem "Sokrates und Alcibiades"), concluding dryly that "beauty and grace are not invariably associated with the feminine, as scholarship is wont to claim" (15). An earlier version of this essay criticized Lawrence Kramer's analyses of Goethe's "Ganymed" for doing just this, pointing out that in his discussion of Hugo Wolf's setting, for example, he asserts: "Nature, Beauty, the Earth—all [are] terms gendered feminine in Western culture" ("Musical Form and Fin-de-Siècle Sexuality," in *Music as Cultural Practice, 1800–1900* [Berkeley: University of California Press, 1990], 167). There is more of the same in "The Schubert Lied: Romantic Form and Romantic Consciousness," in *Schubert: Critical and Analytical Studies*, ed. Walter Frisch (Lincoln: University of Nebraska Press, 1986), 224–33. A reply to this note by Kramer in the subsequent issue of the *Journal of the American Musicological Society* gave me the chance to elaborate on Goethe's sensitivity to a visual tradition representing Jupiter in pursuit of eros, which I bring into my discussion here. Kramer himself also returned to the matter, discerning the influence of Plato's *Phaedrus* in Goethe's poem, in *Franz Schubert: Sexuality, Subjectivity, Song* (Cambridge: Cambridge University Press, 1997), 118–28. He finds an oscillation in gender suggested in "the lovely morning breeze, which would traditionally be personified in the masculine form of a zephyr, and the mythographically feminine nightingale" (121). I am once more struck by the instability of these binary gender assignments. Do we have reason to favor the myth of Philomel over, say, Boccaccio's *Decameron*, where Caterina's young lover "made the nightingale sing" many times over during their night together? When we read that a father opens the balcony door to find his daughter asleep in her lover's arms, the nightingale still in her hand, it is not Philomel that first comes to mind. (On second thought: perhaps it was poetic justice that led the gods to transform the victim of mutilation and rape into a nightingale.) Or how about the argument between Romeo and Juliet in act 3, scene 5? Their lovemaking can go on only if the song they hear is still that of the nightingale, not the morning lark.

Wie im Morgenglanze	How in the morning radiance
Du rings mich anglühst,	You surround me in glow
Frühling, Geliebter!	Spring, Beloved!
Mit tausendfacher Liebeswonne	With thousandfold bliss of love
Sich an mein Herz drängt	Thy eternal warmth's
Deiner ewigen Wärme	Sacred feeling
Heilig Gefühl,	Presses upon my heart,
Unendliche Schöne!	Infinite Beauty!
Daß ich dich fassen möcht	That I might clasp you
In diesen Arm!	With this arm!
Ach, an deinem Busen	Ah, on your bosom
Lieg ich, schmachte	I lie, languishing,
Und deine Blumen, dein Gras	And your flowers, your grass
Drängen sich an mein Herz.	Press against my heart.
Du kühlst den brennenden	You cool the burning
Durst meines Busens	Thirst of my bosom,
Lieblicher Morgenwind!	Sweet morning wind!
Ruft drein die Nachtigall	When the nightingale calls to me
Liebend nach mir aus dem Nebeltal	Lovingly from the misty valley
Ich komme, ich komme!	I come, I come!
Wohin, ach wohin?	Where to? Oh, where to?
Hinauf! Hinauf strebts.	Upward, striving upward!
Es schweben die Wolken	The clouds waft
Abwärts, die Wolken	Down, the clouds
Neigen sich der sehnenden Liebe.	Bow down to yearning love.
Mir! Mir!	To me! To me!
In eurem Schoße	In thy lap
Aufwärts!	Upward!
Umfangend, umfangen!	Embracing, embraced!
Aufwärts an deinen Busen	Upward unto your bosom,
Alliebender Vater!	All-loving father!

Gender identity is gently jostled into place at the very beginning of the poem by the simple transposition of usual word order in the third line. "Der Frühling" is grammatically masculine: had the line read "geliebter Frühling," a merely arbitrary grammatical rule would have called for the masculine form of the modifier. The transposed word order raises the grammatical necessity to a definite designation of gender: spring, the season of budding life and sexuality, *is* the masculine Beloved. A mild ambiguity is brought into play with "Unendliche Schöne!" which may appear at first blush to require a feminine referent—but no feminine subject has been invoked. "Schöne" (as opposed to "Schöner"), however, is not exclusively the feminine form but also an archaic form of "Schönheit," a characteristic that is not innately gender-specific: "Unendliche Schön[heit]" and "Du, Geliebter" both accord with a masculine "Frühling." (The implicit identity of "Frühling, Geliebter!" and "Unendliche Schöne!" is subtly reinforced by the punctuation, which marks both phrases as a form of direct address.) Goethe's extraordinary command of language enabled him to realign conventional heterocentric gender associations by dislodging them from their underlying grammatical support. His poem embraces Ganymede's dawning sexual awareness as a part of nature, not in opposition to her.

A more concealed level of gender signification, crafted for the benefit of connoisseurs, may be at play in the phrase "Deiner ewigen Wärme heilig Gefühl," for as Paul Derks has shown, "Warm" (especially in formulations like "warme Brüder," warme Freunde," or "warme Liebe") was already in late eighteenth-century Berlin a code word for homosexual—or to keep to the language of a contemporary definition: "Herren die sich mit der Päderastie amüsieren werden Warme genennt."[58] Heine, too, uses the word in this way in his attack on Platen. (Not coincidentally, the name of the main character pressed into service in Heine's vicious assault is Hyazinth.) It was most frequently the adversaries of what came to be known as the "Schönheitskult" who brought its veiled forms of expression to public attention, often through sarcastic parody.

Goethe's poem also plays on a visual tradition representing Jupiter in pursuit of eros. The god could assume many forms (turning himself into a swan with Leda, a cloud with Io and Danae or when making love to Hera, an eagle with Ganymede). A pair of paintings from Correggio's *Amori di Giove*, *Io* and the *Rape of Ganymede*, produced at the Mantuan court for Federigo II Gonzaga, a great supporter of libertine art, have been housed in Vienna since the seventeenth century (and copies were displayed in other cities).[59] The openly erotic painting in this pair shows Jupiter, disguised as a great cloud, enfolding a rapturous Io (the two paintings are shown in fig. 6.1). Like the bosom of Spring upon which Ganymede languishes in Goethe's poem, the visage and arm of Correggio's god are not quite obliterated by his disguise.[60] A season personified and a god assuming the form of a cloud appear as cognate images. Goethe's "Ganymed" substitutes clouds for the

---

58. Derks, *Die Schande der heiligen Päderastie*, 86–110. The definition comes from the anonymous *Briefe über die Galanterien von Berlin* of 1782 (Derks, *Die Schande der heiligen Päderastie*, 92), attributed to Johann Friedel. There is a modern edition edited by Sonja Schnitzler, which Robert Tobin discusses. For references, see chapter 2, notes 24 and 28, and my discussion in the same chapter of the phrase "warmes Blut" in Schubert's *Der Graf von Gleichen* and Lessing's *Emilia Galotti*.

59. For a history of the transmission and reputation of these pictures across several centuries, see Egon Verheyen, "Correggio's *Amore di Giove*," *Journal of the Warburg and Coutauld Institutes* 29 (1966): 160–92.

60. A further song points us in the same cultural direction as "Ganymed": Matthäus von Collins's use of *terza rima* and his antiquated turns of phrase in the ballad "Der Zwerg" (D 771) are enhanced by Schubert's Schützian cadence formulas with their last-minute switch to major mode, which coincide with the references to pleasure in death ("doch sterb' ich wahrlich gerne," "jetzt weckt dein sterben einzig mir noch Freude"). The court at Mantua maintained a colony of dwarves.

FIGURE 6.1   Antonio Allegri da Correggio, known as Correggio (1489–1534). left: "Entführung des Gany-med" (GG 276); right: "Jupiter und Io" (GG 274) Kunsthistorisches Museum, Wien. By kind permission.

mythic eagle, thereby intensifying the erotic resonance of the myth even as the clouds and the words "Alliebender Vater" permit an association with the Christian Father in heaven to mingle in. (In any ambiguity one meaning generally predominates, and the Greek tradition has the stronger claim here. Associations drawn from a secondary sphere of reference only make the meaning more complex; they do not erase the first sense.)

Yet another song may help us to understand cultural associations around "Frühling" in Schubert's Vienna. This is the stunning "Blumenballade" "Viola" (D 786) on a poem by Franz von Schober. Heeding the snowbell's call, Viola has emerged too soon from winter's deep sleep to meet her bridegroom, Spring. When Spring comes galloping along many bars later (in a "Galopp" dance pattern), and the rose, lily, and narcissus assemble to greet him, it is already too late for Viola: the ring of Amor's "silver helmet" is transformed into a funeral knell. The name of one figure in this company is set into special relief with striking octave echos in the piano treble that make it resound in memory: narcissus.[61]

---

61. On this remarkable song, see Donald Francis Tovey, "Blumenballade: 'Viola'" [1900], in *Essays in Musical Analysis: Supplementary volume: Chamber Music* (London: Oxford University Press, 1978), 137–41. Schubert's device of repeating a phrase in the piano treble to etch it into memory is similar to his procedure in "Mit dem grünen Lautenbande," the song initiating the second half of *Die schöne Müllerin* (after "Pause"), whose melody and words are later echoed in "Die liebe Farbe."

FIGURE 6.1 (*continued*).

The remaining poems of Platen given in table 6.2 are ones that Schubert may or may not have known; I provide them as further evidence of the centrality of the myths of Hyacinth and Narcissus in Platen's oeuvre. The reference in the first poem—Hyacinth—is unambiguous. The second poem, a celebration of a young man's beautiful form, likens him to Narcissus in the final stanza. Finally, the poem "Tristan"—which Thomas Mann considered Platen's self-portrait—bears numerous traces of the Narcissus myth: he who beholds Beauty will be smitten with a love that can find no satisfaction on this earth and will be doomed to pine away like a spring that runs dry.

There is no doubt that the networks of Greek and Persian images in Platen's poetry are closely linked to his own biography. Yet many of those same images are found in the work of other poets associated with Schubert. The poetic oeuvre of his friend Johann Mayrhofer is deeply steeped in the Hellenizing tradition. He too has a poem on Hyacinth, and the poems from his collection *Heliopolis*, of which Schubert set several, are full of ambiguous eroticism and deep nostalgia for the Greek city of the sun, the mythical destination sought by so many writers of the period. Hölderlin's *Hyperion* (1797) similarly yearns for a mythical Greece; his friend Wilhelm Heinse's scandalous novel *Ardinghello und die glückseeligen Inseln* (1787) ends with the protagonists establishing a utopian community on a Greek island, a community whose defining characteristic is erotic freedom.

TABLE 6.2

Additonal poems by August von Platen. The first was unpublished during the poet's lifetime; the remaining two appeared in *Romanzen und Jugendlieder* (*Gedichte von August Grafen von Platen*, Zweite Vermehrte Auflage [Stuttgart: J. G. Cotta, 1832]).

Den Körper, den zu bilden	This body, to create it
Natur hat aufgewendet all ihr Lieben,	Nature has expanded all her loving,
Den ihre Hand mit milden	This, her hand in sweetest
Begrenzungen umschrieben,	Profile contoured,
Den aus dem reinsten Golde sie getrieben:	This, she drew forth from the purest gold:
O woll ihn rein bewahren,	Oh! let its purity be preserved,
Und laß dich nicht zum eitlen Spiel verlocken,	And let yourself not be enticed by frivolous play,
Zum spiele voll Gefahren,	By games fraught with peril,
Und weiche weg erschrocken,	And draw back in horror
Wenn eine Hand sich naht den goldnen Locken!	If a hand should near your golden locks!
Wiewohl dein ganzes Wesen	For though your entire being
Aus leicht entzündbarn Stoffen scheint zu stammen,	Seems of highly flammable material to stem,
Zur Liebe scheint erlesen,	And for love appears elected,
Laß doch dich nicht entflammen,	Do not allow yourself to become enflamed,
Sonst schlägt die Glut dir überm Haupt zusammen!	Lest impassioned flames engulf you head.
[Und wenn auf weichen Gräsern	[And when upon the soft grass
allein du ruhest unter alten Bäumen,	you rest alone beneath ancient trees,
Und blau vor dir und gläsern	And before you, blue and glasslike,
Des Flusses Wellen schäumen,	The river's waves rise frothing,
Die mit Nymphäen sich und Schilf besäumen:	Its shores lined by nymphs and reeds:
Wenn du so ruhst, so habe	When you thus lie resting, at once
Zugleich nur acht, auf daß du nicht betrogen,	Pay heed that you are not deceived,
Wie jener schöne Knabe,	And like him, that beautiful youth,
Dich spiegelst in den Wogen,	Find yourself mirrored in the waves
Und zu dir selbst dich fühlest hingezogen]*	And to thine own image drawn!]
Einsam und von Schmerz durchdrungen	Lonesome and with sorrow filled
Sitzt der delph'sche Gott und sinnt,	The Delphic god sits musing;
Er beweint den schönen Jungen,	He grieves for the beautiful youth,
Den geliebten Hyazinth.	His beloved Hyacinth.

(continued)

TABLE 6.2 (*continued*)

Könnt ihm doch dein Bild erscheinen,	Should your image appear before him,
Das dir jedes Herz gewinnt,	Which wins you every heart,
Traun! er würde nicht mehr weinen	Believe it! He would weep no longer
Um den schönen Hyazinth.	Over the beautiful Hyacinth.

Tristan

Wer die Schönheit angeschaut mit Augen,	Whoever has beheld Beauty with his eyes
Ist dem Tode schon anheimgegeben,	Is in the care of death already,
Wird für keinen Dienst auf Erden taugen,	Will be fit for no duty on this earth,
Und doch wird er vor dem Tode beben,	And yet he'll tremble when confronting death,
Wer die Schönheit angeschaut mit Augen!	Whoever has beheld Beauty with his eyes!

Ewig währt für ihn der Schmerz der Liebe,	Everlasting will be for him the pain of love,
Denn ein Tor nur kann auf Erden hoffen,	For a fool alone can hope on earth
Zu genügen einem solchen Triebe:	To satisfy a desire such as this:
Wen der Pfeil des Schönen je getroffen,	Whomever the arrow of Beauty has struck
Ewig währt für ihn der Schmerz der Liebe!	Everlasting will be for him the pain of love!

Ach, er möchte wie ein Quell versiechen,	Alas, may he run dry like a spring,
Jedem Hauch der Luft ein Gift entsaugen,	Draw in poison with every breath of air,
Und den Tod aus jeder Blume riechen:	And catch the scent of death from every flower:
Wer die Schönheit angeschaut mit Augen,	Whoever has beheld Beauty with his eyes
Ach, er möchte wie ein Quell versiechen!	Alas, may he run dry like a spring!

*The final two stanzas appeared only in an earlier version of the poem printed in the *Frauentaschenbuch für das Jahr 1825*.

Schubert also sought out the poems of Goethe that flirt with these traditions, most notably "Ganymed," and "Versunken" from the *West-östlicher Divan*, not to mention the passionate love poems addressed to men, like the *Suleika* poems (actually written by Marianne von Willemer) or "Gretchen am Spinnrad," which mark the poetic persona as feminine only through their titles. Interest in the subject of same-sex desire was widespread in nineteenth-century intellectual circles, the discourse rich in mythological and exotic allusion. From opposing standpoints, Ludwig Robert and Thomas Mann both recognized that a language infused with such foreign elements could serve at once to conceal—under the pretense of engaging a historically or culturally remote topic—and to disclose, or perhaps even to shape, forms of feeling unaccepted by society. Its expressive reach was limited solely by the receptive capacity of the audience: while not exactly a coded language, this mode of discourse stands at some remove from everyday usage and takes a certain effort to enter into. And while the range of possible personal relations to the subject is of course vast—interest cannot, after all, be collapsed into identity—Schubert's nuanced settings of August von Platen's poetry have ensured that his voice will be heard in the controversy over same-sex desire that continues to be debated even today. (I note with pleasure that these last words, written some fifteen years ago, are sounding a little quaint today.)

EXCERPTS FROM THE DIARIES OF AUGUST VON PLATEN (1796–1835)

---

14 JUNE 1818

Unter allen diesen Menschen, ich will es nur gestehen, zieht mich eine Physiognomie mehr als alle anderen an. Dies würde nun wenig zu dem stimmen, was ich vergangenen Neunten niederschrieb, allein diese Neigung ist nur das Werk der Phantasie. Mein Alter, mein ganzes Wesen bedarf Liebe. Da ich sie in der Wirklichkeit nicht finden kann noch mag, so suche ich sie im Ideale. Ich glaube nicht, daß jener Jüngling, den ich einstweilen Adrast nennen will, obgleich ich seinen Namen nicht kenne, ich glaube nicht, daß er mir etwas sein könne. Ich vermeide sogar, seine Bekanntschaft zu machen, um mir die schöne Täuschung nicht zu rauben. . . .

Among all these people, I shall admit, there is one physiognomy that attracts me more than all the others. While this would seem to agree little with what I wrote this past ninth, this attraction is solely the product of my imagination. My age, my entire being calls out for love. As I am unable and uninterested in finding it in reality, I seek it in the ideal. I doubt that this youth, whom I shall call Adrast, though I do not know his name, could become something to me. I even avoid making his acquaintance so as not to rob myself of the beautiful deception. . . .

15 JUNE 1818

In diesem Augenblicke ist mir Adrast wieder vollkommen gleichgültig. Diese Neigung ist vielleicht bereits vorüber. Ich kann nicht mehr lieben, wie ehemals. Zuerst bin ich zu kalt, zu überlegt geworden, dann weiß ich, daß ein sträfliches Verhältnis zwischen Männern existieren kann, und dies erregt mir einen unbeschreiblichen Widerwillen. . . .

At this moment I feel wholly indifferent to Adrast again. Perhaps this attraction has already passed. I can no longer love as before. For one, I have become too cold, too deliberate, and for another, I know that a relationship that is punishable by law can exist between men and this arouses the most indescribable repugnance in me. . . .

21 NOVEMBER 1818 (IN A POEM ADDRESSED TO ADRAST)

Hast du, wie Narciß, vielleicht / In der Quelle dich gesehen, / Alles Fremde zu verschmähen, / Was dir nicht an Bildung gleicht?

Have you, like Narcissus, perhaps seen your image in the pool, to disdain all that is foreign, whose likeness [or cultivation?] does not match yours?

22 NOVEMBER 1818 (DIARY POEM)

Holder als die Ros' in Kränzen, / Lächelst du, der Wohlgesinnte, / Duft'ger als die Hyazinthe / Seh ich deine Locken glänzen.

Nobler than the rose in wreaths, you, the well-disposed one, smile, more fragrant than the hyacinth, I see your curled locks gleaming.

25 NOVEMBER 1818 (DIARY POEM)

Gleich dem jungen Ganymede / Fließen duftig die Locken / Von der Stirn, wie Maienglocken, / Und ein Lied ist deine Rede.

Like the young Ganymede, your curled locks drape fragrantly across your forehead, like lilies of the valley, and a song is your speech.

10 DECEMBER 1818

Wenn du mein wärst, welche Reihe von glücklichen Winterabenden! Ich würde dich die südlichen Sprachen lehren, dein schöner Geist erfasste sie leicht. Wir läsen dann Calderón und Ariost zusammen. Deine blühende Stimme würde sich sanft erheben auf den Wogen Spanischer Verse. Kein Geheimnis würde zwischen uns obwalten. Auf die reinste, unbefangenste Offenheit gründet sich die Ruhe der Gemüter. Wir würden nicht sein, was wir scheinen: zwei verschiedene Wesen.

Wir würden unsere Herzen wechselseitig austauschen, wie ihre Namen liebende Otaheiter. Wie könnten wir noch getrennt werden, wenn wir uns selbst nicht mehr unterscheiden könnten? Wenn das Mein und Dein in Geist und Gemüt verschmolzen wären? Wer möchte ein Eigentum haben, wenn er liebt, ein Geheimnis, wenn er geliebt wird?

Später: O Schmerz ohne Ziel und Maß! O unerschöpflicher Jammer! Nie, nie liebte ich, wie in diesem Augenblicke, nie liebte ich so grenzenlos unglückselig. Ich kenne mich selbst nicht mehr ... Wohl sah ich, daß du liebst, aber du liebst nicht mich. ...

If you were mine, what a wealth of joyful winter evenings! I would teach you the southern languages, your beautiful soul would grasp them easily. Then we would read Calderón and Ariosto together. Your resonant voice would rise gently with the undulations of Spanish verse. No secret would obtain between us. For peace of mind is built on the purest, most unreserved honesty. We would not be what we appear: two distinct beings. We would exchange our hearts mutually, like Otaheitians [Tahitians] enamored of their names. How could we ever become separated, if we ourselves could no longer distinguish our separate beings? If mine and yours were melted together in spirit and mind? Who could wish to have a possession when he loves, a secret, when he is loved?

Later: Oh pain without direction or measure! Oh inexhaustible anguish! Never, never have I loved as in this moment, never loved with such boundless agony. I no longer know myself. ... For I have seen that you love, but it is not me you love. ...

7 FEBRUARY 1819

Ich sah ihn Heute mit vielen anderen. Er blickte mich gleichgültig, spöttisch an. In solchen Augenblicken verwandelt sich meine Liebe in Groll und Kälte; dann aber in bittere Thränen. Mir wäre besser, wenn ich nicht wäre. Was blieb mir nun von allen den enthusiastischen Vorspiegelungen unserer künftigen Freundschaft? ...

I saw him today amidst many others. He gazed at me indifferently, disdainfully. At such moments my love is transformed into icy hatred; later into bitter tears. I would be better off if I no longer existed. Then what would remain of all my enthusiastic previsioning [literally: pre-reflections] of our future friendship? ...

25 MARCH 1819

Meine Lage ist fürchterlich. Ich vergieße die bittersten Thränen. Haß und Liebe in meiner Brust vereinigt, zerreißen mein ganzes Herz. ...

My situation is dreadful. I shed the bitterest of tears. Hate and love, united in my breast, tear apart my heart....

10 APRIL 1819

Guter Adrast, du hättest mir viel zu vergelten durch deine Freundschaft, denn du hast mich viel gekostet. So viele Leiden hat mir kaum irgend ein Mensch verursacht. Wenn ich noch an jene Tage des Dezembers und Januars denke, wo mein ganzes Herz zerrissen war. Ich ging so weit mir sogar einen freiwilligen Tod zu wünschen! ...

Dear Adrast, you would offer me considerable compensation by your friendship, for you have cost me dearly. No other being has caused me so much suffering. When I think back on those days in December and January when my entire heart was torn. I went so far as to wish a voluntary death for myself! ...

24 JUNE 1819

Pendant le chemin de retour la conversation tombait sur les formes de civilité des peuples divers, particulièrement sur le vous et le tu. Nous en parlions, mais ni lui, ni moi cependant n'osait encore addresser à l'autre cette seule syllabe de "tu," syllabe très courte en apparence, quoique bien riche en contenu. Elle exprime seul un long ressouvenir de sentiments heureux. J'accompagnais Edouard chez lui et encore là se dévellopait la force de son affection. Ainsi ne puis-je conclure cette journée en m'écriant avec raison: "Vixi!"?

On the way back our conversation centered on forms of civility among diverse peoples, particularly on the use of "tu" and "vous." In speaking to each other, neither he nor I have yet addressed the other with this single syllable "tu," a syllable short in appearance, but extremely rich in content. All in itself it calls up volumes of recollections of joyous sentiments. I have accompanied Edouard back to his place and, once there, the force of his affection continued to unfold. Even so, can I conclude the day exclaiming truthfully to myself: "Vixi!" [I have lived!]?

13 JULY 1819 (PLATEN QUOTES THESE LINES FROM HIS LETTER TO EDOUARD SCHMIDTLEIN)

"Ich übergehe einige Unzartheiten Deines Briefes und ergreife nur den Hauptpunkt, um Dir ein geheimnis ins Ohr zu sagen, das Du zu ignorieren scheinst. Du achtest, sagst Du, Du verehrtest mich, wohl, aber ein Drittes hast Du vergessen, Du liebtest mich. Du liebtest mich, oder Du wärest einer Verstellung fähig, die ich kaum dem schwärzesten aller Dämonen zutraute. Noch gestern spiegelte Deine Liebe in jedem Blick, in jeder Silbe sich, mit jedem Kuß berührte sie meine Lippen."

"I shall pass over several unkindnesses in your letter and come right to the central point, to whisper into your ear a secret which you seem to ignore. You respect me, you say, and revere me, but you have forgotten a third—that you have loved me. You love me or you would possess an ability to deceive surpassing the darkest of demons. Just yesterday your love was reflected in every look, in every syllable, with every kiss it touched my lips."

26 JULY 1819

Hier je ne l'ai pas vu. Aujourd'hui matin nous avons passé quelques heures au jardin de Hutten pour finir la lecture de l'ouvrage de Wagner. Mais je n'étais point heureux; l'amour me dévorait, et lui—dans sa froideur extrême! Je souffre cruellement et plus que je n'ai mérité. Oh pourquoi, pourquoi la Providence m'a ainsi formé! Pourquoi m'est-il impossible d'aimer les femmes, pourquoi faut-il nourrir des inclinations funestes, qui ne seront jamais permises, qui ne seront jamais mutuelles? Quelle impossibilité terrible, et quel sort qui m'attend! Est-il des hommes dont la vie ne sera qu'une longue école de larmes? Je suis tout à fait perdu. Je ne me connais plus. J'oublie tout, mes études, mes amis, mes parents.

Yesterday I did not see him. This morning we spent several hours in the Hutten garden to finish reading Wagner's work.[62] But I was not at all happy; love was devouring me, and he—at his iciest! I am suffering cruelly, much more than I have merited. Oh why, why has providence made me in this way? Why is it impossible for me to love women, why must I nourish such doomed inclinations, which never will be permitted, which never will be mutual? What a dreadful impossibility, and what a fate awaits me! Are there men for whom life is not an endless school of tears? I am altogether lost. I no longer know myself. I've forgotten everything, my studies, my friends, my parents.

19 AUGUST 1819

"Eco y Narciso" [Calderón] est la couronne des comédies mythologiques. C'est vraiment un chef-d'oeuvre. Je n'ai lu aucune comédie en aussi peu de temps. On ne peut dire qu'on y trouvait des passages saillants; mais le tout est d'un effet merveilleux.

"Echo and Narcissus" is the pinnacle of mythological comedies. It truly is a masterpiece. I have never read a comedy in less time. One cannot say that one discovers outstanding passages in it, but the whole makes a marvelous effect.

22 AUGUST 1819

Il me disait pour la première fois qu'il était mon ami (ce qu'il avait nié si fortement dans sa lettre) et je l'assurais, moi, que j'étais le sien. J'ai appris aussi son âge. Il a vingt et un ans. De même ce

---

62. Johann Jakob Wagner (1775–1841), *Naturphilosoph* at Würzburg.

n'était pas pour la première fois qu'il me parlait hier d'un secret, qu'il n'avait pas encore confié à personne et qu'il le rendrait malheureux pour toute sa vie. J'ai deviné ce secret, et je lui ai dit que j'en avais des conjectures. J'y reviendrai une autre fois....

He told me for the first time that he was my friend (which he had denied most strongly in his letter) and I assured him that I was his. I also learned his age. He is twenty-one. But yesterday was not the first time he spoke to me of a secret which he has never confided to anyone and which has made him miserable all his life. I have divined his secret and I told him that I have some conjectures. I will return to this another time....

23 AUGUST 1819

Ce jour a été funeste. Nous nous connaissons l'un l'autre jusqu'au fond de nos âmes, mais sans qu'aucun résultat s'ensuivit. Je me suis rendu chez Edouard à 7 heures du matin après le collège de Wagner. Nous avons passé deux heures ensembles qui peut-être ont été les plus importantes depuis notre première connaisance. Je lui ai dit que je savais son secret et qu'il n'avait plus besoin de dissimuler. Je ne l'ai pas nommé, et il a voulu me tromper encore longtemps. Mais enfin il n'a plus pu nier, que je le comprenais tout-à-fait, comme lui-même il me comprend. Son secret n'est aucun autre que l'impossibilité d'aimer les femmes et l'inclination invincible pour son propre sexe. Ces mots n'ont pas été pronounces, mais il n'y a plus de doute....

This day has been a disaster. We know one another to the depths of our souls, but without anything further resulting from it. I met with Edouard at seven in the morning after Wagner's class. We spent two hours together, perhaps the most important since our first encounter. I told him that I know his secret and that there is no longer any need for him to conceal it. I did not name it, and he continued to try to deceive me for a long time. But finally he could no longer deny that which I had clearly understood, just as he understands me. His secret is none other than the inability to love women and an overwhelming inclination toward his own sex. Those words were not spoken, but there no longer is any doubt....

31 AUGUST 1819 (PLATEN READS BOOK 15 OF OVID'S METAMORPHOSES
*IN ITS ENTIRETY AND COMMENTS ON OTHER BOOKS, INCLUDING THE
STORY OF NARCISSUS)*

PLATE 6.1 Franz Schubert, autograph manuscript, Du liebst mich nicht," D 756, in G♯ minor, C 57 24b. Stift Kremsmünster. By kind permission.

PLATE 6.1 (*continued*).

PLATE 6.1 (*continued*).

PLATE 6.2 Franz Schubert, autograph *Reinschrift*, "Du liebst mich nicht," D 756, in A minor, MH 1862/c. Wienbibliothek im Rathaus. By kind permission.

PLATE 6.2 (*continued*).

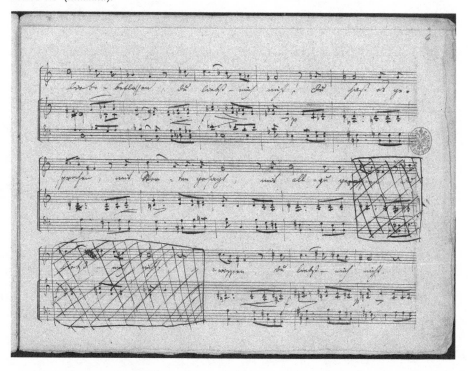

PLATE 6.2 (*continued*).

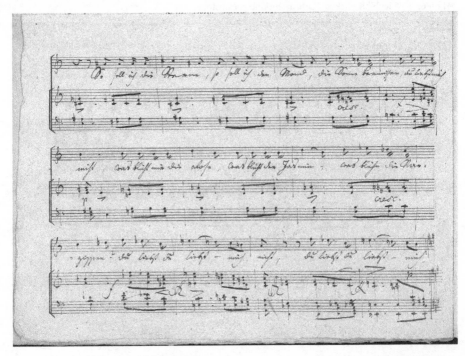

PLATE 6.2 *(continued)*.

NOTES ON THE AUTOGRAPHS FOR SCHUBERT'S
"DU LIEBST MICH NICHT"

"Du liebst mich nicht," D 756 was published in 1826 by Sauer und Leidesdorf, together with the three Rückert songs, "Dass sie hier gewesen," D 775, "Du bist die Ruh," D 776, and "Lachen und Weinen," D 777, as op. 59. While the manuscripts that served as the *Textvorlagen* for this publication have not survived, two earlier autographs for the Platen song are still extant. The earlier of the two is the composition manuscript, dated July 1822, in which the song appears in the key of G# minor. It is shown in plate 6.1 for ease of reference. A facsimile of this autograph, housed in Stift Kremsmünster, had previously only been made available in connection with the Olms reprint of August von Platen's correspondence.[63]

A second autograph is housed in the *Musiksammlung* of the Wienbibliothek im Rathaus as MH 1862/c (shown in plate 6.2). This is a fair copy in which "Du liebst mich nicht" appears, transposed to A minor, as the third song in a double gathering also containing the Rückert song "Greisengesang," D 778 (issued as op. 60, no. 1), and the Schlegel setting "Der Wanderer," D 649 (issued as op. 65, no. 2).[64]

We do not know for what purpose this autograph was prepared—it is unlikely that it served as the printer's *Vorlage* for any of the songs contained in it. But MH 1862/c is a neatly written presentation copy, notated on paper specially ruled for the combination of voice and piano. The version of "Du liebst mich nicht" preserved in this manuscript bears witness to the difficulties

---

63. Platen, *Briefwechsel*, vol. 2, following 320.

64. On the basis of its rare paper type and watermark, Robert Winter places MH 1862/c in 1826, the same year all three songs were published in separate collections. See Robert Winter, "Paper Studies and the Future of Schubert Research," in *Schubert Studies: Problems of Style and Chronology*, ed. E. Badura-Skoda and Paul

Schubert encountered in making the transposition up a half step from G♯ minor. Apparently, this was his first effort to transpose the song, for the text shares many details of articulation with the G♯-minor autograph, and like the earlier autograph, it contains an extra measure in the postlude. There is one major revision: the three measures preparing the cadential arrival on G♭, measures 26 through 29, have been crossed out and renotated as an arrival on F♯. The passage continues in this new enharmonic guise through measure 32. The published text later reverted to the notation of the crossed-out measures, a better preparation for the upcoming climactic return to the tonic via B♭minor, the neapolitan minor.

Two striking departures from the first edition illuminate the extraordinary climaxes at "vermissen" and "Narzissen." Both in the early G♯-minor version and in this A-minor autograph, the singer's highest note (F♯, in A minor) is reserved for the downbeats of measures 43 and 48. The revision in the published text intensifies the drama of these passages, arriving at the highest note simultaneously with the diminished seventh that brings on the tonal rupture. Moreover, Schubert's concern over the appearance of the notes on the page, evident in the earlier crossed-out passage, is also indicated by his notation of these measures. Unlike either the G♯-minor autograph or the A-minor publication, the version preserved in MH 1862/c uses a change in key signature to simplify the notation following the affecting resolution to the major mode in measure 40, and another to signal the return of the tonic minor for the postlude. Sometime before the publication of "Du liebst mich nicht," Schubert returned to the concept of the original G♯-minor autograph, maintaining a single key signature throughout—which has the result that the measures at "vermissen" and "Narzissen" stand in high relief on the page, a dramatic cluster of sharps amassed above a G♯ root.

Branscombe (Cambridge: Cambridge University Press, 1986), 226. Ernst Hilmar had earlier argued for a date of 1822, based on handwriting considerations; see his *Verzeichnis der Schubert-Handschriften in der Musiksammlung der Wiener Stadt- und Landesbibliothek*, Catalogus Musicus 8 (Kassel: Bärenreiter Verlag, 1978), 70. In either case, the decision to transpose the song appears to have been made independently of plans for its publication by Sauer und Leidesdorf.

WORKS CITED

MUSIC EDITIONS, FACSIMILES, AND MANUSCRIPTS

Beethoven, Ludwig van. *Werke. Gesamtausgabe*. Edited by Sieghard Brandenburg and Ernst Hettrich, on behalf of the Beethoven-Archiv Bonn. Munich, G. Henle Verlag, 1955–.

Cherubini, Luigi. *Les deux journées / libretto by Jean Nicholas Bouilly; music by Maria Luigi Cherubini*. Facsimile editions of the printed orchestral score and the printed libretto, with an introduction by Charles Rosen. Score, Gaveaux: Paris, 1800; libretto, Paris: Imprimateur-Libraire, 1800. Photoreprint, New York: Garland, 1980.

Eberwein, Carl. *Ernst, Graf von Gleichen*. Deutsches Nationaltheater, 1824 [Sign. 160]. Thüringisches Landesmusikarchiv, Weimar.

Jahrmärker, Manuela, ed. *Der Graf von Gleichen. Franz Schubert: Neue Ausgabe Sämtlicher Werke*. Edited by Walther Dürr, Michael Kube, and Walburga Litschauer. Series 2, vol. 17. Kassel: Bärenreiter Verlag, 2006.

Mozart, Wolfgang Amadeus. *Neue Ausgabe sämtlicher Werke*. Edited by E. F. Schmid, W. Plath, and W. Rehm. Internationale Stiftung Mozarteum Salzburg. Kassel: Bärenreiter Verlag, 1955–.

Schubert, Franz. *Franz Schubert: Der Graf von Gleichen; Oper in zwei Akten (D 918); Erstveröffentlichung der Handschrift des Komponisten aus dem Besitz der Wiener- Stadt und Landesbibliothek*. Text by Eduard von Bauernfeld. Edited by Ernst Hilmar, with an essay by Erich W. Partsch. Vol. 2 of *Veröffentlichungen des Internationalen Franz Schubert Instituts*. Tutzing: Hans Schneider, 1988.

———. *Der Graf von Gleichen*. Autograph score manuscript in the Wienbibliothek im Rathaus in digital facsimile at http://www.schubert-online.at/activpage/index_en.htm. Accessed 18 August 2010.

———. *Neue Ausgabe sämtlicher Werke* (*NSA*). Issued by the Internationale Schubert-Gesellschaft. Edited by Walter Dürr, Arnold Feil, Christa Landon, et al. Kassel: Bärenreiter Verlag, 1964–.

———. / Richard Dünser. *Franz Schubert: Der Graf von Gleichen* (D 918, completion). Oper in 2 Akten, Score. Bad Schwalbach: Edition Gravis, 1997.

———. *Werke. Kritisch durchgesehene Gesamtausgabe.* Edited by Eusebius Mandyczewski, Johannes Brahms, et al. Leipzig: Breitkopf & Härtel, 1884–97. Reprint, *Franz Schubert's Complete Works.* New York: Dover, 1964–69.

———. *Alfonso und Estrella.* D 732. Piano-vocal score based on the Urtext of the New Schubert Edition by Catherine and David McShane. Introduction by Walter Dürr. Kassel: Bärenreiter-Verlag, 1996.

———. "Du liebst mich nicht." D 756, first version, G# minor, Stift Kremsmünster, C57 24b.

———. "Du liebst mich nicht." D 756, second version, A minor, Wienbibliothek im Rathaus, MH 1862/c.

———. "Muth." Gesellschaft der Musikfreunde, A235.

Schumann, Robert. *Werke.* Edited by Clara Schumann, Johannes Brahms, et al. Leipzig, 1881–93.

Weigl, Joseph: *Die Schweizerfamilie.* Digital facsimile manuscript scores at http://www.oper-um-1800.uni-koeln.de/einzeldarstellung_werk.php?id_werke=339. Accessed 18 August 2010.

———. *Die Schweizerfamilie: Lyrische Oper in drei Aufzügen in Musik gesetzt von J. Weigl, Clavier-Auszug.* Braunschweig: G. M. Meyer, Jr., n.d. [1830s].

DIGITAL ARCHIVES

"Medienrechtsgeschichte" (Austrian censorship statutes from 1781 to 1902). http://www.univie.ac.at/medienrechtsgeschichte/statutes.html. Accessed 18 August 2010.

"Opera in Italy and Germany between 1770–1830." http://www.oper-um-1800.uni-koeln.de/. Accessed 18 August 2010.

"Schubert-online." Schubert materials in the Wienbibliothek im Rathaus et al. http://www.schubert-online.at/activpage/index_en.htm. Accessed 18 August 2010.

"Thüringisches Hauptstaatsarchiv, Weimar" (theater programs, etc.). http://archive.thulb.uni-jena.de/ThHStAW/content/below/index.xml. Accessed 18 August 2010.

DOCUMENTS, BIBLIOGRAPHIES, AND REFERENCE WORKS

Bauernfeld, Eduard von. *Aus Bauernfelds Tagebüchern.* Edited by Carl Glossy. [Reprinted from *Jahrbuch der Grillparzer-Gesellschaft*, 1834.] Vienna: Verlag von Carl Konegan, 1895.

———. 1879 autograph copy of selected entries from his 1820s diaries, prepared for publication. Wienbibliothek im Rathaus, Handschriftensammlung, H.I.N. 13004.

Beethoven, Ludwig van. *Ludwig van Beethovens Konversationshefte.* Deutsche Staatsbibliothek Berlin Series. Edited by Karl-Heinz Köhler, Grita Herre, and Dagmar Beck with the aid of Günter Brosche. 11 vols. Leipzig: VEB Deutscher Verlag für Musik, 1972–2001.

Deutsch, Otto Erich. *Schubert: Die Dokumente seines Lebens.* Franz Schubert, *Neue Ausgabe sämtlicher Werke.* Series 8, suppl., vol. 5. Kassel: Bärenreiter Verlag, 1964.

———. *Schubert. Die Erinnerungen seiner Freunde.* Leipzig: Breitkopf & Härtel, 1957.

———. *The Schubert Reader, a Life of Franz Schubert in Letters and Documents.* Translated by Eric Blom, being an English version of *Franz Schubert: die Dokumente seines Lebens.* Revised and augmented with a commentary by the author. 1st American edition. New York: Norton, 1947.

———. *Thematisches Verzeichnis seiner Werke in chronologischer Folge.* Kassel: Bärenreiter Verlag, 1978.

Enzinger, Moriz. "Franz v. Bruchmann, der Freund J. Chr. Senns und des Grafen Aug. v. Platen: Eine Selbstbiographie aus dem Wiener Schubertkreise nebst Briefen." In *Veröffentlichungen des Museum Ferdinandeum in Innsbruck* 10:117–339. Innsbruck: Museum Ferdinandeum,1930.

———. "Zur Biographie des Tiroler Dichters Joh. Chrys. Senn." *Archiv für das Studium der Neueren Sprachen* 156 (1929): 169–83.

Hilmar, Ernst. *Verzeichnis der Schubert-Handschriften in der Musiksammlung der Wiener Stadt- und Landesbibliothek.* Catalogus Musicus 8. Kassel: Bärenreiter Verlag, 1978.

———. "Zur Schubert-Rezeption in den Jahren 1831 bis 1865—Eine kommentierte Auflistung der Quellen in der 'Wiener Zeitung.'" In *Schubert durch die Brille, Internationales Franz Schubert Institut Mitteilungen* 29:223–25. Tutzing: Hans Schneider, 2002.

Hofmann, Renate. *Clara Schumanns Briefe an Theodor Kirchner mit einer Lebensskizze des Komponisten.* Tutzing: Hans Schneider, 1996.

Kinsky, Georg. *Das Werk Beethovens: Thematisch-bibliographisches Verzeichnis seiner sämtlichen vollendeten Kompositionen.* Completed by Hans Halm. Munich-Duisberg: G. Henle, 1955.

Kunze, Stefan ed. *Ludwig van Beethoven: Die Werke im Spiegel seiner Zeit: Gesammelte Konzertberichte und Rezensionen bis 1830.* Laaber: Laaber-Verlag, 1987.

Litschauer, Walburga. *Neue Dokumente zum Schubert-Kreis: Aus Briefen und Tagebüchern seiner Freunde.* Vienna: Musikwissenschaftlicher Verlag, 1986.

———. *Neue Dokumente zum Schubert-Kreis 2.* Vienna: Musikwissenschaftlicher Verlag, 1993.

Litzmann, Berthold. *Clara Schumann: Ein Künstlerleben: Nach Tagebüchern und Briefen.* 3 vols. Leipzig: Breitkopf & Härtel, 1923–925. Reprint, New York: Georg Olms Verlag, 1971.

Mandelkow, Karl Robert, ed. *Goethe im Urteil seiner Kritiker: Dokumente zur Wirkungsgeschichte Goethes in Deutschland.* Teil 1, 1773–1832. Munich: C. H. Beck, 1975.

Die Musik in Geschichte und Gegenwart: Allgemeine Enzyklopädie der Musik. Founding Editor Friedrich Blume. 2nd ed. Edited by Ludwig Finscher. Kassel: Bärenreiter; Stuttgart: Metzler, 1994–2008.

Pollack, Christian, ed. *Franz Schubert, Bühnenwerke: Kritische Gesamtausgabe der Texte.* Vol. 3 of Veröffentlichungen des Internationalen Franz Schubert Instituts. Tutzing: Hans Schneider, 1988.

Platen, August von. *Der Briefwechsel.* Edited by Paul Bornstein. 4 vols. Munich, 1914. Reprint, Hildesheim: Georg Olms Verlag, 1973.

———. *Die Tagebücher des Grafen August von Platen.* Edited by Georg von Laubmann and Ludwig von Scheffler. 2 vols. Stuttgart: Cotta'sche Buchhandlung Nachfolger, 1896–1900. Reprint, Hildesheim: Georg Olms Verlag, 1969.

Schmidt, Carl, ed. *Theater-Journal und Verzeichniß der im Jahre 1815 auf dem k .k. privil. Theater in der Josephstadt und Meidling aufgeführten Trauer-Schau-Lust-und Singspiele.* Vienna: Felix Stöckholzer von Hirschfeld, 1816.

Schochow, Lilly, and Maximilian Schochow, eds. *Schuberts Liedertexte: Die Texte seiner einstimmig komponierten Lieder und ihre Dichter.* 2 vols. Hildesheim: Georg Olms Verlag, 1974.

Schreyvogel, Josef. *Josef Schreyvogels Tagebücher 1810–1823.* Edited by Karl Glossy. Schriften der Gesellschaft für Theatergeschichte. 3 vols. Berlin: Verlag der Gesellschaft für Theatergeschichte, 1903.

Waidelich, Till Gerrit, ed., with preliminary work by Renate Hilmar-Voit and Andreas Mayer, *Franz Schubert, Dokumente 1817–1830.* Vol. 1, *Texte. Programme, Rezensionen, Anzeigen, Nekrologe, Musikbeilagen und andere gedruckte Quellen.* Vol. 10 of Veröffentlichungen des Internationalen Franz Schubert Instituts. Edited by Ernst Hilmar. Tutzing: Hans Schneider, 1993.

OTHER PRIMARY TEXTS

Adorno, Theodor W. *Beethoven: Philosophie der Musik: Fragmente und Texte*. Edited by Rolf Tiedemann. Frankfurt am Main: Suhrkamp Verlag, 1993.

———. *Beethoven: The Philosophy of Music*. Edited by Rolf Tiedemann. Translated by Edmund Jephcott. Stanford, Calif.: Stanford University Press, 1998.

Allgemeine musikalische Zeitung, no. 26 (June 1824): 423–28.

Aristophanes. *Lysistrata*. Edited with introduction and commentary by Jeffrey Henderson. Oxford: Clarendon, 1987.

Benjamin, Walter. "Goethes Wahlverwandtschaften." In *Illuminationen: Ausgewählte Schriften*, edited by Friedrich Unseld, 63–135. 2nd ed. Frankfurt: Suhrkamp Verlag, 1980.

———. "Goethe's *Wahlverwandschaften*." In Johann Wolfgang von Goethe, *Wahlverwandschaften*, edited by Hans-J. Weitz, 253–333. Frankfurt: Insel Verlag, 1978.

———. "The Image of Proust." In *Illuminations*, edited and with an introduction by Hannah Arendt, translated Harry Zohn, 201–16. New York, Schocken Books, 1969.

———. *Selected Writings*. Vol. 1, *1913–1926*. Edited by Marcus Bullock and Michael W. Jennings. Cambridge, MA: Belknap Press of Harvard University Press, 1996.

———. *Selected Writings* Vol. 2, *1927–1934*. Edited by Howard Eiland, Gary Smith, and Michael W. Jennings. Cambridge, Mass.: Belknap Press of Harvard University Press, 1999.

Chamisso, Adelbert von. *Adelbert von Chamissos Werke*. Edited by Julius Eduard Hitzig. 5th expanded edition. Berlin: Weidmann'sche Buchhandlung, 1864.

———. *Sämtliche Werke*. 2 vols. Munich: Winkler Verlag, 1975.

———. *Sämtliche Werke in zwei Bänden*. Vol. 2. Darmstadt: Wissenschaftliche Buchgesellschaft, 1982.

———. *A voyage around the world with the Romanzov exploring expedition in the years 1815–1818 in the brig Rurik, Captain Otto von Kotzebue*. Translated and edited by Henry Kratz. Honolulu: University of Hawaii Press, 1986.

Collin, Matthäus von. "Über das historische Schauspiel." *Deutsches Museum* 9 (1812): 193–213. Edited by Friedrich Schlegel.

Condillac, Etienne Bonnot de Condillac. *Abhandlung über die Empfindungen* [Traité des Sensations]. Edited by Lothar Kreimendahl. *Philosophische Bibliothek 25*. Hamburg: Felix Meiner Verlag, 1983.

Dommer, Arrey von. *Musikalisches Lexikon*. Expanded edition of H. Ch. Koch. Heidelberg: Mohr, 1865.

Eichendorff, Joseph von. "Die Deutsche Salon-Poesie der Frauen" (1847). In *Werke*. Vol. 3, *Schriften zur Literatur*, 87–101. Munich: Winkler Verlag, n.d.

Falckenstein, Johann Heinrichs von. *Analecta Thuringo-Nordgaviensia* (Worinnen vor diesesmahl vorgestellet wird . . . Klarer Beweis, daß Graf Ernst von Gleichen nicht zwey Weiber zu gleichen Zeit gehabt, mithin kein *Bigamus* gewesen . . .). Vol. 10. Schwabach: Christoph Conrad Zell, 1744.

Friedel, Johann. *Briefe über die Galanterien von Berlin auf einer Reise gesammelt von einem österreichischen Offizier* (Berlin, 1782). Edited by Sonja Schnitzler. Berlin: Eulenspiegel, 1987.

Goethe, Johann Wolfang. *Briefwechsel zwischen Goethe und Zelter in den Jahren 1799 bis 1832*. Edited by Edith Zehm et al. Vol. 20.1–3 of *Sämtliche Werke nach Epochen seines Schaffens: Münchner Ausgabe*. Munich: Carl Hanser Verlag, 1991.

———. *Dramen 1765–1775*. Edited by Dieter Borchmeyer and Peter Huber. Vol. 4 of *Sämtliche Werke: Briefe, Tagebücher und Gespräche 1*. Frankfurt: Deutscher Klassiker Verlag, 1985.

——. *Epoche der Wahlverwandschaften, 1807–1814*. Edited by Christophe Siegrist, Hans J. Becker, Dorothea Hölscher-Lohmeyer, Norbert Miller, Gerhard H. Müller, and John Neubauer. Vol. 9 of *Sämtliche Werke nach Epochen seines Schaffens: Münchner Ausgabe*. Munich: Carl Hanser Verlag, 1987.

——. *Der Junge Goethe, 1757–1775, 2*. Edited Gerhard Sauder. Vol. 1.2 of *Sämtliche Werke nach Epochen seines Schaffens: Münchner Ausgabe*, 37–77 (*Stella 1*). Munich: Carl Hanser Verlag, 1987.

——. *Stella*. Translated from the German of M. Goethe, Author of The Sorrows of Young Werther &c. &c. Absolvent Amantes. London: Printed for Mookham and Carpenter, No. 14, Old Bond Street, 1798.

——. *Weimarer Klassik 1798–1806*. Edited by Victor Lange. Vol. 6.1 of *Sämtliche Werke nach Epochen seines Schaffens: Münchner Ausgabe*, 462–505 (*Stella 2*). Munich: Carl Hanser Verlag, 1987.

——. *West-östlicher Divan*. Stuttgart: Cottaische Buchhandlung, 1819. Reprint, Frankfurt: Insel Verlag, 1981.

Goldoni, Carlo. *Il filosofo di campagna. A comic Opera; As performed in the King's Theater in the Hay-Market*. London: W. Griffin, 1768.

Grillparzer, Franz. *Dramen 1817–1828*. Edited by Helmut Bachmaier. Vol. 2 of *Franz Grillparzer Werke in sechs Bänden*. Frankfurt: Deutscher Klassiker Verlag, 1986.

Hahn, Ludwig Philip. *Siegfried, ein Singeschauspiel*. Strassburg: Joh. Friedrich Stein, 1779.

Hebbel, Friedrich. *Friedrich Hebbel's sämmtliche Werke*. Vol. 12. Hamburg: Hoffmann und Campe, 1867.

Heine, Heinrich. *Historisch-kritische Gesamtausgabe der Werke*. Edited by Manfred Windfuhr. Vol. 8/1. Düsseldorf: Hoffmann und Campe, 1979.

Heinse, Wilhelm. *Ardinghello und die glückseeligen Inseln: kritische Studienausgabe*. With 32 illustrations, documents in reception, commentary and an epilogue. Edited by Max L. Baeumer. Stuttgart: Philipp Reclam Jun., 1975.

Homer, *The Odyssey of Homer: In the English Verse Translation by Alexander Pope, Illustrated with the Classical Designs of John Flaxman*. New York: Heritage Press, 1942.

Jahrbücher der Literatur. Vol. 19. Vienna, 1822.

Kleist, Heinrich von. *Sämtliche Werke und Briefe*. Vol. 2. Munich: Carl Hanser Verlag, 1965.

Kotzebue, August von. *La Peyrouse*. In *Erheiterungsbibliothek für Freunde romantischer Lectüre*. Neue Folge. Vol. 11, 183–238. Vienna: bey Kaulfuß und Krammer, Buchhändler, 1825.

Lessing, Gotthold Ephraim. *Emilia Galotti* in *Werke* II. Edited by Gerd Hillen, 127–204. Munich: Carl Hanser Verlag, 1971.

——. *Emilia Galotti*. Translated by Benjamin Thompson, Es. (London, 1800). In *Four Georgian and Pre-revolutionary Plays*. Introduced and edited by David Thomas, 244–89. New York: St. Martin's Press, 1998.

Lichtenberg, Georg Christoph. *Schriften und Briefe*. 2 vols. Munich: Carl Hanser Verlag, 1968.

Liszt, Franz. *Sämtliche Schriften*. Vol. 5, *Dramaturgische Blätter*. Edited with commentary by Detlef Altenburg, Dorothea Redepenning, and Britta Schilling. Wiesbaden: Breitkopf & Härtel, 1989.

Mann, Thomas. "Chamisso." In *Aufsätze, Reden, Essays* I, 230–253. 1911. Reprint, Berlin: Aufbau Verlag, 1983.

——. *Death in Venice*. Translated and edited by Clayton Koelb. Norton Critical Edition. New York: Norton, 1994.

——. "Platen-Tristan-Don Quichotte" [1930]. In *Thomas Mann Essays*, edited by Hermann Kurzke and Stephan Stachorski. Vol. 3. Frankfurt am Main: S. Fischer, 1994.

Marx, Adolf Bernhard. *Ludwig van Beethoven: Leben und Schaffen.* 2 vols. Berlin: Otto Janke, 1859. Reprint in facsimile, 2 vols. in 1. Hildesheim: Georg Olms Verlag, 1979.

Menzel, Wolfgang. *German Literature.* Translated from the German of Wolfgang Menzel by C. C. Felton. 3 vols. Boston: Hillard, Gray and Company, 1840.

Metternich, Clemens von. *Metternich: The Autobiography, 1773–1815.* Welwyn Garden City, Ravenhall Books, Linden Publishing, 2004.

Montesquieu, Charles-Louis de Secondat, Baron de. *The Spirit of Laws* [1748]. Translated from the French by Thomas Nugent, LL. D; a new edition, carefully revised and compared with the best Paris edition, to which are prefixed a memoir of the life and writings of the author and an analysis of the work by M. d'Alembert. Vol. 1. Cincinnati: Robert Clarke and Co., 1873.

Moratín, Leandro Fernàndez, de. *The Maidens' Consent (El sí de las niñas, 1801).* Translated by Harriet de Onís. Great Neck, N.Y.: Barron's Educational Series, 1962.

Musäus, Johann Karl August. *Volksmährchen der Deutschen: Prachtausgabe in einem Bande.* Edited by Julius Ludwig Klee. Woodcuts after original drawings by R. Jordan, G. Osterwald, L. Richter, and A. Schrödter. Leipzig: Mayer und Wiegand, 1842.

Nestroy, Johann. *Johann Nestroy: Stücke 26/I.* Edited by John R. P. McKenzie. Johann Nestroy Sämtliche Werke, Historisch-kritische Ausgabe, edited by Jürgen Hain, Johann Hüttner, Walter Obermaier, and W. Edgar Yates. Vienna: Jugend und Volk, Edition Wien, Dachs Verlag, 1995.

Peacock, Thomas Love. *Nightmare Abbey and Crotchet Castle.* With an introduction by J. B. Priestley. The Novel Library. London: Hamish Hamilton, 1947.

Platen, August von. *Gedichte von August Grafen von Platen.* Zweite Vermehrte Auflage. Stuttgart: J. G. Cotta, 1832.

———. *Ghaselen.* Erlangen: Carl Heyder, 1821.

———. *Lyrik: Werke.* Edited by Kurt Wölfel and Jürgen Link. Vol. 1. Munich: Winkler Verlag, 1982

Rossi, Joseph. *Denkbuch für Fürst und Vaterland.* Vienna: J. B. Wallishauser, 1814.

Rückert, Friedrich. *Östliche Rosen: Drei Lesen.* Leipzig: F. A. Brockhaus, 1822.

Schlegel, Friedrich. *Kritische Friedrich-Schlegel-Ausgabe.* Edited by Ernst Behler. Vol. 23. Paderborn: Verlag Ferdinand Schöningh, 1987.

Schubert, Gotthilf Heinrich. *Die Symbolik des Traumes.* Bamberg: Kunz, 1814.

Sealsfield, Charles. *Austria as It Is: or Sketches of Continental Courts: By an Eyewitness.* London: Hurst, Chance, 1828. Reprint, Whitefish, Montana: Kessinger Publishing, n.d.

———. *Austria as It Is: or Sketches of Continental Courts: By an Eyewitness.* Edited, with additional documents and a German translation, by Primus-Heinz Kucher. Vienna: Böhlau Verlag, 1994.

Smith, Adam. *The Theory of Moral Sentiments* [1759]. New Rochelle, N.Y.: Arlington House, 1969.

Soden, Julius Reichsgrafen von. *Ernst, Graf von Gleichen, Gatte zweyer Weiber.* Berlin, 1791.

Steig, Reinhold, ed. *Achim von Arnim und Jacob und Wilhelm Grimm. Achim von Arnim und die ihm nahe standen.* Edited by Reinhold Steig and Herman Frierich Grimm. Vol. 3. Stuttgart: J. G. Cotta, 1904.

Strunk, Oliver W., ed. *Source Readings in Music History.* Rev. ed. General editor Leo Treitler. New York: Norton, 1998.

The Harmonicon. Vol. 2. London: W. Pinnock, 1824.

Tieck, Ludwig. *Phantasus*. Edited by Manfred Frank. Vol. 6 of *Schriften*. Frankfurt: Deutscher Klassiker Verlag, 1985.

Triest, Johann Karl Friedrich. "Abhandlung: Ueber reisende Virtuosen." *Allgemeine musikalische Zeitung* 46–48 (1802): 737–49; 753–60; 769–75.

———. "Development of the Art of Music in Germany in the Eighteenth Century" (1801). In *Haydn and His World*, edited by Elaine Sisman, translated by Susan Gillespie, 321–94. Princeton, N.J.: Princeton University Press, 1997.

Vega, Lope de. *The Star of Seville* (La estrella de Sevilla). Translated in prose by Philip M. Hayden. New York: Houghton Mifflin, 1916. Reprint, Whitefish, Montana: Kessinger Publishing, n.d.

———. *The Star of Seville* (La estrella de Sevilla): *A Drama in Five Acts*. By Mrs. Butler. London: Saubers and Otley, Conduit Street, 1837.

Vulpius, A., ed. "Der zweibeweibte Graf von Gleichen und seine Gemahlinnen." In *Curiositäten der physisch- literarisch- artistisch- historischen Vor- und Mitwelt: zur angenehmen Unterhaltung für gebildete Leser*. Vol. 3. Weimar: im Verlage des Landes-Industrie-Comptoirs, 1813.

Wagner, Richard. *Gesammelte Schriften und Dichtungen*. Leipzig: C. F. W. Siegel's Musikalienhandlung, 1904.

Weissweiler, Eva. *Clara und Robert Schumann: Briefwechsel: Kritische Gesamtausgabe*. 2 vols. Frankfurt: Stroemfeld/Roter Stern, 1984–87.

———, ed. *The Complete Correspondence of Clara and Robert Schumann*. Translated by Hildegard Fritsch and Ronald L. Crawford. 2 vols. New York: Peter Lang, 1994–96.

Wiener Theaterzeitung. Edited by Adolf Bäuerle. Vienna: Keck Verlag, 1815.

Wordsworth, William. *Revised Preface to the Lyrical Ballads* (1802). Reprinted in *Wordsworth and Coleridge. Lyrical Ballads*. Edited by W. J. B. Owen. Oxford, New York: Oxford University Press, 1969.

Zeumer, Karl. "Geschichte der Westgotischen Gesetzgebung." In *Neues Archiv der Gesellschaft für ältere deutsche Geschichtskunde zur Beförderung einer Gesamtausgabe der Quellenschriften deutscher Geschichten des Mittelalter*, 32, no. 1, 419–516. Hamburg and Leipzig: Hahn'sche Buchhandlung, 1897.

STUDIES

Agawu, V. Kofi. "Schubert's Harmony Revisited: The Songs 'Du liebst mich nicht' and 'Dass Sie hier gewesen.'" *Journal of Musicological Research* 9, no. 1 (1989): 23–42.

Allanbrook, Wye J. "Mozart's Happy Endings: A New Look at the 'Convention' of the 'lieto fine.'" In *Mozart Jahrbuch* 1984/85, 1–5. Kassel: Bärenreiter, 1986.

Anderson, Bonnie S. "*Frauenemancipation* and Beyond: The Use of the Concept of Emancipation by Early European Feminists" In *Women's Rights and Transatlantic Antislavery in the Era of Emancipation*, edited by Kathryn Kish Sklar and James Brewer Stewart, 82–97. New Haven, Conn.: Yale University Press, 2007.

Appiah, Kwame Anthony. "The Marrying Kind." *New York Review of Books*, 20 June 1996.

Applegate, Celia. "Robert Schumann and the Culture of German Nationhood." In *Rethinking Schumann*, edited by Roe-Min Kok and Laura Tunbridge, 3–14. New York: Oxford University Press, 2010.

Arblaster, Anthony. *Viva la Libertà: Politics in Opera*. London: Verso, 1992.

Bertelsen, Lance. *The Nonsense Club: Literature and Popular Culture, 1749–1764*. Oxford: Clarendon Press Oxford, 1986.

Biba, Otto. "Da Ponte in New York, Mozart in New York." *Current Musicology* 81 (2006): 109–121.

Bode, Wilhelm. *Goethes Schauspieler und Musiker: Erinnerungen von Eberwein und Lobe*. Berlin: Ernst Siegfried Mittler u. Sohn, 1912.

Borchmeyer, Dieter. "Anwalt der kleinen Terz: Goethe und die Musik." In *Beethoven, Goethe und Europa: Almanach zum Internationalen Beethovenfest Bonn 1999*, edited by Thomas Daniel Schlee, 41–61. Laaber: Laaber-Verlag, 1999.

Bormann Alexander von. "Romantische Erzählprosa." In *Deutsche Literatur: Eine Sozialgeschichte*. Vol. 5, *Zwischen Revolution und Restauration: Klassik, Romantik, 1786–1815*, edited by Horst Albert Glaser, 181–84. Hamburg: Rowohlt Verlag, 1980.

Branscombe, Peter. "Schubert und Nestroy (mit einem Seitenblick auf die Familie Unger)." In *Schubert und seine Freunde*, edited by Eva Badura-Skoda, Gerold W. Gruber, Walburga Litschauer and Carmen Ottner, 279–90. Vienna: Böhlau, 1999.

Bretherton, David T. "The Shadow of Midnight in Schubert's 'Gondelfahrer' Settings." *Music and Letters* 92 (2011): 1–42.

Brett, Philip. "Musicality, Essentialism, and the Closet." In *Queering the Pitch: The New Gay and Lesbian Musicology*, edited by Philip Brett, Elizabeth Wood, and Gary C. Thomas, 9–26. New York: Routledge, 1994.

Cone, Edward T. "Schubert's Promissory Note: An Exercise in Musical Hermeneutics." In *Schubert: Critical and Analytic Studies*, edited by Walter Frisch, 11–30. Lincoln: University of Nebraska Press, 1986.

———. "Schubert's Promissory Note: An Exercise in Musical Hermeneutics." *19th Century Music* 5 (1982): 233–41.

Cook, Nicholas Cook. "The Other Beethoven: Heroism, the Canon and the Works of 1813–14." *19th Century Music* 27 (2003): 3–24.

Crutchfield, Will. "Christa Ludwig Sings Schubert's 'Winterreise.'" *New York Times*, 17 July 1988, Arts and Leisure, 27.

Cusick, Suzanne G. "Gender and the Cultural Work of a Classical Music Performance." *Repercussions* 3 (1994): 77–110.

Denny, Thomas A. "Archaic and Contemporary Aspects of Schubert's *Alfonso und Estrella*: Issues of Influence, Originality, and Maturation." In *Eighteenth-Century Music in Theory and Practice: Essays in Honor of Alfred Mann*, edited by Mary Ann Parker, 241–61. Stuyvesant, N.Y.: Pendragon Press, 1994.

Derks, Paul. *Die Schande der heiligen Päderastie: Homosexualität und Öffentlichkeit in der deutschen Literatur 1750–1850*. Homosexualität und Literatur 3. Berlin: Rosa Winkel, 1990.

Dieckmann, Friedrich. *Gespaltene Welt und ein liebendes Paar: Oper als Gleichnis*. Frankfurt am Main: Insel Verlag, 1999.

Dunsby, Jonathan. "Why Sing? Lieder and Song Cycles." In *The Cambridge Companion to Schumann*, edited by Beate Perrey, 109–14. Cambridge: Cambridge University Press, 2007.

Dürhammer, Ilija. *Geheime Botschaften: Homoerotische Subkulturen im Schubert-Kreis, bei Hugo von Hofmannsthal und Thomas Bernhard*. Vienna: Böhlau Verlag, 2006.

———. *Schuberts literarische Heimat: Dichtung und Literaturrezeption der Schubert-Freunde*. Vienna: Böhlau Verlag, 1999.

Dürr, Walther. "Lieder für den verbannten Freund: Franz Schubert und sein Freundeskreis in Opposition zum Metternich-Regime." In *Zeichen Setzung: Aufsätze zur musikalischen Poetik*, 135–40. Kassel: Bärenreiter Verlag, 1992.

——. "Schuberts romantisch-heroische Oper Alfonso und Estrella im Kontext französischer und italienischer Tradition." In *Der vergessene Schubert. Franz Schubert auf der Bühne*, edited by Erich Wolfgang Partsch and Oskar Pausch, 79–106. Vienna: Österreichisches Theatermuseum, 1997. Exhibition catalog.

Dürr, Walther, and Andreas Krause, eds. *Schubert Handbuch*. Kassel: Bärenreiter, 1997.

Elderfield, John. "Seeing Bonnard." In *Bonnard*, by Sarah Whitfield, 33–52. New York: Museum of Modern Art, 1998. Exhibition catalog.

Fichte, Hubert. "I Can't Get No Satisfaction: Zur Geschichte der Empfindungen des Grafen August von Platen-Hallermünde." In *Homosexualität und Literatur 2: Die Geschichte der Empfindlichkeit, Paralipomena I*, 183–234. Frankfurt am Main: S. Fischer, 1988.

Fisk, Charles. *Returning Cycles: Contexts for the Interpretation of Schubert's Impromptus and Last Sonatas*. California Studies in 19th Century Music. Edited by Joseph Kerman. Berkeley: University of California Press, 2001.

Fodor, Jerry. "The Truth Is Not Out There." *Times Literary Supplement*, 16 October 2009.

Frisch, Walter, ed. "Memory and Schubert's Instrumental Music." Special issue with contributions by Walter Frisch, John Daverio, John M. Gingerich, Charles Fisk, and Scott Burnham. *Musical Quarterly* 84, no. 4 (Winter 2000).

Fuerst, Norbert. *Grillparzer auf der Bühne: Eine fragmentarische Geschichte*. Vienna: "Manutiuspresse" Wulf Stratowa Verlag, 1958.

Gallarati, Paolo. "Mozart and Eighteenth-Century Comedy." In *Opera Buffa in Mozart's Vienna*, edited by Mary Hunter and James Webster, 98–114. Cambridge: Cambridge University Press, 1997.

Gardiner, John M. "On the Objectivity of Subjective Experiences of Autonoetic and Noetic Consciousness." In *Memory, Consciousness, and the Brain: The Tallinn Conference*, edited by Endel Tulving, 159–72. Philadelphia: Psychology Press, 1999.

Gay, Peter. *The Bourgeois Experience. Victoria to Freud*. Vol. 2, *The Tender Passion*. New York: Oxford University Press, 1986.

Geyer-Kiefl, Helen. *Die heroisch-komische Oper: ca. 1770–1820*. Tutzing: Hans Schneider, 1987.

Goldschmidt, Harry. *Franz Schubert: Ein Lebensbild*. Leipzig: VEB Deutscher Verlag für Musik, 1976.

Gramit, David. "Orientalism and the Lied: Schubert's 'Du liebst mich nicht.'" *19th Century Music* 27 (2003): 97–115.

Gross, Friedrich. "Zum Nutzen oder Nachteil der Gegenwart? Geschichte in Bildern Schwinds." In *Moritz von Schwind, Meister der Spätromantik*, edited by Siegmar Holsten et al., 33–53. Staatliche Kunsthalle, Karlsruhe. Ostfildern-Ruit: Verlag Gerd Hatje, 1996.

Guralnick, Elissa S. "'Ah Clara, I Am Not Worthy of Your Love': Re-reading 'Frauenliebe und Leben', The Poetry and the Music." *Music and Letters* 87 (2006): 580–605.

Gurewitsch, Matthew. "Why Shouldn't Men Sing Romantic Drivel, Too?" *New York Times*, 6 November 2005.

Hachtmann, Otto. *Graf Julius Heinrich von Soden als Dramatiker*. Ph.D. diss. University of Göttingen: Druck der Univ.–Buchdruckerei von W. Fr. Kaestner, 1902.

Hallmark, Rufus. "Schumann and Other Frauenliebe Songs." Unpublished paper presented at Queens College, 2001.

Hanson, Alice M. *Musical Life in Biedermeier Vienna.* Cambridge: Cambridge University Press, 1985.

Head, Matthew. "Beethoven Heroine: A Female Allegory of Music and Authorship in *Egmont.*" *19th Century Music* 30 (2006): 97–132.

Hilmar, Ernst. *Franz Schubert in seiner Zeit.* Vienna: Hermann Böhlaus Nachfolger, 1985.

Höbelt, Lothar. "The Austrian Empire." In *The War for the Public Mind: Political Censorship in Nineteenth-Century Europe,* edited by Robert Justin Goldstein, 211–38. Westport, Conn.: Praeger, 2000.

Hoeckner, Berthold. *Programming the Absolute: Nineteenth-Century German Music and the Hermeneutics of the Moment.* Princeton, N.J.: Princeton University Press, 2002.

Hofmann, Renate. "Julius Stockhausen als Interpret der Liederzyklen Robert Schumanns." In *Schumann Forschungen.* Vol. 9, *Robert und Clara Schumann und die nationalen Musikkulturen des 19. Jahrhunderts. Bericht über das 7. Internationale Schumann-Symposion am 20. Und 21. Juni 2000 des 7. Schumann-Festes, Düsseldorf,* edited by Matthias Wendt, 34–46. Mainz: Schott, 2005.

Houben, Heinrich Houbert. *Verbotene Literatur von der klassischen Zeit bis zur Gegenwart.* Vol 1. Ernst Rowohlt Verlag, Berlin, 1924. Reprint, Georg Olms Verlag: Hildesheim, 1992.

Howe, Blake. "The Allure of Dissolution: Bodies, Forces, and Cyclicity in Schubert's Final Mayrhofer Settings." *Journal of the American Musicological Society* 62 (2009): 271–322.

Ivanovitch, Roman. "Mozart's Art of Retransition." *Music Analysis* 29 (forthcoming).

Jacobs, Helmut C. "Jean Nicolas Bouilly (1763–1842) und die Genese des Leonorenstoffes: 'Léonore ou L'amour conjugal' als 'Fait historique' der Revolutionszeit." *Archiv für Musikwissenschaft* 48 (1991): 199–216.

Kaiser, Gerhard. *Geschichte der deutschen Lyrik von Goethe bis Heine.* 3 vols. Frankfurt: Suhrkamp Verlag, 1988.

Keiler, Allan. "Liszt and Beethoven: The Creation of a Personal Myth." *19th Century Music* 12 (1988): 116–31.

———. "Liszt and the Weimar Hoftheater." *Studia Musicologica Academiae Scientarum Hungaricae* 28, Fasc. 1/4 (1986): 431–50.

———. "Liszt Research and Walker's *Liszt.*" *Musical Quarterly* 70 (1984): 374–403.

———. "Ludwig Rellstab's Biographical Sketch of Liszt." In *Franz Liszt and His World,* edited by Christopher H. Gibbs and Dana Gooley, 335–60. Princeton, N.J.: Princeton University Press, 2006.

Kerman, Joseph. "An die ferne Geliebte." In *Beethoven Studies,* edited by Alan Tyson, 123–57. New York: Norton, 1973.

Knoespel, Kenneth J. *Narcissus and the Invention of Personal History.* Garland Publications in Comparative Literature. New York: Garland, 1985.

Kohlhäufl, Michael. *Poetisches Vaterland: Dichtung und politisches Denken im Freundeskreis Franz Schuberts.* Kassel: Bärenreiter, 1999.

Kramer, Lawrence. *Franz Schubert: Sexuality, Subjectivity, Song.* Cambridge: Cambridge University Press, 1997.

———. "Musical Form and Fin-de-Siècle Sexuality." In *Music as Cultural Practice, 1800–1900,* 135–74. Berkeley: University of California Press, 1990.

———. "The Schubert Lied: Romantic Form and Romantic Consciousness." In *Schubert: Critical and Analytical Studies*, edited by Walter Frisch, 224–33. Lincoln: University of Nebraska Press, 1986.

Kramer, Richard. "Between Cavatina and Ouverture: Opus 130 and the Voices of Narrative." In *Beethoven Forum* I, 165–89. Lincoln: University of Nebraska Press, 1992.

———. *Distant Cycles: Schubert and the Conceiving of Song*. Chicago: University of Chicago Press, 1994.

———. "Posthumous Schubert." *19th Century Music* 14 (1990): 197–216.

———. *Unfinished Music*. Oxford: Oxford University Press, 2008.

Kravitt, Edward F. "The Lied in 19th-Century Concert Life." *Journal of the American Musicological Society* 18 (1965): 207–18.

———. *The Lied: Mirror of Late Romanticism*. New Haven, Conn.: Yale University Press, 1996.

Kris, Ernst, and Otto Kurz. *Legend, Myth, and Magic in the Image of the Artist: A Historical Experiment*. New Haven, Conn.: Yale University Press, 1979.

Lafite, Carl Johann Sigismund. *Das Schubertlied und seine Sänger*. Vienna: Strache, 1928.

Liess, Andreas. *Johann Michael Vogl: Hofoperist und Schubertsänger*. Graz and Cologne: Verlag Hermann Böhlaus Nachf., 1954.

Lightfoot, Jane. "Matrons without Stains." Review of Ruurrd R. Nauta and Annette Harder, eds., *Catullus' Poem on Attis: Texts and Contexts*. Leiden: Brill, 2005. *Times Literary Supplement*, 22 July 2005.

Link, Dorothea. "The Viennese Operatic Canon and Mozart's 'Così fan tutte.'" *Mitteilungen der Internationalen Stiftung Mozarteum* 38 (1990): 111–21.

Lockwood, Lewis. "Beethoven's Emergence from Crisis: The Cello Sonatas of Op. 102 (1815)." *Journal of Musicology* 16 (1998): 301–22.

———. *Beethoven: The Music and the Life*. New York: Norton, 2003.

Loos, Helmut, ed. *Robert Schumann: Interpretationen seiner Werke*. Vol. 1. Laaber: Laaber Verlag, 2005.

Lühning, Helga, ed. *Leonore: Oper in zwei Aufzügen von Ludwig van Beethoven: Das Libretto der Aufführung von 1806*. Bonn: Beethoven-Haus, 1996.

———. "Schubert als Dramatiker: *Alfonso und Estrella*: Vorurteile, Mißverständnisse und einige Anregungen zu einer Neuorientierung." In *Schubert und das Biedermeier: Beiträge zur Musik des frühen 19. Jahrhunderts; Festschrift für Walther Dürr zum 70. Geburtstag*, edited by Michael Kube, Werner Aderhold, and Walburga Litschauer, 25–43. Kassel: Bärenreiter-Verlag, 2002.

———. "Über die unendlichen Augenblicke im *Fidelio*." *Bonner Beethoven Studien* 4 (2005): 111–20.

Mandrell, James. "Of Material Girls and Celestial Women, or Honor and Exchange." In *Heavenly Bodies: The Realms of* La Estrella de Sevilla. Conference proceedings from an international symposium on *La estrella de Sevilla* held at Pennsylvania State University, 1992, edited by Frederick A. De Armas, 146–62. Lewisburg, Pa.: Bucknell University Press; London: Associated University Presses, 1996.

Marshall, Robert, and Charles Rosen. "What Mozart Meant: An Exchange." *New York Review of Books*, 6 December 2007.

Mathew, Nicholas. "Beethoven's Political Music, the Handelian Sublime, and the Aesthetics of Prostration." *19th Century Music*, 33 (2009): 110–50.

McConkey, James, ed. *The Anatomy of Memory: An Anthology*. New York: Oxford University Press, 1996.

McKay, Elizabeth Norman. "Schubert and Classical Opera: The Promise of Adrast." In *Der vergessene Schubert: Franz Schubert auf der Bühne*, edited by Erich Wolfgang Partsch and Oskar Pausch, 61–78. Vienna: Böhlau Verlag, 1997. Exhibition catalog, Österreichisches Theatermuseum.

McKendrick, Melveena. "In the Wake of *Machiavelli—Razón de Estado*, Morality, and the Individual." In *Heavenly Bodies: The Realms of* La Estrella de Sevilla. Conference proceedings from an international symposium on *La estrella de Sevilla* held at Pennsylvania State University, 1992, edited by Frederick A. De Armas, 76–91. Lewisburg, Pa.: Bucknell University Press; London: Associated University Presses, 1996.

Menninghaus, Winfried. *In Praise of Nonsense: Kant and Bluebeard*. Translated by Henry Pickford. Stanford, Calif.: Stanford University Press, 1999.

———. *Lob des Unsinns: Über Kant, Tieck und Blaubart*. Frankfurt: Suhrkamp Verlag, 1995.

Meyer, Stephen. "Terror and Transcendence in the Operatic Prison, 1790–1815." *Journal of the American Musicological Society* 55 (2002): 477–523.

Morrison, Toni. "Memory, Creation, and Writing." In *The Anatomy of Memory*, edited by James McConkey, 212–18. New York: Oxford University Press, 1996.

Muxfeldt, Kristina. "Political Crimes and Liberty or Why Would Schubert Eat a Peacock?" *19th Century Music* 17 (1993): 47–64.

Nagel, Ivan. *Autonomie und Gnade: Über Mozarts Opern*. Munich: Carl Hanser Verlag, 1988.

———. *Autonomy and Mercy: Reflections on Mozart's Operas*. Translated by Marion Faber and Ivan Nagel. Cambridge, Mass.: Harvard University Press, 1991.

Nalbantian, Suzanne. *Memory in Literature: From Rousseau to Neuroscience*. New York: Palgrave Macmillan, 2003.

Noltenius, Rainer. *Dichterfeiern in Deutschland: Rezeptionsgeschichte als Sozialgeschichte am Beispiel der Schiller- und Freiligrath-Feiern*. Munich: Wilhelm Fink, 1984.

Nottebohm, Gustav. *Zweite Beethoveniana: nachgelassene Aufsätze*. Leipzig, 1887. Reprint, New York: Johnson Reprint Corporation, 1970.

Obermaier, Walter. "Schubert und die Zensur." In *Schubert-Kongreß Wien 1978: Bericht*, edited by Otto Brusatti, 117–26. Akademische Druck- u. Verlagsanstalt: Graz, 1979.

Offen, Karen. "How (and Why) the Analogy of Marriage with Slavery Provided the Springboard for Women's Rights Demands in France, 1640–1848." In *Women's Rights and Transatlantic Antislavery in the Era of Emancipation*, edited by Kathryn Kish Sklar and James Brewer Stewart, 57–81. New Haven, Conn.: Yale University Press, 2007.

Ogris, Werner. "Die Zensur in der Ära Metternichs." In *Humaniora: Medizin – Recht – Geschichte*, 243–56. Berlin: Springer Verlag, 2006.

Ozawa, Kazuko. "*Frauenliebe und Leben*: Acht Lieder nach Adelbert von Chamisso für eine Singstimme und Klavier op. 42." In *Robert Schumann: Interpretationen seiner Werke*, edited by Helmut Loos, 274–80. Laaber: Laaber Verlag, 2005.

Petrobelli, Pierluigi. "Don Giovanni in Italia." *Analecta Musicologica* 18 (1978): 30–51.

Purdy, Daniel. "Sophie Mereau's Authorial Masuerades and the Subversion of Romantic *Poesie*." In *Women in German, Yearbook 13: Feminist Studies in German Literature and Culture*, edited by Sara Friedrichsmeyer and Patricia Herminghouse, 29–48. Lincoln: University of Nebraska Press, 1997.

———. *The Tyranny of Elegance: Consumer Cosmopolitanism in the Era of Goethe.* Baltimore: Johns Hopkins University Press, 1998.

Ramalingam, Vivian. "On 'Schubert, Platen, and the Myth of Narcissus,' Fall, 1996." Colloquy. *Journal of the American Musicological Society* 50 (1997): 530–36.

Reimann, Paul. *Hauptströmungen der deutschen Literatur, 1750–1848: Beiträge zu ihrer Geschichte und Kritik.* Berlin: Dietz Verlag, 1963.

Rolland, Romain. *Beethovens Meisterjahre.* Leipzig: Im Insel Verlag, 1930.

Rosen, Charles. *Beethoven's Piano Sonatas: A Short Companion.* New Haven, Conn.: Yale University Press, 2002.

———. *The Classical Style: Haydn, Mozart, Beethoven.* New York: Norton, 1971.

———. *The Romantic Generation.* Cambridge, Mass.: Harvard University Press, 1995.

Rushton, Julian. *W. A. Mozart: Don Giovanni.* Cambridge Opera Handbooks. Cambridge: Cambridge University Press, 1981.

Russell, Charles C. *The Don Juan Legend before Mozart: With a Collection of Eighteenth-Century Opera Librettos.* Ann Arbor: University of Michigan Press, 1993.

Samuels, Robert. "Narratives of Masculinity and Femininity: Two Schumann Song Cycles." In *Phrase and Subject: Studies in Literature and Music,* 135–45. Oxford: Legenda, 2006.

Saslow, James M. *Ganymede in the Renaissance: Homosexuality in Art and Society.* New Haven, Conn.: Yale University Press, 1986.

Sauer, Eberhard. *Die Sage vom Grafen von Gleichen in der deutschen Literatur.* Strassburg: Druck von M. DuMont Schauberg, 1911.

Sautermeister, Gert. "Lyrik und literarisches Leben." In *Hansers Sozialgeschichte der deutschen Literatur.* Vol. 5, *Zwischen Revolution und Restauration, 1815–1848,* edited by Gert Sautermeister and Ulrich Schmid, 459–84. Munich: Hanser Verlag, 1998.

Schacter, Daniel L. *Searching for Memory: The Brain, the Mind, and the Past.* New York: HarperCollins, 1996.

Schenker, Heinrich. *Der Tonwille.* Edited by William Drabkin. Team-translated. 2 vols. New York: Oxford University Press, 2004–5.

———. *Der Tonwille: Flugblätter zum Zeugnis unwandelbarer Gesetze der Tonkunst.* Vol. 1. Vienna: Universal Edition, 1921.

Schmidt, Heinrich. *Erinnerungen eines weimarischen Veteranen aus dem geselligen, literarischen und Theater=Leben.* Leipzig: Brockhaus, 1856.

Schumann, Elisabeth. *More Than Singing: The Interpretation of Songs.* New York: Boosey and Hawkes, 1945.

Schwab, Heinrich W. "'Mir ist so wunderbar.' Zum Kanon auf der Opernbühne." In *Von der Leonore zum Fidelio: Vorträge und Referate des Bonner Symposions 1997.* Bonner Schriften zur Musikwissenschaft 4. Edited by Helga Lühning and Wolfram Steinbeck, 235–248. Frankfurt: Lang, 2000.

Schwartz, Peter J. "Why Did Goethe Marry When He Did?" *Goethe Yearbook* 15 (2008): 115–30.

Siegert, Christine. "Brüderlichkeit als Problem: Zur Rezeption von Luigi Cherubinis *Les deux journées.*" In *Early Music: Context and Ideas II.* International Conference in Musicology 11–14 September 2008. Edited by Zofia Fabiańska, Alicja Jarzębska, Wojciech Marchwica, Piotr Poźniak, and Zygmunt M. Szweykowski, 306–55. Kraków: Jagiellonian University, 2008.

Sisman, Elaine Sisman. "Memory and Invention at the Threshold of Beethoven's Late Style." In *Beethoven and His World*, edited by Scott Burnham and Michael P. Steinberg, 51–87. Princeton, N.J.: Princeton University Press, 2000.

Skrine, Peter. "Matthäus von Collin and Historical Drama." *Modern Language Review* 78 (1983): 597–98.

Smith, Colin. "'Ma in Spagna son già mille e tre': On Opera and Literature." *Modern Language Review* 91 (1996): 27–39.

Solie, Ruth. ed. *Source Readings in Music History*. Edited by Oliver W. Strunk. Revised edition, general editor Leo Treitler. Vol. 6, *The Nineteenth Century*. New York: Norton, 1998.

———. "Whose Life? The Gendered Self in Schumann's *Frauenliebe* Songs." In *Music and Text: Critical Inquiries*, edited by Steven Paul Scher, 219–40. Cambridge: Cambridge University Press, 1992.

———. "Whose Life? The Gendered Self in Schumann's *Frauenliebe* Songs." In *Das Andere: Eine Spurensuche in der Musikgeschichte des 19. und 20. Jahrhunderts*, edited by Annette Kreutziger-Herr, 247–70. Hamburger Jahrbuch für Musikwissenschaft. Vol. 15. Frankfurt: Peter Lang, 1998.

Solomon, Maynard. "Franz Schubert and the Peacocks of Benvenuto Cellini." *19th Century Music* 12 (1989): 193–206.

———. *Mozart: A Life*. New York: HarperCollins, 1995.

———. "Schubert: Family Matters." *19th Century Music* 28 (2004): 3–14.

Steblin, Rita, with Erich Benedikt, Walther Brauneis, Ilija Dürhammer, Herwig Knaus, Michael Lorenz, and Gerhard Stradner. *Die Unsinnsgesellschaft: Franz Schubert, Leopold Kupelwieser und Ihr Freundeskreis*. Vienna: Böhlau Verlag, 1998.

Steinberg, Michael. *The Concerto: A Listener's Guide*. New York: Oxford University Press, 1998.

Strauss, Joseph. "Normalizing the Abnormal: Disability in Music and Music Theory." *Journal of the American Musicological Society* 59 (2006): 113–84.

Szondi, Peter. "Friedrich Schlegel and Romantic Irony, with Some Remarks on Tieck's Comedies." In *On Textual Understanding and Other Essays*. Translated by Harvey Mendelsohn, foreword by Michael Hays, 57–74. Theory and History of Literature Series, no. 15. Minneapolis: University of Minnesota Press, 1986.

Tettau, Wilhelm Johann Albert Freiherr von. *Über die Quellen, die ursprüngliche Gestalt und die Allmählige Umbildung der Erzählung von der Doppelehe eines Grafen von Gleichen: Ein kritischer Versuch*. Erfurt: Verlag von Carl Villaret, 1867.

Thayer, Alexander Wheeloch. *Thayer's Life of Beethoven*. Revised and edited by Elliott Forbes. Princeton, N.J.: Princeton University Press, 1967.

Tobin, Robert D. "In and against Nature: Goethe on Homosexuality and Heterotextuality." In *Outing Goethe and His Age*, edited by Alice A. Kuzniar, 94–110. Stanford, Calif.: Stanford University Press, 1996.

———. *Warm Brothers: Queer Theory and the Age of Goethe*. Philadelphia: University of Pennsylvania Press, 2000.

Tovey, Donald Francis. *Essays in Musical Analysis: Symphonies and Other Orchestral Works*. London, 1935. Reprint, London: Oxford University Press, 1981.

———. "Blumenballade: 'Viola' [1900]." In *Essays in Musical Analysis: Supplementary Volume: Chamber Music*. London: Oxford University Press, 1978: 137–41.

Verheyen, Egon. "Correggio's Amore di Giove." *Journal of the Warburg and Coutauld Institutes* 29 (1966): 160–92.

Vetter, Walther. *Der Klassiker Schubert*. 2 vols. Leipzig: Peters, 1953.

Waidelich, Till Gerrit. *Franz Schubert: Alfonso und Estrella: Eine frühe durchkomponierte Oper. Geschichte und Analyse*. Tutzing: Hans Schneider, 1991.

———. "'Diese in Tönen geschriebene Liebesgeschichte, welche wie keine mehr den Namen einer deutschen *Volksoper* verdient': Zur Rezeptionsgeschichte von Joseph Weigls *Schweizer Familie* in Biedermeier und Vormärz." In *Schubert: Perspektiven*, 2, 180–81. Stuttgart: Franz Steiner Verlag, 2002.

———. "Joseph Hüttenbrenners Entwurf eines Aufsatzes mit der ersten biographischen Skizze Schuberts (1823) und zwei Fragmente eines ungedruckten Schubert-Nachrufs (1828)." *Schubert-Perspektiven* 1 (2001): 37–73.

Waidelich, Till Gerrit, and Ilija Dürhammer, eds. *Schubert 200 Jahre*. Heidelberg: Braus, 1997.

Weinmann, Alexander. "Zwei neue Schubert-Funde." *Österreichische Musikzeitschrift* 27 (1972): 75–78.

Wiesner, Adolph [Dr.]. *Denkwürdigkeiten der Oesterreichischen Zensur vom Zeitalter der Reformazion bis auf die Gegenwart*. Stuttgart: Verlag von Adolph Krabbe, 1847.

Winter, Robert. "Paper Studies and the Future of Schubert Research." In *Schubert Studies: Problems of Style and Chronology*, edited by E. Badura-Skoda and Paul Branscombe, 209–76. Cambridge: Cambridge University Press, 1986.

Wirth, Julia. *Julius Stockhausen, Der Sänger des deutschen Liedes nach Dokumenten seiner Zeit dargestellt von Julia Wirth, geb. Stockhausen*. Frankfurt am Main: Englert und Schlosser, 1927.

Worrall, David. *Theatric Revolution: Drama, Censorship, and Romantic Period Subcultures 1773–1832*. Oxford: Oxford University Press, 2006.

Yates, W. E. *Grillparzer: A Critical Introduction*. Cambridge: Cambridge University Press, 1972.

———. *Theatre in Vienna: A Critical History, 1776–1995*. Cambridge: Cambridge University Press, 1996.

Youens, Susan. "Schubert and the Poetry of Graf August von Platen-Hallermünde." *Music Review* 46 (1985): 19–34.

———. *Schubert's Late Lieder: Beyond the Song Cycles*. Cambridge: Cambridge University Press, 2002.

INDEX

Page numbers written in italics denote illustrations.